BELIEFS

and the world

they have created

JAMIE
CAWLEY

Matador
9 Priory Business Park
Kibworth Beauchamp
Leicestershire LE8 0RX, UK
Tel: (+44) 116 279 2299
Fax: (+44) 116 279 2277
Email: books@troubador.co.uk
Web: www.troubador.co.uk/matador

ISBN 978 1784622 510

British Library Cataloguing in Publication Data.
A catalogue record for this book is available from the British Library.

Printed and bound in the UK by TJ International, Padstow, Cornwall
Typeset in Aldine by Troubador Publishing Ltd

Matador is an imprint of Troubador Publishing Ltd

To Diana

Contents

Foreword

Some years ago it dawned on me that, for almost half of recorded history, no one ever went to a church or temple. Temples were places where godlets lived, not where people went to worship. No one then 'worshipped' in the way Western Beliefs now do. I thought people should know about this.

I looked around for brief summaries of religions and found there were none at all. There are some good books – Diarmaid MacCulloch's *A History of Christianity* is stunningly good, but it is also 1,100 pages long. There are brief introductions to Buddhism, but they left me knowing less about the subject than before I read them. So I decided I had to write a brief, comprehensive introduction.

I have studied religions and ideologies since I was as young as thirteen, when I first read the Qur'an, an odd occupation for a child of Church of England background. I remember the shock of surprise at finding the first chapter called 'The Cow' and a chapter called 'Mary' in praise of Jesus' mother. I even got an O-level in religious knowledge before going on to study Philosophy at Oxford.

I have no faith myself, but find Beliefs interesting and have sought to present them clearly, simply and without bias. All have both a good side and a bad side and I have tried to be balanced between these. I am, if anything, more intolerant of aggressive atheists, whose proudly held ignorance of the topic enables them to miss the point without even noticing.

I hope you find the characters you meet here interesting: Hilkiah, the Chief Priest 'finding' the Jewish law while the Temple was being refurbished; Socrates, who was illiterate as well as a crashing bore, despising those who could read; the emperor Ashoka, vigorously promoting peaceful Buddhism after he had fought to power; Jesus' four brothers, James, Joses, Simon and Judas; Origen, who castrated himself while deciding what went into the Old Testament; Mohammad's beloved employer and wife, Khalifa; St Augustine, mouthing each word he read; Napoleon, creating nation after nation; Karl Marx, boasting of his wife's noble birth, playing the stock market and getting the maid pregnant. I hope I have conveyed something of the interest I find in the subject of Beliefs.

Jamie Cawley, Beijing, China

.1.

BELIEFS

This book seeks to describe in brief all the world's major Beliefs, all ten of them, so that everyone can better understand them and their effects. The Beliefs that have had more than 100 million followers are, in the order that they first started: Polytheism (including Hinduism and Shinto), Judaism, Buddhism, Confucianism, Daoism, Christianity, Islam, Nationalism, Communism and Environmentalism[1].

A Belief, capital 'B', is a structure of thought, behaviour, tradition and practice, based on ideas a group hold to be true: a collective conviction. Everything called a religion or an ideology is a Belief. Both Communism and Christianity are hugely powerful Beliefs that have swept countries and empires away, thrilled their supporters with the excitement of their revelation and led them to heroism and self-sacrifice. Christianity has a

---

[1] The largest of the current smaller religions, not dealt with here, are Sikhism and Ba'hai and, depending on whether they are seen as separate Beliefs, Mormonism, the Alawites, the Druze, Jehovah's Witnesses, Christian Scientists, Rastafarians and Seventh Day Adventists. Other '-isms' are discussed in endnote ii.

personal God and Communism sees an impersonal force of history; but this is a small difference among great similarities. Not all 'religions' have a God: Buddhism has no God in its official Theravada form (although it can have thousands in its Mahayana form) and Confucius, who founded the dominant Chinese ideology or religion, did not believe in a God. Nor do modern ideologies avoid all supernatural ideas: the Nationalist 'Spirit of the Nation' or the Environmentalist 'Gaia' are as supernatural as Amun of Egypt and, well, Gaia, the Greek goddess. We understand 'religions' and 'ideologies' better if we put them all together as Beliefs.

Beliefs have huge power to create and an appalling ability to destroy. Beliefs can bring sublime happiness and they can provide comfort in adversity. Beliefs have stimulated the greatest productions of art, architecture and music. But they have also held peoples in misery and in guilt, and prompted torture and killing on a huge scale.

Beliefs are not the same as faith. Every Belief has a core of faith; that is, members of the Belief are required to accept some propositions as true through commitment, not evidence[i]. Nothing said here is a reflection on the truth of the central propositions of religion, faiths, or whether the hopes of religious people are well founded. Religious faith, that God or godlets exist and their wishes have been revealed, cannot be shown to be either true or false. Nor does understanding a Belief reflect on its faith: Beliefs can change their character completely with no change in their faith at all. Faith is what people hold to be true by conviction; Beliefs are what these convictions make them do. Christianity is a Belief that, before 1700, often encouraged its followers to persecute and sometimes to kill people with different religious views, whether they were Christian or not. Since then, it has disapproved of killing for reasons of religion and promotes charity towards people, whether they are Christian or not. This change had nothing to do with the faith of Christians in the divinity of Jesus: that did not change. Nor did Christianity's sacred writings alter by a syllable between the bloody and the peaceful phases. It was the Belief that changed, not people's faith. This book is not about issues of faith, the purpose of mankind's existence, the search for justice or the need for sustainability: it is about understanding the social, political and human phenomena that are Beliefs. There are no answers here to the questions of whether God or historic destiny exists: the explosion of a suicide-bomb or the ripping-out of a still-beating heart are not affected by these issues of faith. These things were and are determined by Beliefs. Beliefs are not faith in God's existence, they are not patriotism, nor concern for the poor, nor care for the future. Beliefs are not these ideas; they are the strange things that form round these ideas; half corporation, half crowd-dynamics.

As well as faith we cannot discuss personal revelation. The writings of mystics show that language fails at this task. Explaining personal revelation is like trying to explain colour to the blind. Such writings can only be understood poetically, more as feeling than meaning. But, as with poetry, what is communicated depends as much on the receiver, the listener or reader, as on the words themselves. So, inevitably, the details of mystic sects, such as the most abstract Sufis or Kabbalah enthusiasts, remain mysterious.

The relationship of Beliefs to their faith can be compared to the relationship of corporations to their products. Corporations have cultures, rules, traditions, histories and practices that are largely unconnected to their products and markets. You can compare corporations as organisations without needing to think about their output, even if the products are very different. The strengths and weaknesses of a pharmaceutical company can be compared to the strengths and weaknesses of an aircraft company, without their very different products mattering greatly. Similarly, we can compare Beliefs independently of their faiths. Beliefs are immensely powerful. They can induce someone to selflessly sacrifice their own life or persuade them to kill others mercilessly. Yet, despite their importance and the threat they sometimes present to us, Beliefs are not well understood and are virtually never studied together. We need to understand these things better.

Beliefs, capital 'B', are much more than just things people believe to be right. Some believe it is right to smack naughty children; others do not. Both sides can be passionate, but this is a belief about the best means to an end: successfully raising children, not a Belief about the whole meaning of life. This is why only Nationalism, Communism and Environmentalism are 'Beliefs'; although there are so many more modern '-isms', only

Nationalism, Communism and Environmentalism form complete ideologies, comparable to religions, as part of Beliefs (for a more detailed explanation see endnote[ii]).

Over the last hundred years, Beliefs have become the biggest killer of young people in the developed world, overtaking infectious disease for the first time in history. We understand that all infectious diseases have common characteristics, their likely arrival can be anticipated, their epidemiology can be studied and action can be taken to limit their spread. We address the challenge of infections as one subject, with scientific research and international co-operation and with increasing success. In contrast, we often fail to connect problems caused by a Belief to their cause. Few see that the Nazi mass killings were an effect of the Nationalist Belief. Even when we do link a problem with the Belief that caused it, say the 9/11 terrorist attack on America, many muddle Belief with faith. So they look for the cause of 9/11 in the particularities of the Islamic faith. But it is not because Islam is an unusual Belief that caused 9/11: it is because it is a typical Belief. All long-established Beliefs have had periods when they generate mass murder. The Aztec massacre of hundreds at the dedication of a new temple and Mao Zedong's accidental killing of millions during the 'Great Leap Forward' are similar effects arising from the same basic cause: Beliefs. When we understand that these terrible events all have the same cause, we can understand them better and, by understanding them better, we may be able to limit their destructiveness in the future. Our task is to understand the critical part

Beliefs play in our lives and in our societies in an objective way, to show that the cruel effects of Joseph Stalin and Osama bin Laden are not separate products of different causes but similar results of the same cause: Beliefs.

Some things come into focus only when seen from a distance. Looked at closely, Beliefs can be infinitely complicated in a way that conceals their similarities. Distance from the subject can simplify and enable the overall structure to be seen much more clearly. The theory of plate tectonics, for example, is the idea that continents drifted apart over geological time. It seems an almost obvious idea when you look at the shape of the continents either side of the Atlantic on a world map. But, close up, when you look out at the Atlantic from a towering and very fixed cliff, the same idea seems ridiculous. Yet it is the view you get from the distance of the map that is correct, the detailed picture from the cliffs that is wrong. So it is with Beliefs. Mohammad and Marx each ignited Beliefs, Islam and Communism, that fired the passions of idealists in their societies. They both announced revelations that went on to profoundly influence the subsequent history of the whole world. But this similarity between them would be hidden, rather than revealed, by giving extensive information on their backgrounds, Mohammad's in seventh-century Arabia, Marx's in nineteenth-century Europe. This book looks at Beliefs the way you look at a landscape from an airplane: the main structures – and the deep structures – show up clearly when the detail is too small to see. Even if the landscape is already familiar, getting an aerial view of it changes how you understand it and puts the familiar features together in a new way. Even the most familiar Belief can have new light shed on it by looking at it from a distance.

But perhaps too much detail is included? Why include Communism at all? Its last, few, ageing true believers will soon be gone. In countries such as China and Vietnam, where it is used as a term for the ruling organisation, it has become a word that implies no more than concern for the common person, more Community Party than Communist Party, and almost all connection with the original Communist Belief is lost. Where Communism's name and symbols are still attached to current organisations, they have become historical curiosities – as relevant as a Latin motto. So why not let Communism fade into history, unlamented? Equally, we might ask how telling the story of Judaism's origins in the sixth century BCE can add anything relevant today.

But Beliefs can only be understood when their full variety is seen. The meaning of the very category of Beliefs can only really be taken in when you see all its contents. Moreover, older Beliefs do not imply quieter beliefs; it was only after 1,500 years that Christianity entered its most deadly phase. Our current set of Beliefs are changing and mutating in ways we can understand better after we have seen how Beliefs have previously altered – and the changes they went through that made them too dangerous. Moreover, all Beliefs are connected, later Beliefs learning from earlier Beliefs. Judaism gave birth to Christianity and Islam and, in turn, Christianity is the stepparent of Communism and Environmentalism. To understand any Belief as it is now, we need to fit it into a general understanding of other Beliefs, both as they are now and as they have developed in the past.

So the risk of being seen as a superficial potboiler, muckraking through religions and high principles for scandal, is as necessary as the risk of being seen to waste time on ancient, bookish irrelevancies.

This book is not about the peoples who hold each Belief, except incidentally. It is about the major Beliefs themselves: their history, the way they affect us now and how they may affect our future. We explore the history of Buddhism, not of Buddhists; of the Belief of Nationalism, not the development of Nations. Islam had a huge political impact immediately after it was founded, driving the creation of a vast Arab Empire, so this history is important to understanding how the Belief developed. Later, in the fifteenth century CE, there was a second great expansion of the area controlled by Muslim rulers, as the Ottoman Turks and Moghul emperors built their empires. But this expansion of the size of the area controlled by Islamic rulers was virtually unconnected to the religion of Islam itself and so is only mentioned in passing, as we move on to the more significant challenges facing the Islamic Belief today.

As you go through the Beliefs covered here, you will see that the number of Beliefs has grown over time – only one before 600BCE, seven by 750CE, ten today. Over this time the number of people involved in Beliefs has grown even faster and continues to expand their membership today. The newer Beliefs also allow an individual to hold two Beliefs at the same time: someone can be Christian-and-Nationalist or Muslim-and-Environmentalist. Although Beliefs are so important, so gigantic in our lives, they have not previously been brought together and compared, like with like. Understanding them will be vital to our future peace, so we must try to see them for what they are. Tens of thousands are still killed every year by Beliefs. We must find ways to stop this, to fight the malign effects of Beliefs and to prevent the disasters that they caused in the twentieth century happening again this century.

Unless the trends change dramatically, membership of Beliefs will continue to grow. Inevitably, it seems, with more Beliefs and with memberships of Beliefs growing, some Beliefs will develop deadly mutations. But we often do not see the danger because we do not yet understand the nature of Beliefs. We look back at the slaughter of the Thirty Years' War, in which one-in-three of the population were killed, and hope and believe that sectarian warfare is a thing of the past. Yet we are building up to a Sunni/Shi'a holocaust. We have looked at the millions killed in Stalin's collectivisation of the farms and said, 'Extremist Communism is dead, that will not happen again.' But it did, in China and in Cambodia. We looked at the gas chambers of Auschwitz and said, 'Extreme Nationalism will not recur', even as Bosnians were massacred at Srebrenica in 1995. Each atrocity is seen as having a different cause, so they are not linked together to provide lessons relevant to us today. There is every reason to expect Beliefs to cause atrocities again, unless we learn to recognise them, understand them and put their worst aspects behind us.

If we don't get beyond Beliefs, what will we do to ourselves next?

.2.

POLYTHEISM: THE DEFAULT BELIEF

Many tribes, countries and peoples believe that invisible beings with magic powers, godlets, exist and that they can be persuaded to use those powers to help individuals and groups get what they want; this is Polytheism. Although the people who believe this are often completely unconnected with each other, the fundamental Belief of all Polytheism, from ancient Peru to modern Japan, is the same. Polytheism is about a completely different aspect of life to any other Belief. All the other Beliefs, from Judaism to Environmentalism, concentrate on two basic questions: 'What is right and wrong?' and 'How do I live a good life?' Polytheism, in contrast, does not exist to find a meaning for life or to understand the nature of the universe; it exists to get things done, to improve the weather, to win battles, to cure diseases. Ceremonies, requests, spells and sacrifices are designed to work, to get favours delivered, to achieve something.

The Belief of all Polytheisms, from basic Animism to

elaborate Hinduism, is simple: faith in the existence of 'godlets' and belief that if you beg a godlet to help you, or if you conduct appropriate ceremonies and flatter them, you can, sometimes, get their help. But the most likely way to get what you want is to give them a present. The way you give them presents is the same in all Polytheism: by sacrificing. Also, if bad things happen to you or your group, it is because you have offended these invisible beings. They are using their magic against you and you probably need to sacrifice to get back in their favour.

A complicating factor is that, in some periods, some of the other major Beliefs have lost their founding principles and turned into Polytheism in all but name. Medieval Christianity, in a period where literacy was low and the sacred texts were in a language, Latin, that no one spoke (as a native tongue), treated 'saints' exactly as polytheistic godlets. For many years, Islam treated its saints, 'Walis', in exactly the same way, venerating them and bringing them presents. The 'Bodhisattvas' of Mahayana Buddhism are exactly the same as godlets. The acid test for Polytheism is sacrifice: if supplicants sacrifice in the hope of favours, their Belief is Polytheism, whatever the branding above the door. It seems that, when literacy is low, the driving compulsion of humanity to embrace Polytheism takes over other Beliefs, even when the polytheistic element is in direct conflict with the Belief's ethics and understanding of the world. From time to time, this has led to violent struggles to remove the polytheistic 'parasite' from these other Beliefs – the

Christian Reformation and the austerity of the Wahhabis in Islam are two examples of this discussed below.

Today, Polytheism officially commands the allegiance of roughly one-third of the population of the world, most notably in the Hinduism of India. To this can be added Shinto in Japan and the mixture of traditional Polytheism and Buddhism, loosely followed by many people in China and Southeast Asia. In addition, even today, in Beliefs like Christianity, Communism and Environmentalism, there are still strands that are very close to Polytheism in all but name, as we shall see. The polytheistic way of understanding and attempting to influence the world seems hard-wired into human society – a default Belief that returns whenever other Beliefs fade. So let us look at the ingredients of this near-compulsory Belief.

Polytheism sees the godlets as larger, invisible versions of tribal leaders or kings and works on them in the same way. If you give them something, there is a chance you might get what you want. Only a chance, though – the godlets are fickle – but at least you have done what you can. Perhaps you might also wait for a special day to give your gift to the godlet, the right moment to make your sacrifice. Godlets, like the Mafia godfather, are known to be more receptive on certain days. Not that most requests are specific. Some are, but most of the people participating in ceremonies or placing small donations of flowers in front of a shrine are doing so with a vague hope of general good luck, of continued good health, of reasonable weather for harvest, and so on.

Perhaps their expectations are even less: they just want to avoid the problems that can happen when the godlets feel they are being ignored or forgotten.

Powerful men have more influence with godlets in the same way as they have more influence with kings. They can get favours from godlets more easily than mere peasants can. So can holy men. When children in the village of Beth-El mocked the Prophet Elisha's baldness, his simple curse was all that was required for the godlet Yahweh (Judaism at the time accepted the existence of many godlets) to send two bears to maul forty-two of them[iii]. Godlets are not expected to provide answers to metaphysical questions. If these questions arise – 'Why are we here?', 'What is right and what is wrong?', 'What does my life mean?' – the answers are not sought from the godlets. They are amoral, selfish and venal beings. If anything, they are less ethical than mankind. Looking to them for the answers to the great questions of existence would be as logical as looking for the answers to such questions in car repair manuals – it is not their job.

You can ask the godlets to do either good or bad things for you: polytheistic gods don't care whether a favour is to hurt an enemy or to help a friend. But the bigger the favour you want, the bigger the sacrifice, and the more elaborate the ceremony needed to get it. This idea is a universal part of the polytheistic mind-set. So is the idea that human sacrifice is the biggest sacrifice. At the furthest extreme, the sacrifice of the king, mass human sacrifice or the sacrifice of your own (first-born, male) children is sometimes required. While human sacrifice was central to the Aztec religion, with hundreds reportedly slaughtered on special occasions, almost every variety of Polytheism has some record of human sacrifice. There are sub-cults in Hinduism that conducted human sacrifice. It happened in early Chinese history. It was common in Greece before the classical period and, although rare, it also occurred in early classical Rome[iv] too. Human sacrifice is often seen as needed only for very important favours and rarely to be used, for example, only at the start of a war or to stop a natural disaster. But when it is necessary, it is done. Culture after culture, faced with a natural disaster, turned to human sacrifice in an attempt to appease the godlets and so avert the worst consequences. The Bible says that many of Judea's kings in the historical period, long after the semi-mythical David and Solomon, conducted human sacrifices[v]. It is also accepted without question in the Torah, Bible and Qur'an that Abraham's willingness to sacrifice, that is, kill and burn his only legitimate son, was a sign of exceptional devotion to a godlet, a sacrifice worthy of earning exceptional favour. Western Christianity believes that the human sacrifice of Jesus was required to remove the otherwise indelible stain of human original sin.

Polytheistic godlets come in all sizes: from small domestic and personal godlets, through to larger tribal or 'national' godlets, and then up to godlets representing themes like the sea or sun until the king or head of the godlets is reached. Each social unit, from family to empire, has its own patron godlet. The larger the social unit, the more important and powerful is its patron godlet. This works both ways: where patron godlets help their tribes or towns to win battles, both tribe and godlet become more powerful as a result. While lesser or family godlets may only have small domestic statues or pictures kept in the home, more important godlets will have public statues and their own temples to live in. Sacrifices and celebrations relating to the godlet are centred on these temples.

Even relatively tidy pantheons (collection of godlets) still have many godlets that do not fit in. The Greek godlets are a neat group compared to the complete confusion of the Egyptian godlets, but, even so, many don't fit any pattern. Hephaestus, the godlet of fire, Demeter, the godlet of food and the harvest, Dionysus, the godlet of alcohol and dissipation, Eros, the godlet of sexual love, the Moirai (Fates), the inscrutable godlets of destiny, the Mousai (Muses), the divine beings that inspire art: none of these fit in with the 'mainstream' crowd of godlets headed by Zeus on Mount Olympus. There is very little consistency.

The character, the powers and the description of these godlets varies from tale to tale. Sometimes they are very human-style individuals; sometimes they are more like personifications of natural forces. In Scandinavian Polytheism, in one tale the godlet Thor is a hammer-wielding warrior with extra magic powers; in another tale, Thor is closer to being the spirit of the storm, of thunder and of nature's power.

Polytheisms are not exclusive and accept other

people's godlets. Some foreign godlets are seen as just different names for existing godlets or the new godlet is simply added to the existing pantheon. A good example of the political role of a godlet was shown by the actions of Cyrus the Great (Kurus), after he conquered Babylon. He went to the temple to sacrifice to the Babylonian's main god, Marduk. This was seen, not as a religious gesture (in modern terms), but as a gesture of respect to the symbols of Babylon. It showed his intention to respect the culture of the city and its people (which he did).

Despite all the sacrifices, the flattery and the grovelling, the powers of the godlets in the human world are tightly restricted. They are limited to influencing matters that could go one way or the other, matters of chance. Sacrifices and prayers are often made in the hope that the godlets will make an ill person get better, or that they will help to win a forthcoming battle, or so that they will make a season well watered. But requests to change the structure of nature are not often recorded: few people were ever sacrificed at a temple in order to grow wings and fly. Such things never happen, and so were clearly beyond the powers of the godlets. Polytheism can only work if what is requested might happen anyway, so that the sacrifice or prayer sometimes results in what you requested actually happening.

Another restriction on the powers of the godlets is destiny. Polytheistic legends presume that there is a sort of 'script' to life past, present and future and that the godlets are just as embedded in this script as we humans are. There is rarely any attempt to rationalise where the godlets' power to influence the future stops and where inexorable fate takes over. In general, their powers to alter the script, change destiny or avoid fate are limited to local and short-term changes. In consequence, polytheistic societies have completely independent systems for telling the future, for reading ahead in this script, systems that act as though the godlets did not exist. The Babylonians used the stars, the Romans looked for clues in the livers of sacrificed animals, the ancient Chinese studied the cracks on bones heated in fires and the Mayans had complex mathematical systems.

But such forecasting systems are outside the core of Polytheism, which is that there is a mechanism for obtaining supernatural favours. Because it is the process, the ritual and the gifts that matter, not the logic behind it, Polytheisms are not tidily structured; they are inconsistent, contradictory composites of multiple different elements. Stories, folk-legends, historical incidents, tales from other peoples, vague communal memories and beliefs are all mixed up together. They are put together into legends and traditions in much the same way as plants are put into flowerbeds: not because they make sense together but because they look good together.

In Polytheism, most myths of the godlets and heroes are treated purely as stories and have a limited impact on people's daily lives and thinking – much as our novels or films today have only a limited impact on us. Some polytheistic myths do relate to fundamental themes of existence and morality and a few, like the Bhagavada Gita, a section of the Hindu collection of legends known as the Mahabharata, put forward an entire philosophy of life. But even these are of little importance in Polytheism, compared to the central belief that doing certain actions can result in favours being given and failing to do them can result in 'bad luck'. The essence of Polytheism is that randomness and pointlessness are removed from life; things happen for a reason, they are caused by godlets to happen that way. Because there is a reason for things happening, we may be able to influence the course of events. We are not powerless victims of cruel chance; we are actors in a very human drama with the ability to have a part in determining our fate.

Collections of myths link the godlets to earthly heroes and earthly events. So legendary Hindu heroes such as Krishna and Rama are earthly forms of the godlet Vishnu, known as avatars. While godlets can take human form, heroes like Hercules can also become godlets when they die. All pre-literate civilisations have long and complex myths, stories that were only written down after centuries of elaboration in their verbal form. Often they are exceedingly long, bringing together different tales told over many years. The Indian Mahabharata and the Tibetan Epic of Gesar are many times longer than the Epic of Gilgamesh, the oldest legend we have, and longer than the Judean and Babylonian myths collected in the early books of the Bible. These, in turn, are far longer than the Greek *Iliad* and *Odyssey*. All these stories and collections were written down at least 400 years after the events they are based on happened, some after much longer. With all these myths, there are elements of historical fact mixed with elements that cannot be literally true. Arguing about which bits have some element of fact in them and which don't keeps scholars and writers of speculative histories in business.

Polytheisms have ceremonies for life-events such as birth, death and marriage, as well as for communal annual events, like the harvest or mid-summer. Daily, monthly or annual events are linked to godlets and their legends. These rituals often have a practical purpose and are frequently associated with the agricultural calendar. May Day in England was the main celebration of the old, pre-Roman Polytheism that continued long into the Christian era. The people danced round a phallus – the Maypole – with ribbons in the hope that the male sky-god would therefore fertilise the female earth-goddess with his rain[2]. In many Polytheisms these annual rituals are linked to a re-enactment of the core event in a godlet's mythical adventures. But Polytheisms do not have weekly services, nor do they have churches; polytheistic temples are houses for godlets to live in, not for congregations. The idea of a 'service' and a congregation only came with the exile of the Jews in Babylon, although some Hindu temples are beginning to adopt the idea from the monotheisms.

The polytheistic universe is normally divided into

---

[2] This practice continued widely in England until it was banned by the Puritans of Oliver Cromwell's time.

three layers: at the top, sky or heaven, where the godlets live; in the middle, the earth and sea, where mankind lives; and at the bottom, the underworld or Hell. Almost all Polytheisms have tales of how the world started (known as 'cosmogonies'). Often the ancestors of the main gods created the world. But these legends are never central to the Polytheism; they just sit alongside the many other legends.

As well as being a tool to deliver benefits, each Polytheism is the unifying cultural forces that define the group, the shared tales, traditions and ceremonies that define the group. Often the temples of the godlets are a town's main public buildings and their symbols become the symbols of the tribe or town. The godlets and their temples are the personification of the group, the tribe or the city. In the case of India, the Polytheism defines the state.

Polytheism does allow some variation within its strongly determined pattern. Simple hunter/gatherer tribes tend to have a simple Polytheism. Everything – each tree, stone, stream, etc. – has its own spirit/godlet. We call these types of Polytheism 'Animism'. Shamans or witch doctors that work by cursing or 'putting the evil eye' on individuals dominate some of these relatively unstructured Polytheisms. Voodoo is such a Polytheism, cursing or 'blessing' of individuals with only a minimal mythology. At the other extreme, Hinduism, with its long history and vast population, has an almost infinite complexity of myth, belief and practice.

Some Polytheisms have been much bloodier than

others, not only in human sacrifice but also in the 'instructions' of the godlets on the treatment of those captured in war and other prisoners. Sometimes this has a clear causal link. When a society experiences a sudden worsening of conditions – earthquakes, floods, etc. – the logic of Polytheism says that the godlets need extra strong pacification. That is, they need humans to be sacrificed to them. If conditions continue to deteriorate, this may become mass sacrifice, or sacrifice of especially valued people. But in other cases it seems that occasional human sacrifice or mass slaughter of the defeated was just part of the way things were done[3]. In these cases it is normally the least valuable people, prisoners-of-war and slaves, who are sacrificed.

Polytheisms differ in their views of life after death. Many see the soul continuing in the afterlife, much as it does in this world. To keep and serve their soul after their death, leaders in many polytheistic societies have their goods – and sometimes their servants – buried with them. We see this pattern across several completely disconnected early peoples in Europe, Asia and Africa, as well as on into the historical period in both Egypt and China. In India, however, it has long been taken for granted that the spirit is endlessly reborn in this world,

---

[3] In the Bible, for example, during the early polytheistic phase of belief, the Prophet Samuel instructs King Saul to kill every single member of the Amalek tribe, including women, children and animals (1 Samuel 15:3). Because Saul (initially) spared the king, Agag and some of the animals, the Lord decided to deprive him of his kingdom (1 Samuel 15:28), even though Samuel then 'hewed Agag in pieces before the Lord'.

although as a 'higher' or 'lower' person or creature. In China it has been assumed that the dead continue to exist and interest themselves – from time to time, at any rate – in this world. They can affect events to some degree as well, so they need to be kept on side by the living. In the Mayan and Roman Polytheisms, there is only a vague shadowy half-life after death – except for the elite, who can become godlets. But, even in the way they approach death, no Polytheism seems to speculate much on the purpose of life, either in this world or the next. In India, and in a few other Polytheisms at times, there is an idea of good deeds increasing your chances of a good afterlife or rebirth. This idea is referred to as 'karma', but, as with the systems for forecasting the future, there seems very little link between this idea and the other aspects of the Polytheism.

All Beliefs keep some polytheistic aspect: some magic delivery of worldly benefits, even if it embarrasses their intellectual followers. Catholic Christianity still retains a strong polytheistic aspect. The faithful hope that, by burning candles (which used to be very expensive), chanting prayers of fawning flattery and giving presents of various sorts to the Virgin or saints, they will bring their supernatural intervention to help the petitioner in this world. For a considerable period, until the criticism and violence of Wahhabi thought, the same veneration of saints (Wali) and symbols was common in Islam. Nationalism's reverence for symbols, Communism's reverence for early prophets, such as Marx and Lenin, and Environmentalism's fondness for linking disaster to previous indulgence, all have a strong smell of Polytheism about them. Going the other way, some modern polytheistic religions also have sects that have taken a more spiritual turn, such as those Hindu sects that put the spiritual poem of the Bhagavada Gita at the centre of their religion. But this overlap should not blur the principle that Polytheism is about achieving favours from supernatural beings, while the God religions focus on the purpose to life.

Before turning to the important issues of priests, there is the odd reflection that Polytheism is the principal precursor not of other Beliefs, but of science, which, in its focus on achieving results in this world, it more closely resembles. There is a clear line of progression from wizardry, to alchemy, to chemistry, for example. It may be unexpected, but the polytheistic faith, that everything has a comprehensible cause, is the same as the central proposition of science. Science is based on the belief that there is a reason for things happening and that, by studying and understanding these reasons, we may be able to influence them. Science is distinguished from Polytheism, not by its fundamental proposition, which is the same, but by its methods, its care and its honesty. Consequently, following the rigorously tested ideas of science is far more effective in changing the world than following the tales of Polytheism. Because science and Polytheism are about the same things, that is, about the material world and what happens in it, they are in conflict. It is only where there are polytheistic remnants in other Beliefs, such as Christianity, where they still offer magic, that science has come into conflict with contemporary Beliefs. Science has no conflict with the ethical or spiritual teaching of any Belief.

Polytheism has two different types of religious leaders: in some, the religious leaders are just seen as normal people, whose religious authority comes from their post. Greek/Roman Polytheism had such religious leaders; the head of the Roman religious, known as the 'Pontifex Maximus', was a political/administrative job, much like any other. In other strands of Polytheism, there are people who have extra powers that make them different to normal people, intermediaries between the godlets and mankind called 'priests'. For these forms of Polytheism and for the later Beliefs that keep priests, only priests can successfully conduct religious ceremonies. If non-priests conduct them they are invalid and do not 'work'.

Although priests were developed originally in Polytheisms, they carried on through into some later Beliefs. Originally, priests existed independently of any particular Belief; in Polytheism their special powers or special knowledge gives them influence with some or all godlets. The priests of Iran, known as the Magi, came before the Zoroastrian religion they were later associated with and seem to have been flexible about what religion they served when politically necessary and, even today, the Magi tradition of priestly dominance remains with the Shi'a priesthood of Iran. In the early Biblical legends, when the ancestors of the Jews felt that the traditional tribal godlet, Yahweh, was not delivering, they looked for a new godlet and created a golden calf to worship. But Aaron, the High Priest, remained High Priest for this godlet as well. The Pope, the head of the Catholic Church, keeps and still uses the title 'Pontifex Maximus' from the Roman polytheistic head priest.

People become priests by heredity or by initiation or both. In ancient Israel and Judea, for example, the priesthood was hereditary in the Levi family, with the Chief Priest required to prove descent from Aaron himself. Today, both types of priesthood continue: Hinduism and the Ismaili form of Shi'a Islam have hereditary priesthoods, while Catholic Christianity creates priests purely by initiation.

Priesthoods inevitably have their own agendas, especially if they are hereditary, promoting issues that affect them as a caste. Much of Hinduism is organised to maintain the privileges and pay of the Brahmin caste of priests. Some of the old Indian religious texts are only supposed to be read by Brahmins (and most certainly should not be read by women). Chiefs and aristocracies have often supported the idea of a priesthood, because having special and different religious people makes having special and different chiefs and aristocracies more understandable. But there is also a history of struggle between priests and aristocracies. The priests of Egypt often contended for power with the pharaohs – some claim that Akhenaten's extraordinary attempt to introduce some form of one-God belief around 1320BCE was, in part, an attempt to recapture power from the priesthood. Even today, in India, priests have managed to build a caste for themselves and their families that stands above all others. The Magi in Iran were in a constant power struggle with secular rulers and the tradition of clerical involvement in politics is still central to Iran today, even though the Belief involved has changed from the original Polytheism through Zoroastrianism to the Shi'a form of Islam – so much so that the only country where priests officially wield supreme power today is Iran (apart from the Vatican City). But in other countries the political power of priests can be considerable. The Saudi royal family are all descended from the founder of the extremist Wahhabi movement and so are something like hereditary Chief Priests.

But it is not only in Islamic states that priests may gain power. In Ireland, for much of the twentieth century, the Catholic priesthood held a position of power above the law. In the USA, priests have constantly sought power at the level of the states and have had some notable successes. The US Constitution guards against religious take-over, but priests have used the issue of abortion (on which the Christian faith itself has no defined position) as a proxy to avoid the prohibition on religious politics. Tibet had (mostly) religious rulers, although Buddhist priestly rule in Tibet was often rackety, violent and autocratic. But in 1951 it was taken over by the Communist Party of Mao Zedong, and the religious feudal system, slavery and serfdom were all abolished.

Polytheism has an immensely powerful gut attraction to many ordinary people, promising them a way they can influence the forces that control their lives. But it has a very weak appeal to reason, as thoughtful people are well able to see that there is no link greater than chance between polytheistic sacrifices and the outcomes they are supposed to influence. People like Confucius and Aristotle had little time for the legends of Polytheism as long ago as 500-400BCE, except as part of their common cultural heritage. But, at the same time, many sceptics retained a nervous respect for polytheistic practices, much as sophisticated people today may avoid flying on the thirteenth of the month or walking under a ladder.

Simple Polytheism is in decline today. Most Hindus happily go along with their traditional, polytheistic practices, seeing them as their cultural heritage, but draw on elements of the tradition – and there are many of them in Hinduism – that emphasise the allegorical nature of worshipping the traditional Gods as a means to a more profound insight. Shinto in Japan and Chinese traditional religion are almost entirely seen as cultural traditions in the same way. In the West this same visceral, mild Polytheism is retained in Christian traditions included in other Beliefs. At one level this is the simple magic of rural Christianity.

At a more disturbing level, though, the polytheistic urge for human sacrifice to avert disaster or to atone for a failing appears to continue below the surface even today. Was the slaughter of the Jews (and others) by the Nazis, partially, a human sacrifice to prevent the repetition of or atone for the death of millions of Germans of the First World War? Did the catastrophic death of millions in the Soviet collectivisation of the farms in 1927–30 generate a polytheistic need for the atonement of human sacrifice, met by the purges of Communist party officials in the

Great Terror after 1934? Could the destruction of intellectuals in the Chinese 'Cultural Revolution' from 1965 be, in part at least, a similar polytheistic sacrifice/atonement for the slaughter of the 'Great Leap Forward' that ended in 1961? Perhaps not, but the three twentieth century pairings of mass deaths followed by ritualised human slaughter make an odd coincidence.

Some Environmentalists also have polytheistic-style beliefs, seeing great storms as the punishment for failing to placate the (spirits of the) environment. Others seek the construction of wind-turbines, which are known to be wholly ineffective at a practical level but, as polytheistic symbols of our concern, could work to stave off the anger of Nature at being disregarded. The true extent of the polytheistic urge to sacrifice someone or some people after a catastrophe is hidden at the moment and will only be seen in the response to major disasters.

Written religion, science and scepticism have left everyday Polytheism as little more than tradition. However, whenever a catastrophe is followed by the hunt for 'the guilty', it looks, in part at least, like the polytheistic urge to human sacrifice returning. While we can be grateful that there have been few major catastrophes to test this in living memory, one will come; and then the human polytheistic desire for human sacrifice may again be unstoppable. What disaster will trigger the next Great Terror, the next Holocaust or the next Cultural Revolution and what excuse will be given this time?

Postscript: Why write?

It seems that, without writing, Polytheism is the only Belief that humanity can retain. Pre-literate people must have thought about the metaphysical questions and issues of right and wrong, but, until they started writing about them, we cannot know what their thoughts were. It may seem odd to us now, but people didn't start to write about the questions of existence or of right and wrong for two thousand years after writing itself was developed – apart from the limited amount that can be gleaned from legends, royal boasting and the occasional poem. However, this becomes more understandable when we start asking who pays for the writing.

Writing first emerged in the Middle East from symbols used to mark ownership. By around 3000BCE the first 'writing' was used in accounting records, with numbers linked to pictures. An early use was to list the land and animals owned by the temple; for example, the number 23 followed by an ox's head. The ancient Semitic word for ox was 'Aleph' and the ox's head symbol rapidly became stylised to make it faster to draw. Later it mutated into the Greek letter 'Alpha', our capital 'A', indicating an 'ay' or 'ah' sound. The 5,000-year-old ox head symbol led directly to the shape of our capital 'A' today.

For around 2,000 years after its invention in ancient Iraq, writing was only used for matters of record: official writing such as deeds of ownership, laws, diplomatic treaties, commercial agreements and proclamations of victories. In addition, 'temple writing' was important: the words of magic prayers, incantations and songs that had to be got right to make them 'work'. Writing was used only when something needed to be recorded – needed in the sense that someone was willing to pay handsomely for it to be recorded. This is not surprising when we think about the cost and time needed to make one copy of a document, let alone a copy of a book. The first five books of the Bible, known as the Torah ('Instruction') to Jews, are still today sometimes hand-written on a scroll for use in synagogues. It typically takes about 2,000 hours – a year's work – for a trained scribe to complete. So, in today's money, one copy of the Torah would cost around £30,000.

Scribing – reading and writing – was a profession, like carpentry. Probably, no one thought that a king's or lord's child should be taught to scribe any more than they thought to teach them woodwork. Unless you were a scribe yourself, you had to pay a substantial sum to get something written down. Certainly anything longer than a letter would cost a lot. So writing done for ordinary people, as opposed to official or temple writing, was almost entirely limited to property deeds, letters and epitaphs for rich men's tombs.

In the Middle East, the first area to develop writing, all of it was 'official' writing, with a very limited number of exceptions we have found before 800BCE. A document known as the Maxims of Ptahhotep, written in Egypt before 2000BCE, is a long list of conservative sayings, addressed from an older man to a younger man, although that makes it a bit like both law and liturgy. (It is pleasing that a key theme of the first popular writing – and it was popular enough for several copies to have survived the millennia – is that 'young people don't respect their elders anymore'.[4]) There are also one or two instruction manuals, for example, on the care of horses. There is a particularly lengthy tale of Pharaoh Tuthmoses III (1490–1436BCE) campaign on the walls of the Temple of Amon-Re at Karnak that almost forms a narrative. In addition, there are a few letters, love poems and occasional comments on the back of official papers that seem to have been written by scribes in their down-time. In general, though, it took a very long time before people wrote down their myths or philosophic thoughts. This applies equally to Chinese writing. Although the use of characters in inscriptions and oracles is very old – and it may be older than the first Sumerian writing – the first examples of continuous writing of more than just a few characters date from no earlier than the Warring States period (475–221BCE). Both Indian and American writing arrived a little later.

We must also not run away with the idea that people read fluently as we do now, even if they were professional

---

[4] The Maxims of Ptahhotep have an amazing similarity in feeling and subject matter to the much later Chinese Analects of Confucius. Perhaps it is unsurprising that older folk, desiring to make the young responsible and thoughtful, adopt the same line and tone. Doubtless, they were equally effective.

scribes. Before printing was developed, virtually no one read fluently – even the best readers read one word at a time, speaking it out loud. Books were always rare and extremely expensive. We forget that our fluent reading takes several years to acquire in a world filled with writing in books, on screens and on signs. In the ancient world much of the reading done was aloud to groups, where the written word acted as an aid, jogging the memory of a long-practised and rehearsed piece, rather than being read word by word. Even the classical Greeks used the term 'hearing' for getting information from a book. As late as 383CE, St Augustine, a literary giant himself, was so amazed at seeing someone read without sounding the words that he told everyone about it in his autobiography. *'When he read,'* said Augustine, *'his eyes scanned the page and his heart sought out the meaning, but his voice was silent and his tongue was still.'*[5]

When only professional scribes can read or write, who is going to pay for stories, history or philosophy to be written? Stories can be told and ideas discussed with no need for writing. Writing is slow and expensive. Before printing, once your story or thought was written, you have only one copy and what use is that? It just contains material you know yourself. You would have to be very confident to send your one expensive copy to

---

[5]   This was Ambrose, Archbishop of Milan, who had had the most expensive education in the last period of widespread European literacy before the reformation

someone else, and they would probably have to pay a scribe to read it to them. To get another copy made takes the same time and the same cost again. Moreover, the material to write on is often itself expensive – like vellum – or heavy and brittle – like clay slabs. On top of all this, only specialist, trained scribes could read what was written anyway. Finally, assuming that you have the skill to write, or the wealth to pay a scribe to do so, what benefit is it to you to write, apart from occasional letters or legal business? Few can read and even fewer can afford a book, and there are no author's royalties. You know hardly anyone outside your town or area anyway, so there are very few people you can't either speak to personally or send a messenger to with a verbal message.

By contrast, the art of memorising stories and of professional storytelling was well established. All the ancient civilisations had wandering storytellers who made a living telling the great tales to the people in the long, dark nights. This art is largely lost today, although there are still people who memorise the whole Qur'an (77,701 words) and earn the title 'Hafiz'.

On top of all these barriers to writing stories or thoughts there is the conceptual block. Because writing was created and existed only for legal and accounting matters, it seemed completely unfitted to the task of recording narrative material. If we had only the example of legal and accounting writing, the idea that we could tell a tale with these tools would seem as unlikely as telling them with numbers. Might as well ask a chartered surveyor to paint the *Adoration of the Magi*.

So, before widespread literacy, there were many reasons not to write down long stories. Yet it did, finally, happen, more than 2,000 years after the first writing in Sumer. The Judeans and the Greeks, separately, started writing down their stories, legends, histories and philosophy. The first stories of the Bible/Torah were written down shortly after 800BCE, followed quite quickly by the writings of the Judean prophets. The *Iliad* and *Odyssey* of Greece were written down slightly later, we now think around 760–710BCE. Both these documents recorded earlier oral sources, possibly much earlier. The reasons why the Judeans and Israelites wrote their legends down at this particular time are suggested in the next section. The reason for writing the *Iliad* and *Odyssey* down is less clear, although it may have been because they were intended to be performed by a cast, rather than as previously by one 'rhapsode', professional storyteller, thus also starting the Greek enthusiasm for plays.[vi]

Although the Epic of Gilgamesh, or parts of it, is immensely old – there are references to it that date before 2000BCE – it was only written down for the library of the bookish King Ashurbanipal of Babylon (c.685–627BCE). No other material is in the competition for earliest written legend; for example, the Hindu Vedas, which may also be very ancient, remained in the oral tradition until they were written down around 300BCE at the earliest.

The existence of these first narrative writings seems to have encouraged literacy to spread beyond just professional scribes in both Judea and Greece. Indeed, the existence and huge popularity of these early literary writings can be said to have made the idea of 'Greece' itself come into being, by standardising the Greek language and providing common cultural references. Without such written sources, languages drift apart, accents become dialects and develop separately on to mutual incomprehensibility. By 500BCE, literacy was common among Greeks, so exactly the same language was used across a wide area, producing the great flowering of classical Greek writing but also making Greek the language of trade across the eastern Mediterranean. Without the anchor of the *Iliad* and *Odyssey* it is doubtful whether the Greek culture could have spread so far or dominated their cultural world so much. Even then, some illiterate people, like Socrates, opposed it. Plato quotes him[vii]: '*Their* [literate people's] *trust in writing, produced by external characters that are no part of themselves, will discourage the use of their own memory within them.*'[6]

So powerful was this common language and culture that the two empires that conquered classical Greece were both culturally assimilated into the Greek world, even before their conquest of the country. The

---

[6] Socrates obviously could write nothing, but Plato was from a wealthy family, so could afford to have his version of Socrates' conversations written down. By being the first to have his thoughts put in writing, Socrates has gained a reputation for wisdom, despite coming across in the actual writing as a crashing bore with extreme right-wing views.

Macedonians struggled, but finally became accepted as 'Greeks', even as they politically absorbed Greece. Under Alexander the Great, the Macedonians/Greeks conquered as far as India but always found that Greek language and culture had gone before them, at least in trading cities. While the Romans never took on the Greek language in Rome itself, they adopted it for the eastern half of their empire, modified their pantheon of gods to match the Greek pattern, one for one, and devised stories of how the Roman people came originally from Troy, a city within the historic area of Greek culture.

So the first books of the Bible, the Torah, and the *Iliad/Odyssey* are, by a long way, the earliest writing of legends or history and, probably because of this, they are also, by far, the most influential collections of stories ever written. It is fair to say that almost every aspect of European culture derives directly from the cultures of the first two story-writings: Judea's Torah and Greece's *Iliad*. The reward for being the first to take writing outside its earlier, limited use is for the early Jews and classical Greeks to be jointly credited with the foundation of Western thought and for their writings to be treated as holy writ.

Writing had another key effect on Beliefs. Long before the first stories were written, prayers, holy songs and magic incantations had been set in writing. Because these holy words are in a specific language – presumably the language the relevant godlets speak – it seemed wrong to translate them. Ancient Sumerian continued to be used as a religious language for more than a thousand years after it had stopped being spoken in everyday life. The same preservation of a holy language, incomprehensible to the ordinary faithful, happened many times: in Western Christianity with Latin, in Egyptian Christianity with Coptic, in Russian Christianity with Old Church Slavonic[7], in the Sanskrit of the Hindu Vedas, the Hebrew and Aramaic of the Talmud, the Avestan language of the Zoroastrian Gathas, and the Buddhist Sutras in Sanskrit and old Chinese. Such specialist religious languages can be used to keep the holy writing away from the inspection of non-priests and potential sceptics. Sometimes this subtle concealment allows even the oddest material to be accepted as holy.

The ability to read, and especially the ability to read the holy language, became a key source of authority and power for priests of all kinds and, in the case of China, also for government. The ability to read at all, in an almost entirely illiterate society, is close to magic, let alone the ability to read holy mysteries buried in an incomprehensible tongue. The monopoly possession of this power was a key way in which priesthoods were able to demonstrate their difference and superiority. When the words written and read out are also incomprehensible, because they are in a different language, the power and separateness of those who can understand this material is greater indeed, while the incomprehensible noises of

[7] The Greek Orthodox Church got around the problem that many scriptures are in a language comprehensible to its congregation by requiring that they be spoken 'inaudibly' (kryptikos) in the liturgy.

the ritual language can embody a feeling of unworldliness that common speech cannot match. Many English-speaking Christians today find the antique language of the King James Version of the Bible more 'holy-sounding' than more immediately comprehensible translations.

So writing and reading are fundamental to Beliefs. The founding of the first new religion itself was a direct result of the first narrative writing...

.3.

JUDAISM:
THE STUBBORNNESS
OF THE HILL PEOPLE

Judaism is a term that covers three generations or iterations of a Belief. The first generation was 922–587BCE and confined to the small kingdoms of Israel and Judea. It was a period when one of the godlets, Yahweh, was selected not just to be the main godlet of Judeans but their *only* godlet. The second generation of the Belief arose in Babylon after 587BCE and was the first religion to have regular services, religious buildings other than houses for the godlets and worship other than sacrifices and requests. The third generation came after the destruction of the Jerusalem Temple in 72CE, with the creation, again mostly in Babylon, of the Talmud, a gigantic compendium of holy books that ramble on about every aspect of a Jew's life. A fourth phase possibly started with the foundation of Israel in 1947.

Not only were the Judeans and their sister people, the Israelites, the first in the world to write down the oral traditions of the tribe, but they did it twice, with both versions written at much the same time. It seems that there was a competition between the two countries' temples, each with its own priesthood, each at the centre of the two kingdoms. The main Israelite Temple was at their capital, Samaria; the main Judean one was at their capital, Jerusalem. This unusual arrangement of two competing kingdoms sharing the same religion/culture, seems to have prompted the idea of writing down their tribal legends in the first place. Each wrote a version of history showing that Yahweh, the tribal godlet they shared, favoured their particular kingdom/capital/priesthood/style of worship. Writing the stories down gave each side a version of the long-established, main stories to support their case.

So all the early stories of the Bible, the gripping legends that still resonate today – the Garden of Eden, Noah's flood, the escape of the Israelites from Egypt, etc. – were written twice: once from a Judean point of view, where the godlet is known throughout as Yahweh, and once from the Israelite point of view, where the godlets are called 'Elohim' and the chief godlet 'El', until he reveals his name to Moses (the Judean version is known as 'J', the Israelite one as 'E'). These stories were edited together in Judea after the Kingdom of Israel was defeated by the Assyrians in 722BC and their country reduced to a dependency of the Assyrian empire. The 'editing' was unusual in that both versions were chopped into bits and then stuck together, interwoven with each other, but with very little deleted – to make a curiously repetitive and, sometimes, contradictory merged document.

Although they were written twice, none of these legends appear to be supported by evidence any more than any other ancient legend from any country. Despite much study, no evidence for the existence or actions of Abraham, Isaac, Joseph, Moses, David or Solomon has ever been found, any more than it has for Achilles, Lord Rama or Thor. In these stories, the exact status of Yahweh[8] varied, as it tends to do in all Polytheisms. He was generally accepted in the wider region as one of the second-rank godlets, married to Asherah and junior to the leader of the godlets, El. The name Israel (Yisra-el) itself means 'persevere with El'. Originally, Yahweh was far from being the exclusive godlet of Israel and Judea. According to the Bible, Solomon, the legendary last King of the combined Israel and Judea, built a temple dedicated to Yahweh on the top of Mount Zion (Jerusalem); he also built altars dedicated to Ashtoreth, Goddess of Sidon, and the godlets Chemosh and Moloch on other mountaintop sites[viii] like any other normal king of the time.

In 722BCE the kingdom of Israel fell to the Assyrians and, in a move common at the time, the Assyrians sent the leadership of the defeated Israelite kingdom, around 27,000 people, into exile in another part of the empire, in what is now south-eastern Turkey[ix]. But the vast majority of Israelites remained where they were, worshipping and sacrificing to Yahweh at his temple in

---

[8] Written in Hebrew as YHWH. Early written Hebrew has no vowels.

Samaria as they had done for centuries and would continue to do so for many centuries to come. The idea that there were ten 'Lost Tribes of Israel' is unfounded and their later history is given briefly below[9].

Judea had escaped conquest by the Assyrians in a campaign shortly after the one that defeated Israel (720BCE) and retained some small independence, paying tribute as an Assyrian client state. Yahweh, the main godlet of the Jerusalem Temple, was credited with this escape and his status took a big turn upwards as a result. The king who held off the Assyrians was Hezekiah (715–686BCE) and thereafter determinedly supported Yahweh as the only godlet of Judea and during his long reign.

It is difficult to overstate the insignificance of this statelet of Judea. The people, who, all together, would not have filled a modern major sports stadium even half-full, scraped a living in the dry, demanding hills because they did not have the power to move to the richer, flat land that lay between them and the Mediterranean Sea. Another tribe, called the Palestinians or Philistines, occupied these lands – the words 'Philistine' and 'Palestinian' are different translation spellings of the same word[10]. Not only did they have better agricultural land

---

[9] The idea of the ten lost tribes comes from the Book of 2 Esdras, an Apocryphal and very dodgy composite Jewish/Christian apocalyptic book written by several hands sometime around 600 years later.

[10] Yes, groups under the same two names are still fighting and shouting over the same bits of land today, 2,600 years later. They had been at it for at least 400 years before this as well.

but also the Palestinians sat on several key trade routes both on land and sea, and so had much more contact with the wider world than the hill people. Ironically, most of the original area of Judea now forms the southern part of the current Palestinian 'state' and the original area of the Palestinians is now mostly in Israel.

Returning to King Hezekiah, he focused Judea heavily onto the cult of Yahweh and made the temple at Jerusalem the only legal place to sacrifice. During Hezekiah's rule, not only were the two previous versions of the legends 'J' and 'E' combined (or 'redacted') together but a third version, called 'P', was also written. 'P' also included the priestly rules and tribal lists that had been written down earlier (typically, rules and accounting documents were written long before narratives). It was during this period that Judean prophets first started writing down their prophecies. These, the first writing with known authors, are Amos, Hosea, Isaiah and Micah. They are not unusual for being prophets – indeed, at one point Amos denies that he is a member of the Prophets Union[x], so they were not scarce – but it is unique that their thoughts were written down and shows how the idea of literacy had become part of Judaic life.

But after Hezekiah, his son and grandson reverted to normal Polytheism and included several godlets in their religious activities. Under their rule, more than fifty years combined, the temple at Jerusalem had devotional statues for several different godlets[xi], following the older traditions.

After their death an eight-year-old came to the throne

and this young king, Josiah, swung heavily to support the 'Yahweh-only' group again. During his long reign of thirty-one years this had a powerful effect on the religion of the Judeans. Together with Yahweh's chief priest, Hilkiah, he set about destroying the hill-altars of the other godlets, renewing Yahweh's temple in Jerusalem, and removing all non-Yahweh material from it. As you might expect for such a small group, the temple, originally built by Solomon, was not very large, around 30 metres long by 9 wide and 13.5 tall – similar to a smallish church perhaps.

During the course of refurbishing the temple[11] Hilkiah 'found' a crucial scroll, hidden in the walls but exposed, he said, by the works[xii]. This lost scroll, apparently written centuries earlier by Moses, a legendary hero of the tribe, held the law Yahweh had given him. It also threatened that the tribe would be thrown out of their land if they allowed sacrifices to be made to any other godlet. This scroll was some or all of what became the Biblical book of Deuteronomy (the writer of this is known as 'D'). Following its discovery, the ceremony of Pesach (Passover) was celebrated for the first time as a central part of the new practice. (The Bible actually says Pesach was celebrated for the first time since the period of the Judges some 4–500 years earlier.[xiii])

Tradition also has it that Hilkiah wrote the history of

---

[11] Some of the supposedly 'lost tribes of Israel' contributed to the repairs. 2 Chron 34:9.

Judea, which we now have in the Bible, called the Book of Kings and the books of Joshua, Judges and Samuel. These, unsurprisingly, make the international role of the kings of Judea appear a great deal more important than it was in fact and stress the theme that sacrifice and attention to Yahweh alone bring success and victory in battle. So, by the end of Josiah's reign, the material of the Torah, the first five books of the Bible, was all in existence, albeit in three separate books: the combined books of J and E, P and D. In addition, a library of other matters – the histories called the books of Samuel and Kings and the first prophets – existed. All these pointed to Yahweh as the only godlet for the Hill People of Judea.

There was a problem, however, with the idea that Hill People were the chosen people of Yahweh as, transparently, other peoples, such as the Assyrians, were more powerful than them. Did this imply that their godlets were more powerful than Yahweh? The answer was no; Yahweh was just angry at the repeated betrayals of his people going off after other godlets. The Book of Kings is critical of the repeated deviation of the people and their kings 'whoring' after other godlets, and sees clearly that the wrath of Yahweh causes the failures that kept Judea so weak. It is worth noting that at no point is it suggested that other godlets do not exist; it is clearly assumed that they do – just that Judeans should avoid them and stick exclusively with their tribal godlet, Yahweh.

Perhaps emboldened by his record of strict devotion to Yahweh, in 610BCE Josiah decided to take on the

Pharaoh of Egypt, who was moving his army north along the coast to support the Assyrians who were fighting in Iraq. Josiah was defeated and killed.

Perhaps Josiah's reforms would not have made much difference had his kingdom stayed together. Later kings might again have reverted to Polytheism after what happened to him, or the kingdom could just have puttered on until the distinctive people vanished without trace as the Israelites did 900 years later (see below). But the kingdom did not carry on. Thirteen years after Josiah's death, Judea fell to the King of Babylon, Nebuchadnezzar, who had earlier taken over the Assyrian Empire.

Following their victory, the Babylonians made a unique, bizarre and hugely significant decision. Leading citizens of Judea who might make trouble were, as usual, selected for exile, just as had happened to the Israelite leaders 125 years before. But Nebuchadnezzar decided to exile the Judeans to his capital, Babylon, rather than, as usual, to some remote part of the empire. For some unknown reason, the hillbillies of Judea were being sent to the largest, oldest and richest city in the world.

At this stage Babylon was already over 1,500 years old. Its famous law-giving king, Hammurabi, had flourished over a thousand years before the Judeans arrived. It was the centre of the most civilised part of the world. It already had a longer history as a major city than London or Beijing has today. It was a genuine city as well, possibly the only one in the world at the time. Estimates of its population at the time vary a lot – but only from 200,000 upwards.

The Babylonians left one of Josiah's grandsons as

tributary king of a shrunken Judea. He revolted a few years later and, in 589BCE, nine years after his first siege, Nebuchadnezzar again re-entered Jerusalem. This time he destroyed Jerusalem utterly and it seems to have remained uninhabited. More of the people were exiled to Babylon. In addition to the exiles in Babylon, much of the rest of the population of Judea fled to Egypt during these prolonged wars. As a result, most of the population of the hill country appear to have left their tribal area and gone to live in the two most civilised and developed powers of the world. Would they vanish into the local populations in their areas of exile as those Israelites who had been exiled earlier had done?

You might have thought that the defeat of their king, the destruction of their capital and temple, and the scattering of their people might shake the Judeans' faith in themselves as the chosen people of Yahweh or in Yahweh's power; but it did not. On the contrary, with their temple gone, they clung to and developed their religion to suit their position as a separate tribe that found itself in the long-established, sophisticated and rich urban contexts of Babylon and Egypt. Before the temple in Jerusalem was destroyed, the people of Judea could simply go to the temple to make a sacrifice. Now all they were left with was their writings and with these they were able to form a new kind of Belief: the second generation of Judaism.

The 'exiles' did well in Babylon, despite the laments recorded in the Bible. Many Jews, as we may now call them, settled in a suburb of Babylon called Springhill,

'Tel Aviv' in Hebrew, and many of them prospered – the city of Tel Aviv in modern Israel is named after it. There was an important Jewish community in Babylon for over a thousand years, through many vicissitudes – it was also in Babylon later that the third phase of Judaism was based with the creation of the Talmud (see below). Then, when Baghdad became the capital of the region, 1,300 years later, it inherited the large Jewish community. They remained there for another thousand years, until the 1940s, when the Jewish community was forced to move to Israel. The final ending of the original 'exile' was in living memory.

Returning to the start of the Exile, after 589BCE, the first five books of the Bible, the Torah (it means roughly 'Teaching'), were edited together in Babylon in the early years of the Exile[xiv] by pulling together the existing three documents, the already combined J/E, P and D. The new Jewish belief started in Babylon, tailored to the new needs of exile, largely from Hilkiah's scroll (D), found so shortly before.

The other group of Judeans, who had fled to Egypt, also settled there. They formed another substantial and long-lived community in the only other ancient, urbanised part of the world. From this time on, the majority of Jews, as we may now call them, have lived outside Judea. They are known as the Jewish 'Diaspora', from the Greek word meaning a scattering. This situation, as an urban minority, explains why the religion they developed was so distinctive and different to any previous religion: a unique response to a unique situation.

In both centres of the Diaspora, in Babylon and in the city later called Alexandria in Egypt, the Jews retained their identity and their religion developed. With the guidance of figures like Jeremiah in Egypt and Ezra in Babylon (and, later, in Jerusalem), the scriptures were refined and finalised. The core of the old religion had been typically polytheistic – animal sacrifices at hill temples. These had now been removed from them, so the laws and writings became the new core of their religion. The new religion defined the Jewish people and excluded non-Jews. It made them a chosen people, a people who must observe rules of behaviour and diet that keep them separate. The law forbade sharing in the ceremonies of godlets, even the godlet of the city, although the exclusivity was not perfect, as the traditional 'Jewish' name, Mordechai, shows – it means 'Servant of Marduk', the main Babylonian godlet. The new religion also set up the complex and restrictive rules surrounding the day of the Sabbath. Without a temple, the community met in a special building on the Sabbath, meetings that became the world's first regular communal religious services in the first ever congregational religious building. The first 'Belief of the Book' had been created.

Not only was much of the material of the early Bible pulled together for the first time in Babylon, but also the writing itself developed. For the first time marks were added to show the vowel sounds. Previously only consonants had been written and writing had acted more as an aid to memory of existing songs, rules, etc., rather than providing new information. The lack of defined vowel sounds did not matter when people knew which word was referred to from the context and how the word was pronounced from its daily use in spoken language. With the new writing, you could tell how to pronounce a word even if you had not previously heard it – important when the laws needed to be unambiguous and because Hebrew was rapidly becoming only a second language for many Jews. It was about this time that the Jews also stopped using the name 'Yahweh' for their godlet, preferring to simply use titles such as 'Lord' ('Adonai' in Hebrew) to refer to him.

Much of the older written material from Judea consists mainly of lists of the members of the tribes (the Book of Numbers) and old rules for the priesthood (the Book of Leviticus) that were included in the 'P' source. These books show the primitive quality of the older religion before Deuteronomy and the Exile. For example, with sacrificed animals, Leviticus demands that you must burn the *'two kidneys and the fat which is on them'*. Kidney fat is mentioned in Leviticus chapter 3, verse 4; and twice in verse 9, and twice in verse 14, and twice in verse 15 and again in verse 17, and in several other chapters as well. Not the most spiritual of documents.

The ancient legends of the Middle East, as well as the tales of other peoples of the region, provided 'J' and 'E' with stories that now form the first part of Genesis, the first book of the Bible – stories such as the tower of Babel and Noah's flood. Among these is the story of the creation (from 'P') that forms the first two chapters of the Bible – the ones that start, in the King James Version:

'*In the beginning God created heaven and earth.*' The Bible was originally written in Hebrew and the word used here is 'Elohim', a plural word meaning 'the godlets'. The Hebrew word for a single godlet is 'El' (also used for the chief godlet). The –im ending was and is (masculine) plural in Hebrew and all related Semitic languages.[12] A lot of special pleading has been used to try to justify treating 'Elohim' here as the singular 'God'. In writings of a later period it is sometimes used as though it were singular, but, here, the end of the passage removes any doubt that it is intended to refer to the 'Gods', plural; in the King James Version it reads, '*Let us make man in our image…*'[xv] So the Bible in English should start '*In the beginning the Gods created heaven and earth…*' giving a much clearer picture of Judaism at this period as a religion linked to one godlet, while accepting the existence of many.

The alternative story of the origin of humankind comes from the writer of 'J'[xvi]. This is the story of Adam, Eve, the serpent and the Tree of Knowledge in the third chapter of Genesis and comes more directly from the ancient tradition – it is one of the only two stories in the Bible to have talking animals[13]. It provides a better idea of how much, in the old religion before the Exile in Babylon, Yahweh was seen as a traditional, human-with-

---

[12] For example: Cherub-Cherubim, Goy-Goyim, in Hebrew, Bedu-Bedouin in Arabic.

[13] The other is the story of Balaam's ass.

super-powers godlet. Yahweh is walking in the Garden of Eden '*in the cool of the day*' when Adam and Eve hear him and hide amongst the trees. So Yahweh shouts, '*Where art thou?*' They come out and Yahweh discovers that Adam and Eve have disobeyed him by eating the fruit he had forbidden them to eat and he curses them with the many evils of life, including, for women, birth pains and domination by men and, for men, poor soil. Mysteriously, though, he also makes them clothes and says, '*Behold, the man is become as one of us, to know good and evil...*'

Returning to the story of the Jews, they now have their new Belief largely complete, and are generally making a good living in the suburbs of the largest and richest city in the world. Forty-eight years after the start of the Exile in Babylon, in 538BCE, the opportunity came for the exiles of Babylon to move back to Jerusalem. This was after the Persian king, Cyrus the Great (Kurus), took over the Babylonian Empire and allowed all previously exiled people to return if they wanted to[14]. But very few Jews were willing to abandon Babylon to return to the remote hills of their parents and grandparents. So it was only a small party that made the journey back to Judea the following year, getting to the ruins of Jerusalem in 537BCE. The locals already in the area were mostly Israelites, who still worshipped Yahweh at the temple in

---

[14] A contemporary cylinder seal of this announcement is in the British Museum.

Samaria, the former capital of the Kingdom of Israel. They offered to help the newly returned Jews to build a new temple on Mount Zion but were told to go away, as they were not Jewish.[xvii] After that, the Israelites saw the incoming Jews not as returnees but as colonisers, planning to take away their land. Despite this, the new temple was completed, to exactly the same specifications as the old, in 516BC, twenty-two years after the first return and seventy years after the destruction of the first temple.

The Jews back in Judea continued to look down on the Israelites, refusing to use the name 'Israelites' and calling them 'Samaritans', after their capital at Samaria. Even 500 years later, Jesus could use 'Samaritan' as a by-word for an inferior or tainted person in the parable of the 'Good Samaritan'. Unsurprisingly, they still called themselves Israelites. They numbered in the millions in the Roman period but suffered badly in the Samaritan wars of the sixth century CE. There are still officially around 700 of them today.

Despite the rather rickety return to Jerusalem, the centre of Judaism continued to be Babylon and the towns that succeeded it as capitals of the area we now call Iraq. Here it continued for the next 2,500 years, a sophisticated, literate, book-based religion of city dwellers.

Back in the hills, fifty years after it was completed, the temple in Jerusalem was in trouble. The local hostility of the Israelites/Samaritans and their lobbying against the incoming Jews with the Persian king had had their effect. So the Jews in Jerusalem asked for help from their Babylonian co-religionists. This appeal was heard by the king's cupbearer, who was a Jew called Nehemiah. He got together with a noted Jewish scribe called Ezra and, together, they raised a lot of money from Babylonian Jews and a small expedition was sent off to reinvigorate Jerusalem.[15] When they got there Ezra was shocked at the degree of backsliding from Judaism, as he understood it. He got all the local (male) Jews together and read out the law from 'morning until midday' in the rain, which seems to have surprised many of them. (It is symbolic of the change from Yahweh worship to Judaism that Ezra was not a prophet announcing revelations but a scribe reading the law.) The people – that is, the men – were told to get rid of their non-Jewish wives. Apparently, they did this right away and, with the help of the Babylonian money and the new arrivals, the walls of Jerusalem and the Judaism inside them were rebuilt.

Despite these efforts of Ezra and others, though, there continued to be differences between the Jews of the Diaspora, mostly in Babylon and Egypt, and the Jews of Jerusalem. The Diaspora culture was urban, sophisticated, literate and often influenced by the writings of other religions, such as Zoroastrianism. Diaspora Jews could not have 'priests' who sacrificed animals, because, according to their rules, priests and

---

[15] There are some questions about the timing of this expedition and whether it may have been two expeditions, one led by Nehemiah, one by Ezra, but it makes little practical difference.

sacrifices were only possible at the temple in Jerusalem. Instead, they had 'Rabbis', Hebrew for 'teachers', who conducted their meetings and ceremonies and expounded the law. Diaspora groups had regular weekly meetings in buildings set aside for the purpose, buildings called 'synagogues', which means 'meeting house'. Tellingly, it is a Greek word, reflecting the international language of the eastern Mediterranean, not a Hebrew one. Nothing like this had happened with any religion previously – polytheistic temples are houses for the gods and the key activity is sacrifice, not 'worship'. The Jews had invented the religious service, with readings from the scrolls, congregational prayers and singing, held together with a liturgy. The Diaspora Jewish Belief did not have a king or kingdom and was largely separated from political issues. The motor of the Diaspora Jewish Belief was to keep the urban Jewish people separate from the surrounded crowds of non-Jews and to keep them following their distinct rules of eating and behaviour.

The Jews who had returned to Jerusalem and its surroundings, in contrast, had the temple served by priests as the centre of their faith. For them, animal sacrifice was again their central religious act[xviii]. The temple surround had a complex drainage system to remove all the blood produced by the huge number of sacrificial animals slaughtered there. The temple authorities also became heavily involved in the issues of power and rule in the land. As time moved on, the walled city of Jerusalem, together with its surrounding land of Judea and its people, inevitably became a political unit as much as a religious one. The overlords of the region changed from the Persians to the Greeks after Alexander the Great overthrew the Persian Empire in 333BCE and, in 165BCE, the Jews of Judea rose in revolt against the Greek (Seleucid) king. Under Judah Maccabee (Yehuda HamMakabi), they achieved a short-lived independent kingdom again. A period of huge political complexity followed as Greek Seleucids (from the north), Parthians (from the east), Egyptians (from the south) and Romans (from the west) all got involved. When there were pauses between these forces, the Jews of Judea took the opportunity to engage in civil wars, largely between different members of the same family who occupied the positions of both high priest and king. When the dust settled, most of the area formerly occupied by Israel, Judea and the Palestinians was a Roman province called Judea, ruled through tributary kings. Horos, known to us as Herod 'the Great' (74–4BCE), is the best known of these.

Unsurprisingly, the two very different traditions of the Judean Jews and the Jews of the Diaspora clashed, especially when Diaspora Jews returned to visit Jerusalem from their cities elsewhere. The sophisticated, literate and spiritually focused Jews of the Diaspora found a very different and, to them, cruder religion in Judea, as well as a priesthood caught up in politics. These conflicts crystallised under Roman rule into constant friction between the Sadducees[xix], the temple-based Judean aristocracy, and the Pharisees (the term means 'set apart'), who represented the Diaspora style of thinking and worship that later became known as Rabbinic Judaism.

But, despite these differences, both Jewish groups, the Diaspora and the Judeans, prospered in the years before 66CE.

The Diaspora was largely split between two powerful and largely peaceful empires: the Parthians, in the east, who ruled over the largest city of the Diaspora, Babylon, and the Romans in the west, who ruled over the second city of the Diaspora, Alexandria. The Jews were a significant, respected and growing religious group in both empires.

In the Parthian Empire, which ruled the modern areas of Iraq and Iran and beyond, the Jews had important teaching and study centres, numerous synagogues and an empire-wide leader known as the Exilarch. They converted both individuals and groups to Judaism. The largest of the groups to be converted in Parthia at this time was Adiabane, a tributary kingdom some way north of Babylon. The king converted to Judaism around 50CE, bringing a substantial proportion of his population with him. The Jewish community of this empire prospered peacefully for hundreds of years, going smoothly through the transition of the empire from Parthian to Sassanid rule.

Diaspora Judaism had also spread widely in the Roman Empire. There was the long-standing and substantial population of Jews in Alexandria, said to be nearly half the population of the city. Many of them, as with Jews throughout the eastern Mediterranean, had lost their Hebrew and could speak only Greek. It was in

Alexandria that much Hebrew literature, including the Torah, was translated into Greek. There were often several synagogues in the major towns in the eastern half of the Roman Empire and they actively recruited converts. Synagogues in these towns had two congregations: fully-fledged Jews, including full converts, and supporters ('god fearers' or 'theosebes'), people who followed Judaic religion and practice but would not complete the conversion, largely because of the requirement for circumcision. Circumcision is the ritual cutting off of the foreskin of the penis required of male Jews. Normally this is done to a newborn child in Jewish and, later, Muslim households, but it is a very off-putting idea for adult men in an era before anaesthetic or antiseptic.

But even outside the two empires, Judaism flourished. There were important Jewish tribes across Arabia and there is evidence of Jewish areas in the Caucasus and Central Asia. Judaism at this time was a lively, dynamic and growing religion, with impressively decorated synagogues, much less intense rules and very little of the exclusivity it later adopted. It is important to understand that Judaism, as a religion, suffered no persecution during this long period, although the tangled politics of Judea itself ensured that the minority of Jews living there had plenty of troubles.

These were yet to come. Under Herod, who himself came from a recently converted Arabian Jewish family, the temple precinct had been greatly developed and ornamented and became famous for its grandeur. Although Diaspora Jews had mixed feelings about the priesthood in Jerusalem, they enjoyed the prestige the religion got from the wealth and power of Jerusalem and its nominally independent Jewish king, as well as the benefit of the peace enforced by his Roman overlords.

But politics, mixed with a religious expectation of a new 'King of the Jews', a Messiah, was to bring down the Judean Jews. Messiah means 'the anointed' and refers to the tradition of pouring oil on the forehead of the early kings of Israel who were sometimes therefore referred to as 'Messiahs' in Hebrew, which translates into 'Christos' in Greek. In 66CE there was a revolt against the Roman rule of Jerusalem and its surrounding area. By a series of unfortunate events, this resulted in five years of grim fighting before the Romans re-established their rule. The Romans were putting down the revolt in their usual speedy and thorough manner, under their general, Vespasian, when the emperor, Nero, was killed with no obvious successor. While Vespasian went off to Rome (in the event, to become emperor himself), the Jews were left alone to engage in a furious and brutal civil war amongst their different factions until the Romans returned to sort things out under Vespasian's son, Titus. In the defeat of the Jewish rebels in Jerusalem in 70CE the temple and its surrounding sacred precinct were completely destroyed by fire, probably by accident.

In 132CE there was another revolt, led by Simon bar Kokhba, who was acclaimed as Messiah. This deteriorated into guerrilla warfare and took four years to put down. After this the Romans levelled much of Jerusalem to the ground, changed its name to Aelia Capitolinus[16] and banned Jews from entering the city. They also changed the name of the province from Judea to Palestrina. Although banned from Aelia Capitolinus, most of the local Jewish population stayed in Palestrina. The local Jews developed a tradition of, once a year, assembling on the Mount of Olives, across the valley from the site of the temple, and loudly bewailing the loss of their capital and temple.

The destruction of the temple in 70CE and the complete destruction of Jerusalem in 136CE meant the end for the temple priesthood, the Sadducees. Judaism after that is the product of the Diaspora, Philistine, tradition only. This series of disasters in the traditional centre might have been a knockout blow for many religions. But, for the second time, not for Judaism. The second destruction of Jerusalem prompted some Jews to seek to write down their oral traditions, the ideas the Pharisees had developed over the previous 500 years in the Diaspora. This formed a book known as the 'Mishnah' (which means something like the 'Review'). Over the next 300 years this was commented on and added to, until it was finally pulled together in Babylon to form the Talmud ('Instruction' or 'Teaching')[17], the central book of subsequent Rabbinic Judaism sometime about 500CE. This is the start of the third stage of

---

[16] Some suggest that the Romans changed the name before the revolt, possibly triggering it.

[17] There is a less authoritative Talmud, called the 'Jerusalem' Talmud, which is believed to have been collected together in northern Palestrina.

Judaism, now as a highly bookish, scholarly Belief, completely rule-bound, yet with almost no theology.

The core of the Talmud, the Mishnah, is a miscellany of material: rulings and guidance on behaviour and tradition, sage advice, detailed instructions on the ritual to be used in the sacrifices at the no-longer-existing temple (written by people who had not seen them), stories of the great Rabbis and arguments about aspects of practice. This was written in both Hebrew and Aramaic. Round this hodgepodge of the Mishnah are later comments and expositions, followed by still later comments that, put together, complete the Talmud. These later comments are written, quite literally, round the Mishnah, the words of each layer of comment being written in onion-like layers going outwards on each page from the centre or bottom corner.

This Talmud is a gigantic collection of stuff – over 6,000 pages in normal print – much of it rules and comments on rules that affect every aspect of Orthodox Jewish life thereafter: food, sex, clothing, attitudes to disease, death, servants, masters, children – everything. Consequently, being an Orthodox Jew is, for many, a full-time occupation. The rules affect everything, every minute of the day. The rules are so complex and conflicting that they need Rabbinic help in their interpretation. The rules create guilt, because the rules cannot all be followed, all the time, and failure to follow them can lead to disaster for the whole family and community. Finally, the rules enforce complete social separation from non-Jews, as you cannot follow all the rules and mix. Although Judaism continued to have its annual festivals, its feast days, its stories from the Torah and its weekly services in a very similar manner to its earlier form, its character was dominated by the length and depth of these rules. Much of the challenge for each Jew since has been the extent to which they attempt to follow all these rules or the extent to which they adopt a broader, less finicky method of following a Jewish life.

Although, in the very long run, Judaism became synonymous with Talmudic orthodoxy, for many centuries a large body of Jews did not accept the authority of the Talmud. During this time Judaism split into two sects: the Rabbinic school and the Karaite school. The Karaites claimed to be seeking to return to a simpler interpretation of the Torah, ignoring the additions of the Talmud, but giving attention to sections of the Tanakah (Old Testament), such as the prophets, that Talmudic Rabbis largely ignore. This school flourished during the Abbasid period and produced the definitive version of the Jewish 'Old Testament', the Masoretic Text around 700CE. The Karaites continued for many years alongside Rabbinic Judaism – in the seventeenth and eighteenth centuries there was a well-known Karaite population in Poland/Lithuania – but, when Lithuania came under Russian control and there was widespread persecution of the Jews, they seem to have faded back into Rabbinic Judaism. In the Islamic world, Karaite congregations seem to have declined steadily, becoming largely confined to Egypt by the beginning of the twentieth century. Over the last fifty years much of this population has emigrated to the US and Israel, where small Karaite congregations continue. While the name 'Karaite' is almost extinct, the spirit of Karaite Judaism is very much alive in Liberal Judaism today.

When the Emperor Constantine started the process to make Christianity the Roman Empire's official religion after 313CE, there was a great deal of pressure on Jews in the Roman Empire to convert. Many of the Jews that 'converted' to Christianity and, later, to Islam, saw these two as descendants of the ancestral Jewish religion as much as the Talmudic orthodoxy that now formed Rabbinic scholarship. The pressure to convert to Christianity was eventually the last straw for the Israelites (Samaritans), who revolted in 484CE after considerable persecution[18]. In a series of wars, their numbers were reduced drastically, from a large community of around a million to a small minority that suffered further abuse after the destruction of the short-lived Jewish kingdom of Judea 614–29(?) (See below).

However, even in this period, the process was not all one way. Sometime around 400–500CE the King of Himyar, now known as the Yemen, in the southwest corner of the Arabian Peninsula, converted to Judaism[19]. Himyar remained actively Jewish, persecuting Christians with considerable vigour, until the (Christian) King of Ethiopia removed the dynasty in 525CE and 'converted'

---

[18] Some say the persecution came after the initial revolt.

[19] His conversion was through contact with the Jews of Yathrib, later Medina, who were later to be so important in the story of Islam.

the country to Christianity. It remained officially Christian until the coming of Islam.

There were extended wars between the Sassanid and Byzantine empires from 602 to 628CE that produced an unexpected opportunity for the Jews. During these wars the Sassanid shah recruited a special Jewish army, partially from his own population, but, promising to give them Judea to rule if they conquered it, he also raised a Jewish revolt within the Byzantine Empire itself. This joint force of Sassanid army and Jewish troops entered Jerusalem with great slaughter after a siege in 614CE, destroying all the Christian churches and monuments. The son of the Sassanid Empire's Jewish Exilarch, Nehemiah ben Hushiel, was made King of Judea, subordinate to the Sassanid shah. Under him, a predominantly Jewish kingdom existed for a period of around ten to fifteen years. Details are missing but the area was repossessed by the Byzantines after around 625CE and there was a massacre of the Jews and most of the remaining Samaritans/Israelites (629CE?) before it was overrun by the Muslim Arab armies in 638CE.

The Muslims who conquered Judea also defeated and took over the whole Sassanid Empire in Iran and Iraq, as well as areas in the south and east of the Roman Empire, including Egypt. At first, they did not seek to convert non-Arab people to Islam. Indeed, for the first century or so, they made it more or less impossible for any non-Arab to become Muslim; you had to be accepted into an Arab tribe before that was possible. But, from the first, there was an incentive to try to convert in order to avoid a tax only applied to non-Muslims and other rules that made Muslims superior citizens. This incentive became very attractive after 760CE, once the incoming Abbasid caliphs relaxed the rules for conversion. This, combined with Islam sharing so much practice and history with Judaism, made Jewish conversion to Islam common over the following centuries. Despite these losses to Islam, Judaism flourished as a separate and respected minority religion through and beyond the ninth-century Islamic 'Golden Age', when the Abbasid caliphs ruled the Muslim world from Baghdad. The caliphs treated the leader of the Jews, the Exilarch, as a dignitary commanding considerable respect.

While Jews were under pressure to convert away from Judaism in the two empires, the Abbasid Islamic Caliphate and the Christian Byzantine Empire, the opposite occurred in what is now southern Russia. There were already rather mysterious but apparently long-established rural Jewish communities in the area. Some, known as the Mountain Jews, were based in what is now Chechnya, others in what is now Georgia, and there were urban Jewish communities in the cities of the Black Sea coast. Then, around 750CE, the Kagan (king) of Khazaria converted to Judaism. This was a large region that extended from north of the Caucasus Mountains on the east to the mouth of the Danube on the west. Judaism, both Rabbinic and Karaite, remained the religion of Khazaria for the next 200 or so years, until the kingdom fell. Orthodox Rabbinic Jewish practice prevailed in the Khazar court, and there was considerable cross-fertilisation with Judaism elsewhere. Many Jews from other areas, where they faced persecution by Christians, moved to Khazaria, which had developed a rich and sophisticated culture between the Byzantine Christian and Abbasid Muslim empires. At its peak, Khazaria had a large and peaceful empire, going as far as the Aral Sea, trading between the Middle East, Europe and China. The Khazar Kagan took upon himself to champion Jewish interests throughout the known world, matching the Byzantine position as champion of Christians and the Abbasids as champions of Muslims. It was during this time that the Prince of Kiev, deciding to adopt a new Belief to replace his ancestral Polytheism, faced a fairly even choice between the three empires, each representing one of the three great Abrahamic religions. (He chose the Orthodox Christianity of Byzantium.[20]) But after around 900CE the Khazar Empire gradually shrunk and fell apart, with outside incursions and internal uprisings. In 960CE, the Russians of Kiev defeated the Kagan and Khazaria was absorbed into the, now Christian, Russia. But many of the people retained their Jewish Belief and went on to form much of the Jewish population of Russia and Eastern Europe (Ashkenazi Jews).

After the development of the Talmud around 500CE, the Jewish religion remained remarkably consistent for

---

[20] Russians love to tell the story that the prince, Vladimir, sent out ambassadors to all three empires. Islam was ruled out because it banned alcohol, which the Russians loved, and Christianity was chosen because the beauty of Agia Sophia in Byzantium with the choir singing was like heaven. Much would have been different if the Kagan had built a better synagogue.

over a millennium. This constancy is despite, or because, all Jews have lived in minority communities in countries dominated by other religions between the fall of Khazaria in 960 until the foundation of Israel in 1947. The history of the Jewish population under Islamic, Christian, Nationalist and Communist rule is a mixed pattern of tolerance, persecution, acceptance and mass-murder. But this complex, turbulent, dramatic and profoundly tragic saga did not significantly affect the character of the Belief itself. As we shall see from Christianity and Islam, Beliefs have periods of development and then centuries when nothing much changes. Apart from the minority developments noted below, Orthodox Judaism changed its character very little between 960 and 1947.

During the history of Rabbinic Judaism there have been several experiments in mysticism. Kabala is a medieval development that revels in noting coincidences of words and numbers – the number of names of God or of books of the Bible, etc. Most regard it simply as making magic numbers out of coincidences, but it became an important part of Hasidic mysticism.

Hasidic Jews (from the Hebrew word meaning 'pious') are noticeable for their traditional dark costume, beards and hats, and are sometimes referred to in consequence as 'Ultra-Orthodox'. In reality, they have mystical views many Jews regard as distinctly unorthodox. Hasidism arose around 1740, in part as a response to the dryly academic nature of Orthodox Judaism, in part as a response to the grim life being experienced at the time by the Jewish community of Poland, Lithuania and, especially, Russia. It emphasises the personal relationship of the individual with God, enabling ordinary Jews to see themselves as equal in value to religious scholars and as mattering to God, regardless of their lack of learning and unhappy lives. Hassids have developed extra rules that keep them separate from non-Hassids, Jewish or not. They also split into different dynasties or congregations, with quite distinct, and not always popular, views: some Hassids disapprove of the State of Israel, even though they live there.

Around 1850 a new form of Judaism arose in America called Reform Judaism (or Progressive, or Liberal Judaism). Reform Judaism now accounts for the majority of American Jews and a significant minority elsewhere. Reform Judaism follows the Nationalist-influenced redefining of Jews as a 'People' or tradition, as opposed to a Belief defined by its scripture, and takes the view that the rules need to adapt to the needs of the people, rather than the other way around. Hence, at its core, Reform Judaism requires only monotheism and an acceptance of the unique character and history of Jews and their relationship with their God. Naturally, much of the history, traditions and writing of Judaism is kept, but, in the Karaite tradition, the specifics and details of the Talmud are largely ignored. The arrival of Progressive Judaism allowed Orthodox Judaism to harden its edge as a rule-dominated system.

So Judaism sprang from a typical polytheistic religion with a local patron godlet called Yahweh. Under Hezekiah and Josiah it was changing into a one-godlet-only religion ('Monolatry') and key aspects of the Belief were written down. That structure was quickly modified by the unique experience of a hill tribe that turned into a city-based minority population (the Exile). The first five books of the Bible (the Torah) were then edited together in Babylon and Egypt. The Judaism it created kept the Jews separate from the larger, urban and literate population by developing special religious meeting places, religious services, and restrictions on diet and behaviour. Over the following ten centuries an extensive, but largely verbal, commentary on the Torah was developed in Babylon. With the destruction of the Jewish state of Judea in 132CE, this commentary was written down, commented on and turned into the Talmud, the foundation of the third, Rabbinic, phase of Judaism. The Belief had completely changed from a typical tribal Polytheism, through a long period as a lively and growing religion of ceremony, legend and tradition, to a formal and scholarly minority Belief, fighting dissolution from both assault and assimilation with a wildly complex set of all-encompassing rules.

The nature of the Jewish godlet changed much less. If you look at the Jewish scripture, the Torah, it refers to the tribal godlet of Judea/Israel, always taking the existence of other godlets for granted. The first of the Ten Commandments reads, for example, *'You shall have no other gods before me.'*[21] The seventh and eighth lines of the Shema, the main Jewish prayer used to this day, translate as *'Beware, lest your heart be deceived and you turn and serve*

---

[21] There are other versions of the exact words of the First Commandment but all of them have the same meaning.

other gods and worship them.' The perception of one 'God the Creator' comes only from reading the Bible with Christian/Islamic pre-conceptions. The Talmud, the other sacred Jewish source, does not deal with the metaphysical nature of the Jewish God but with Jewish laws, traditions, practices, etc. and the sayings that relate to them.

In the other parts of the Old Testament, which in the Jewish Tanakah do not have sacred status, there are only a few, rather suspect places where it is claimed that the Jewish God is pre-eminent, even to non-Jews. The clearest example is in the later chapters of the book of Isaiah. These are not written by Isaiah but by an unknown and excitable writer early in the period of the Exile. He wants to stress that the Jewish godlet is so powerful that his powers work even outside Judea and so he can still help the newly exiled Jews in Babylon. In his enthusiasm he makes wild claims for the Jewish godlet's unique power and importance and even goes so far as to call Cyrus of Persia the 'Messiah'[xx]. But nobody much listened to Second Isaiah, as he repeatedly wails. Another odd source for the idea of there being only one God is in the Book of Job, a morality play/story where the god referred to appears to be God the Creator and Judge. But this God also has children, has a bet with Satan and tells Job off from inside a whirlwind. Other unexpected ideas are also put forward in Job and it is not taken very seriously as a theological guide.

But whether the Jewish godlet/God created the world or not affects the way he is seen in Judaism very little.

Judaism really doesn't do theology on the exact nature of God. What matters is that he is their God and they are his people. The reason some Jews have tacitly accepted the idea of their God being the same as the universal God the Creator is probably because they don't want the Jewish God to look smaller than the Christian/Islamic God. Other Jews are reluctant to accept this universal God because it implies that they have to share their God – a bit – with other peoples.

Judaism has succeeded in keeping a following remarkably well, often against great hostility: the religion was born in stubbornness after complete defeat and reborn in stubbornness after another major defeat and remains true to this aspect of its origin. It has maintained its followers as small and separate groups in many different environments. Often its followers have been discriminated against and sometimes terribly persecuted. Its focus has had to be on maintaining the distinctiveness and cohesion of the tribe. The exact nature of faith is unimportant compared to keeping the law. There are many, many, many books on what it 'means' for a person to be a Jew but remarkably few on what God means to Jews.

The Belief of Judaism has, for many years now, been principally about descent – are you born of Jewish parents or not? – and, for the Orthodox, about observing the rules of the law in daily life. The question for Jews has been how much they 'assimilate' into the culture that surrounds them and how much they maintain the detailed rules of Kosher and Sabbath that keep them separate. Kosher is the word meaning 'fitting' and is generally used to refer to food allowed by the rules. Sabbath is the day on which no work must be done. Both have rules that are followed with pettifogging attention to detail in Orthodox households. For example, building a fire is work and, according to the Rabbis, electricity is fire, so an Orthodox Jew cannot switch on electricity on the Sabbath because it is work and work is forbidden on that day. Orthodox Jews cannot drive or be driven on the Sabbath either. For food to be Kosher milk products have to be rigorously separated from meat and, if this is not assured, neither can be eaten. Both restrictions serve to create a powerful separation between Orthodox Jews and other peoples in modern society.

After Nationalism came to prominence during the 1800s (see chapter 6), it started to turn Judaism from a Belief into a 'Nation'. Because Judaism is generally passed down in families, it has always had a dual character, mixing Belief and descent. (This is true of most Beliefs, but it is more conspicuous in a minority religion.) But, until the dramatic advance of Nationalism, the emphasis was on the religious aspect. Even characters as exotically Jewish by descent as Benjamin Disraeli, twice prime minister of the UK, had all legal and many social disabilities removed because he was Christian by religion. But Nationalism provided a new basis for excluding those of Jewish descent, whatever their stated religion. The popularity of Communism among Jewish groups, who had often been prevented from moving up the social ladder by religious discrimination, put many Jews in political opposition to Nationalists. Nationalism also created a desire for a Jewish 'Nation-State' among a few Jews and political groupings, known as Zionists, and were set up to advance that ambition. The only location for a Jewish Nation-State that had any resonance was the area around Jerusalem. As the twentieth century started, Jewish settlers started to arrive in the area with the mission to found the Jewish Nation-State there. They were strongly supported by money and political lobbying from some European Jewish organisations.

After the First World War, the French and British were given control of the area, which had previously been a part of the (Turkish) Ottoman Empire and drew the boundaries of new phantom nations for reasons and in ways that verged on the whimsical. In 1920, the British re-created the area of 'Palestine', for the first time in 1,000 years, by carving it out of the previous Ottoman province of Syria. While part of the British motivation for this was to provide the basis of a Jewish Nation-State, by the weird 'logic' of Nationalism (see chapter 6), creating a new state also created a new 'Nation'. This new 'Palestinian' people was made up of the Muslims and Christians[22] who lived in the area but not the Jews who lived there because they

---

[22] At the time of the creation of Palestine, about 10% of the population were Christian and around 10% Jewish, most of the remainder being Sunni Muslim. The majority of Christians living in the former province of Syria lived to the north. There, the Lebanon was created by the French as a country to ensure a Christian majority, with similar divisive effect.

were already being seen as a different 'Nation', albeit one as yet without a Nation-State.

The transformation of Jewishness from the Judaic Belief into a 'Nationality' was completed when, during World War II, millions of Jews, defined as a Nation, not as a Belief or by place of birth, were slaughtered by the Nazis. At the same time this showed the catastrophe of a Nation in a Nationalist world with no Nation-State, borders or guns to defend itself. It also brought to that Nation the pity and support of many. A new Nation-State was founded in the area of the former state of Judea/Palestrina for the Jewish Nation. It was called Israel – rather surprisingly, given that the Jews had previously despised the Israelites in the area (the ones they called Samaritans). The inconsistent and complex mixing of the Belief of Nationalism into Judaism has had more effect on it than any other factor in 1,500 years, dragging even the most reluctant Jews into a political stance.

Since the foundation of the Jewish state in Israel in 1947, the situation has come to resemble the way it was after the original return to Jerusalem from Babylon exactly 2,600 years earlier. Then, the incoming people called themselves 'Jews' and fell out with the people previously on the land, people who called themselves 'Israelites'. The incoming people of recent times call themselves 'Israelis' and have fallen out with the people previously on the land, people who call themselves 'Palestinians'. History echoes in this part of the world.

Today Judaism is again divided between a very political Jewish state, centred on Jerusalem, and Diaspora

Jews, living as a minority in other states and defined by descent. This relationship between the Jewish Diaspora and the Jewish state resembles the last period that the two co-existed in simmering animosity from 165BCE to 72CE. More echoes. But, this time, the Jewish Belief is mixed with the Nationalist Belief. The Nationalist Belief manages to make a difficult situation impossible. It gives Diaspora Jews two nationalities, of descent and of geography, Jewish Nation and birth Nation. At the same time, it provides two 'Nationalities', Israelis and Palestinians, with the same land as their Nation-State, implying an endless zero-sum conflict, as a gain on one side is a loss on the other. Until we can address the absurdity of the Nationalist Belief, the conflicts must remain.

The Jewish Nation-State itself, Israel, is in an area with few undisputed 'natural' or traditional borders and 5,000 years of recorded conflict. The current position in the region is one of fractal aggression: every group opposing another group is made up of smaller groups, whose mutual distrust and dislike is prevented from breaking into war only by the presence of larger conflicts. Should any of the larger conflicts be resolved, the smaller groupings will, with relief, turn to attacking each other.

It now seems impossible to delink the Nationalist view of Jewishness from the Belief of Judaism, which causes profound problems for both the Diaspora, whose National loyalties can be questioned, and for the Israelis, who have their own second-class citizens, non-Jews, and no apparent way to soften the lines of distinction with the countries that surround them. The problem for the Jews used to be that their Belief offended Christians; now it is that it fits unusually badly into a world defined by Nationalism. Until aggressive Nationalism goes the same way as aggressive Christianity, the fundamental problem for Jews and Judaism will remain.

It seems likely that the stubbornness of the Hill People will be tested again.

Postscript: The Mystery of the Fire

One religion challenges Judaism's claim to be the first to go beyond Polytheism: Zoroastrianism. This is the ancient religion of Iran that still has a few followers in both Iran and India. Zoroastrian ideas had a profound impact on the development of Judaism, Christianity and Islam. Nailing down the beliefs and practices of early Zoroastrianism, however, is like nailing jelly to the ceiling: both challenging and futile.

Although its founder, Zarathustra or Zoroaster, lived sometime before 600BCE (probably), no Zoroastrian material was written down for 800 years, so Judaism's claim to be the first religion of the book is unscathed. The Magi, the priests of the region, are said to have feared that writing down the hymns would be to risk losing their secrets and their power, so they learned them by heart. (The Magi are best known in the West as the 'wise men from the east' that visited the baby Jesus in Matthew's Gospel.) So, for the period from at least 600BCE to 200CE, Zoroastrianism was maintained through rigorously learned and repeated priestly recitations. Unfortunately, by the time they were written down, after 200CE, the language of the recitations, Avestan, was no longer spoken in normal life and was poorly understood. Moreover, no written Avestan existed, so a special alphabet was created to write down the key recitations, known as the Gathas. Not only had these been recited for hundreds of years in a formulaic and extreme style but also the Magi had been involved in several major political upheavals and had, at times, been banned. On top of that, the Greeks, under Alexander, had invaded and occupied the region and Zoroastrianism had declined almost to invisibility before reviving later. The credibility of the written form of the Gathas is further undermined because they are clearly influenced by Indian writings from a period later than Zarathustra.

So it is remarkable that the written Gathas have any credibility at all as resembling the teaching originally given by Zarathustra himself. They have some credibility because they are not the sort of thing you would make up – one of the Gathas is a record of the wedding of Zarathustra's third daughter, which would be an odd idea to include, were it not part of an original text. The whole feeling of the Gathas is of a wilder, more anarchic, violent and bleaker world than that of second-century Iran when they were written down. But when matters get less tangible, when the Gathas move from talking about the plains or the wedding guests and move on to talking of God or godlets, the extent to which the Gathas are Zarathustra's original words is questionable. Even if they are his exact words in Avestan, it is impossible to determine what they mean with any precision, simply because no one spoke Avestan at the time of writing and we have no other Avestan writing to compare them with. Translators have to guess by comparison with the meanings of 'similar' words in 'similar' ancient languages. On top of all this, Zoroastrianism before

200CE was also anti-images, so we have minimal statuary or painting to help guide us.

Some very extravagant and creative ideas have been put forward for the original message of Zarathustra. (Be particularly cautious about internet searches in this area.) So anything said about Zoroastrianism before it started to be influenced by other religions must be considered as a view, rather than a fact. It seems that Zarathustra claimed that Ahura Mazda (which probably means 'Lord Wisdom', but may mean 'Light Wisdom'. Or it may mean something different), originally a leading godlet of the Iranian polytheistic religion, was both the only God and the maker of all good things. It has been said that early Zoroastrians had to recite, 'There is no God but Ahura Mazda and Zarathustra is his prophet.' However, this leaves the problem that evil exists. Zarathustra, or his later successors, saw evil as caused by the bad godlet, Angra Mainyu. This rather undermines claims that Zoroastrianism is the first monotheism, although, in the end, it appears that Ahura Mazda will triumph. Many contemporary references to Zoroastrianism saw it as a dualist religion, with two contending gods, one of good and another of evil. This aspect of Zoroastrianism influenced Judaism while the Jews were in Babylon under Persian rule. It is from this time that there are references in the Bible to Satan (meaning 'Opponent' in Hebrew).

A factor that complicates our understanding of Zoroastrianism is the role of the Magi (singular, a Magus). This appears to have been a largely hereditary priesthood – Zarathustra seems to have been one himself –

something like the Brahmins of India. They definitely had their own agenda, which was not necessarily to preserve the exact original beliefs. So, although Zoroastrianism may originally have been either monotheistic or dualist, when the written form of Zoroastrianism was created, around 220CE, it had reverted, almost completely, to the shape of a standard Polytheism. It had a complete hierarchy of Gods, monsters and myths.

In this highly polytheistic version of Zoroastrianism, there are the six 'divine sparks' that the creator made first and who then made the world (there are echoes of Plato's ideas in this). These may be the 'Amesh Spenta', meaning the 'Bounteous Immortals' who then created the 'Yazatas', which probably means 'Worthy of Veneration', and their leader, Ohrmuzd, who may or may not be the same as Ahura Mazda. There are also bad godlets to be rejected and other 'Ahuras', unspecified. There may also be a human saviour that will help usher in the triumph of Ahura Mazda. Or that may have been added later and, anyway, it is not generally accepted. As can be seen, there is very little that is different to Polytheism about this stage of Zoroastrianism, certainly very little one can be sure of as coming from Zarathustra himself.

A variant of Zoroastrianism called Zurvanism appears to have held that Ahura Mazda and Angra Mainyu were twin brothers, one good, one bad, under a father god, Zurvan.

Despite the confusions, Zoroastrianism seems to be the source of two ideas that became important later in Christianity. However confused it may have become, there was always, somewhere in Zoroastrianism, the idea of the Creator God as the source of all good, even if there was difficulty about fitting this with the existence of evil. There was also a strong theme of judgement in the life after death in Zoroastrianism. Souls of the departed crossed a bridge that gradually became narrower. Those who fail the judgement fall into the fire below; those who pass over go on to eternal joy.

The practice of Zoroastrianism is famous for the presence of fire in Zoroastrian temples and the elaborate and lengthy Fire service. There is also the long tradition amongst Zoroastrians known as the 'sky burial'. They put their dead on high places or pillars so that carrion birds eat their remains.

Zoroastrian ideas were undoubtedly part of the rich mixture into which Christianity was born and its focus on one God must have had some influence on the Christians, helping to add the idea of God the Creator to the Judaic focus on their one godlet.

In the second century of the Current Era, a religion called Manichaeism arose, following a prophet called Mani. Mani, who started as a Christian, brought together themes from Zoroastrianism, Buddhism and Christianity into a religion that spread widely through the Roman and Persian empires. The key theme was the battle between Light and Darkness; man was born to light but falls into the darkness of the material world. But a saviour will be sent to rescue man from the endless round of rebirth in darkness.

Mani travelled to Iran, the home of Zoroastrianism,

where the king supported his religion. But, after the king's death, the Magi reasserted their power and put Mani in prison, where he died. Manichaeism was suppressed by the Magi in Iran and, later, by the Christians in the Roman Empire – although Saint Augustine was originally a Manichaean before he converted to Christianity – and, over several centuries, vanished from view as a separate religion there. But it continued in Asia and Manichaeism was adopted as the national religion of the Uighur people of central Asia in 763CE, gaining some converts in Tang China, before vanishing under the weight of Buddhism and Islam, although unexpected remnants, such as remote Manichaean monasteries, hung around the Middle East for many years.

The underlying 'dualistic' idea of Manichaeism was closely connected to some parts of the Christian Church, originally called the 'Gnostics', who went on in various forms until their more or less final suppression in the 'Albigensian Crusade' (see chapter 4) ending in 1229CE. These groups saw the God of the Old Testament as the evil creator of the wretched material world in which they lived, sometimes using Plato's term, the Demiurge, for this figure. He fought for the souls of mankind against the good God of perfect forms and spirituality revealed by Jesus. Not much more detail is available on these beliefs, as the Christian Church destroyed any material it could find relating to them.

After the conquest of Iran by the Arabs in 744CE, Zoroastrianism was treated as a 'religion of the book'. This meant it was respected and protected, but the religion declined in the face of the prestige and success of Islam. Despite this, there may have been up to 300,000 Zoroastrians in Iran until recently but many fled following the revolution of 1979. They still have one seat in the Iranian parliament. There are also thought to be around 110,000 Zoroastrians in India where they are called Parsees (meaning Persians).

.4.

CHRISTIANITY: THE MANY WAYS TO THE ONE GOD

The Christian Belief was formed during a fortunate period for the countries surrounding the Mediterranean Sea. The Roman Empire was at its height and was to remain so for at least 350 years, generally keeping the peace and limiting excessive corruption. To the east, the long-lived and largely peaceful Parthian Empire, based in Iran, had excellent trading and cultural links with its western neighbour.

The state religion of Rome was a dull and unconvincing Polytheism. To quote Gibbon, '*The various modes of worship which prevailed in the Roman world were all considered by the people as equally true; by the philosopher as equally false; and by the magistrate as equally useful.*' The Romans tolerated all religions so long as they were long established. Most regions of the empire had their own religions, many of them minor variations on standard Polytheism. New cults were not legal, but the Romans were very reluctant to persecute anyone much for their religious views. Generally, they refused to do so unless the cult members made the most ostentatious nuisance of themselves. So, although the early Christian father, Justin Martyr, was determined to die for his religion he had to wait until the age of sixty-five, after many years of seeking trouble, before the Roman authorities co-operated and beheaded him.

In this peaceful period, many people had the leisure to consider the meaning of life and explore new ideas. There were mystery religions, such as the cult of Isis, connected to very ancient tales from Egypt, and the cult of Dionysus, associated with alcohol and drug-taking. The old religion of Iran, Zoroastrianism, was in a moribund phase but had thrown up the idea of a single god and of the world as a battleground between the force for good and the force for bad. The cult of Mithradatism, popular in the Roman Army, seems to have been derived from an offshoot of the Zoroastrian religion. Buddhist ideas came all the way from India.

But the most powerful influences on spiritual thinking and theological speculation were Judaism and Greek Philosophy. Judaism was famous throughout the Roman Empire for its ancient writings, the uncompromising nature of its practices, and the grandeur of the temple precinct built by Herod round its famously empty temple: a temple without statue or symbol in it. Greek Philosophy had huge prestige amongst the literate and many were attracted to the Platonic ideas of an ideal, perfect world we are only the imperfect reflection of. A satisfactory answer to giving meaning to life would need to unite these very different themes. This would be a new Belief that would combine the intellectual allure and prestige of Greek Philosophy with the historical prestige and fierce character of Judaism. Bringing these together would unite the head and the heart, analysis and tradition, the adult and the child, the clean purity of abstract analysis with the complex depth of cultural heritage.

Christianity takes as its central story the short period of Jewish revival preaching of a man called Yeshua, before his execution in around 30CE and his subsequent brief reappearance to his followers.

Yeshua was the name of the person we call Jesus, the same name as the Old Testament prophet we call Joshua. Over time, this name was slowly changed in translations into 'Jesus'. The Greeks have no letter for the 'sh' sound, so it became an 's' (sigma) and they couldn't say the 'ua' sound, so it became a 'u', changing Yeshua to 'Iesu' or 'Jesu', pronounced 'Yea-zu'. To fit Greek and Latin grammar, a final '–s' was sometimes added (which became fixed in English translations), changing it to Jesus, pronounced Yea-sus. English changed the pronunciation of the 'JE' in 'Jesus' from 'Yea' to 'Gee', arriving at the name we use now. Jesus had only one name as far as we know.

'Christ' comes from the Greek word 'Khristos', which was used as the translation of the Hebrew 'Messiah'. 'Messiah' and 'Khristos' have the literal meaning of one who has been ceremonially touched with sacred oil (anointed). It was a title used frequently for the early kings and high priests of Israel who had oil put on their heads in their enthronement ceremonies and it later became synonymous with a righteous prophet or king. Samuel, Saul, David and Solomon are all referred to as Christs and, in the Book of Isaiah, Cyrus of Persia is referred to as Christ. Three verses in the (fairly whacky) Book of Daniel tell of the arrival of a 'Messiah/Christ the Prince', in a context that could mean more or less anything. The first time the title is used for Jesus is in Paul's letters (which were written before the Gospels) and he uses it constantly, often in the format 'Christ Jesus', sometimes just as 'Christ' alone[23]. There is, however, no record of Jesus being anointed and Paul never explains why he thinks Jesus was anointed. It has been suggested that the stories in the Gospels of a woman pouring costly oil over Jesus' head (in Mark and Matthew) or his feet (in Luke and John) counts as an 'anointing'[xxi]. Alternatively, some have suggested that Jesus' ceremonial immersion in the River Jordan by the preacher, John the Baptist (Johanan), was the equivalent to a ceremonial anointment with oil. On balance, it seems that Paul simply decided the title seemed a good one and so gave the Belief its name.

All we know about Jesus comes from the 'Gospels', brief biographies written many years later by members of the groups that followed him after his death, probably

---

[23] The very first written use of 'Christ' for Jesus we have is probably in Paul's first letter to the Thessalo-nians written in 51CE.

working from notes and conversations with his original followers. There is no independent reference to him during his life or until long afterwards.

Jesus came from a large Jewish family – both Mark and Matthew name his four brothers: '...*his brethren James, and Joses, and Simon, and Judas? And his sisters are they not all with us?*'[xxii] The Gospel of John also mentions them.[xxiii] They were the children of a carpenter who lived in the town of Nazareth in the area called Galilee. This is in the north of Judea, the predominantly Jewish Roman province that included all the area of ancient Judea, Israel and Palestine. There are one or two stories of Jesus' childhood reported in the Gospels, but nothing is known of his adult life until he was, we guess, about thirty to thirty-three years old, at which point he joined the followers of John the Baptist, a revivalist preacher, by being symbolically washed in the river. After John the Baptist was arrested and jailed, Jesus started his own preaching mission with a group of followers.

He preached for either one year or three years (we don't know which) along lines similar to those of many other Jewish Diaspora-style teachers of the time. They emphasised that the ethical teaching of Jewish law was more important than the dietary/Sabbath rules. In line with many of the revivalists that were burgeoning during this period, Jesus forecast the imminent end of the world. But it seems that he was a relative moderate in the Jewish revivalist movement, expressing less anti-Roman sentiment than some other preachers and not demanding the hair-shirt austerity favoured by others. The Gospels also record Jesus performing a number of rather low-key miracles, but only the last Gospel, named after John, reports him making any public claims of divinity. Eventually, he travelled to Jerusalem, fell foul of the temple authorities there and was executed by the Roman governor[xxiv]. His execution was in the style the Romans used for criminals: nailing them to a wooden cross and allowing them to die slowly, in full view of the public. After his execution he briefly reappeared to some of his followers.

Almost everything we know of the period after the Gospels finish comes from the book called the Acts of the Apostles and from the Letters (Epistles) in the New Testament section of the Bible. After Jesus' death, his followers continued as a small Jewish sect. The new sect was known as the Nazarenes after Jesus' home district and was led initially by Jesus' brother, James, and one of his followers from Nazareth, Peter[24]. This sect was subject to some persecution. A member of the group called Stephen was stoned to death after he made an inflammatory speech. Saul, a member of the Pharisee group, seems to have led the persecution. However, Saul was miraculously converted from the persecutor of the Nazarenes to Paul, the missionary of Christianity. Many Jews at the time used both a Hebrew name and a Greek name and he is referred to as Saul (Hebrew) before he made his first convert to Christianity and Paulos (Greek)

---

[24] For the record, Peter, held to be the first Pope, was married. Matthew 8:14, 1 Corinthians 9:5.

afterwards^xxv. Paul and others travelled around the eastern Mediterranean encouraging Jewish synagogue members and would-be Jewish synagogue attenders to join this sect. The not-fully-Jewish synagogue attenders were called 'theosebes' – god-fearers. They followed most Jewish practices but were unwilling to be circumcised; the new religion gave them full membership without this painful and dangerous operation. The Nazarenes shared a regular weekly meal, which included a re-enactment of the events of Jesus' last meal before his death. They also acted as a mutual aid group, supporting each other. At this early stage they were seen as a Jewish sect – of which there were several – but Paul is quite clear that non-Jews (he calls them all 'Hellenes', Greeks) were to be admitted to his group.

Paul returned to Jerusalem and met James, the brother of Jesus, who led Jesus' followers there, but then he was attacked in the temple by people saying that he had allowed a non-Jew to enter the temple precinct and had to be rescued by Roman soldiers[25]. Paul had the title of a Roman citizen, so he could demand to be judged by the emperor. After considerable delay, he was sent to Rome for judgement. We don't know what happened to him after he arrived in Rome, but the silence suggests he was executed or died. Despite this, James' group withered

---

[25] The Acts of the Apostles hints that the crowd may have been stirred up by some of James' group. They profoundly disagreed with Paul's acceptance of gentiles and had required that he make a penance for it. Some may have felt this not enough.

away and Paul's congregations went on and developed into the new Belief.

The new cult had a wealth of sources from which to derive its theory and practice. Apart from the verbal traditions of the early followers, there were the Gospels, the Letters, Platonist ideas and the Old Testament.

No one wrote a biography of Jesus' preaching and life until at least thirty years after his death. This may have been because he had prophesied that the world would end before his followers' deaths[xxvi], so there was no need to record his words and deeds. Over the next decades, however, a number of brief biographies of Jesus were written and Christianity accepts four of these. These were written in Greek and are called the Gospels (Good News). We don't know who wrote them, but three of them, known by tradition as the Gospels of Matthew, Mark and Luke, all tell similar stories.

Mark is the shortest and earliest Gospel. Despite its centrality to the Belief Paul built, Mark gives a remarkably limited account of Jesus' appearance to his followers after his execution – 435 words in the King James Version of the Bible. The Gospels of Luke and Matthew use the same central information as Mark but add bits from other sources, as well as providing a different perspective on some of the stories also found in Mark. Matthew appears to be writing for those who know the Old Testament and adds in many references to Biblical prophecies. Luke seems to have a gentile (non-Jewish) audience in mind and writes with many more pro-gentile and anti-Jewish passages.

The fourth Gospel, John, was written noticeably later than the other three. It is a much less historical presentation and has more commentary and editorial material. John presents a quite different account of Jesus' mission, much more based around Jerusalem and less in northern Judea. It is also markedly anti-Jewish. Of all the Gospels, only Mark could have been written by an eyewitness of Jesus' life, but the majority of scholars believe that it was pulled together from a collection of earlier notes.

More important to the development of early Christianity were the open letters of Paul and others to the congregations of the new churches they had just founded. These are called the 'Epistles', Greek for 'letters', in the King James Bible. These give religious and practical guidance and explain the faith as (mostly) Paul saw it. The Letters were written before the Gospels and appear to refer to a quite different Belief to the reformed and revived Judaism the Gospels say Jesus talked about. Although he was much the same age as Jesus, Paul never met him and seems to have known virtually nothing about him, his life or his teaching. Paul only once indisputably quotes what Jesus said, and then only the words of the last supper ceremony[xxvii]. For Paul, the fact of Jesus' death and resurrection is all we need to know and there are no references in Paul's writing to any other events in Jesus' life.

For Paul, the resurrection is the central, symbolic miracle of the religion. It is Paul who explains Jesus' death as a human sacrifice to erase humanity's previous sins. The Letters contain not only advice but also much theology, especially in Paul's letter to the Romans, which summarised his thinking about the religion. This long letter not only provided the basis for Augustine's gloomy Catholic theology but Luther's Protestant 'justification by faith alone' (both outlined later). 'Romans' is probably closer to being the foundation document for Christianity than any other text. It is also Paul who introduces many of the ideas of Greek Philosophy into Christianity.

In doing this, Paul, half-accidentally, introduces the concept we now have of God: the single Creator, Lawgiver and Judge.

Paul, as a Jew, naturally started with the Jewish concept of one godlet, exclusive to the Jews, who had laid down the laws for the Jews to follow and who judged them accordingly (and whose name had, by now, not been used for 500 years). The Jewish godlet at this time was far from the only godlet that existed; it was central to Jewish Belief and history that their people were constantly being tempted to follow other godlets[26]. But Paul wanted non-Jews to adopt Christianity as well. *'Is he the God of the Jews only? Is he not also of the Gentiles? Yes, of the Gentiles also,'*[xxviii] said Paul. This meant that Paul's godlet had to be God and Lawgiver for everyone in the world, not just the godlet of the Jews. For Paul, it seems to have followed automatically that this one God must

---

[26] It will be remembered that the creation story in the Bible/Torah unequivocally states that the world was made by the gods, plural, in Hebrew. See 'Judaism' above.

be the same as the one that made the world, so other godlets were irrelevant or non-existent. Paul says so, and appears to have been aware that he was among the first to say so[xxix]. To this new vision, Paul added in the idea of the life after death, possibly originating in Zoroastrianism but long held by the Jewish Pharisee movement, a movement of which Paul was a proud member.

Although Paul's specific concept of God the Creator, Lawgiver and Judge was original to him, similar ideas were in the air at the time. Philo of Alexandria, another leading Jewish scholar of the period, also put forward a vision of a universal God, based on the Jewish tradition. These composite views of God linked the key ideas from the three most respected sources at the time: the Greek God-the-Creator, the Jewish God-the-Lawgiver and the Zoroastrian Judgement-after-Death. This concept of God, with a capital 'G', introduced first by Paul's Christianity, was to become the founding concept of Islam and, after that, on to Sikhism and is the basis of every sizeable Belief and sect until 1792CE. So powerful is this idea of One-God-Creator-and-Judge that it has been back-projected into subsequent readings of the Old Testament, despite numerous and clear references to other godlets, god walking in the cool of the evening, god wrestling with Moses, etc. Even atheists see Paul's God as the one that they don't believe exists.

But, for many, the problem of the existence of evil in the world had meant that the idea of a single, good creator God could not work. How could God who created the world be good, if evil – sometimes entirely random and naturally caused evil – exists in the world he created? Zoroastrianism had stumbled on this problem and had (apparently) changed its view to see the world as a battle between two opposing godlets, good and bad, as the solution. Fortunately, the Neo-Platonist school of Greek Philosophy had already developed the idea that evil is not an entity on its own but is simply an absence of good, just as darkness is not a thing in itself, just an absence of light. The answer the Christians got from the Neo-Platonists is that God is all good and all-powerful, but the existence of evil in the world shows that there are places, including many a human heart, where the spirit of God is absent. Paul clearly knew of these ideas and uses similar thoughts in his approach to the issue of God and evil.

The speculative thoughts of the Greeks, the third source of the Christian thinking, provided much more than a solution to the problem of evil. Well before Jesus' time, the idea of a composite creator, often seen as having three elements, was being discussed. Among these ideas was the three-fold separation of 'the One', the original spiritual creator; 'the Word', the transmitter of wisdom and insight; and 'the Builder' that built the physical world (these are the *Monados*, the *Logos* and the *Demiourgos* in Greek). Various other patterns of trinities were also put forward, but the idea of 'the Word' as a transmitter of Godliness/wisdom became very powerful as indicated by the first chapter of the Gospel of St John, which begins *'In the beginning was the Word and the Word was with God and the Word was God'*.

The fourth source for Christians was Jewish literature – most of which was later combined into one book, the Old Testament. The first five books of the Bible, known as the Torah to the Jews and their core holy texts, had been available in Greek for around 300 years before the Christian religion started. The rest of what we now call the Old Testament was being translated up to about 100CE. Many early Christians spoke Greek and very few of them spoke Hebrew, so this provided them with access to this huge and long-established body of writing.

So, with the Old Testament, the Letters, the ideas of Greek Philosophy and the Gospels, there were three alternative, rich and complex sources for the new Belief. When Christianity separated from Judaism, probably after the destruction of the temple in Jerusalem in 73CE, it became seen as a new cult, and therefore illegal in Roman law. Because Christianity was illegal, no Church authority in the early days could be very effective in controlling ideas. So this new cult, with its one creating and judging God, was launched, unconstrained, into a rich ecosystem of competing religions, philosophies, cults and ideas. Over the years, many different ideas about Christian theology and practice were considered. Branching groups split off, bickered with each other, reunited and split again, but, gradually, a core of orthodox thinking and practice developed among the Christians of the Roman Empire, along with a hierarchy of priests, deacons and bishops.

Christianity outside the Roman Empire developed

very differently and ideas such as the Divinity of Jesus and the Trinity were either not accepted at all or were seen very differently. Simplifying considerably, most of these churches saw Jesus as a (very important) human prophet, avoiding a mountain of theological complexity. This was the Christianity the Prophet Mohammad knew. For the sake of simplicity and because it has now been reduced to a tiny rump Belief, we will follow a long Western tradition and ignore this. All the discussion below relates only to the Christianity connected to the Roman Empire and its European successors.

So before Christianity became an official national religion of the empire, there was an extended struggle in the early Church between competing ideas about God, different ideas for religious services and alternative versions of scripture. This Darwinian struggle led to the survival of the fittest form of Belief; the survival of the ideas that made Christianity able to convert and convince, to expand and adapt, over 2,000 years and to meet the spiritual, social and psychological needs of millions of people in widely varying circumstances. But the complexity that makes it so adaptable also makes Christianity appear in many varied forms, as emphasis has shifted from one aspect of Belief to another. This complexity and adaptability has made it today the second largest Belief after Nationalism.

What held the many and varied forms of Belief together under the Christian label during this time in the Roman Empire was its illegality. Despite their huge variations of opinion and practice, all Christians looked to copy the Jewish tradition and refused to participate in any activity that involved godlets. But the Jews had been granted a special exemption from these duties because theirs was a Belief pre-dating the foundation of Rome and this exemption did not apply to Christians. This meant that all forms of civic or military advancement were closed to them. Every governmental post required some polytheistic ceremony that Christians refused to participate in. This gave a feeling of community and directed their energies into their religion. While the danger to life and limb from persecution was, in practice, generally remote, it certainly existed and could reawaken at any time. Roman persecution was intermittent and often less than thorough, but, periodically, some Christians did die for their religion. This 'persecution lite' is one of the great promoters of dissident movements, as many governments have found to their cost, and so it worked for Christianity. Martyrdom was seen as one of Christianity's glories and a willingness to suffer a martyr's death a sign of great holiness. The refusal to accept the ceremonies or practices of other religions became a central essence of Christianity, almost its defining characteristic, in the Roman Empire before 313CE. So, when Christianity moved from an illegal sect and became the official religion, it had a steely intolerance built in. Indeed, as soon as Christianity became the official religion of the Roman Empire, persecution of Christians who deviated from orthodox belief became much greater than persecution of Christians had ever been under the Greek/Roman Polytheism.

A bizarre mirror image of this history occurred in Iran. Christianity had faced only limited challenges from the Zoroastrian priesthood before 313 CE and had spread widely throughout the region. After Christianity became the official Roman religion, however, Christians were seen as enemy spies and severely persecuted, with hundreds of official executions of priests and bishops a year after 313CE. The pendulum swung, however, and by the middle of the next century, the Christian-on-Christian persecution of those who deviated from the approved line in the Roman (Byzantine) Empire was so strong that the Iranians were welcoming fleeing Christians for their fiercely anti-Roman attitudes.

The six key ideas that define the Christianity that emerged, after the conversion of the emperor Constantine, as the legal religion in the Roman Empire were:

Belief in one God: Creator, Lawgiver and Judge

This is Paul's powerful concept, despite its central problem that so many events seem both random and evil. But God the Creator is, for many, too remote a figure, too grand for individuals to relate to at a personal level. Something that created the infinity of time and space is awe-inspiring but seems unreachable. People wonder if he could be interested in individuals and the petty affairs of their behaviour. You can't easily ask the All-Powerful, Eternal Creator of the Universe to help your children in their exams. People also need a personal God who cares about what happens to them and what they do.

Belief that Jesus was the human form of God

Christians see Jesus as the human form of Paul's God, known as his Son (or as his divine messenger). Christians believe that Jesus told humanity about the important rules and practices to follow, albeit sometimes obscurely, building on older Jewish revelations. He also allowed himself to be killed but returned to life briefly. For many Christians, God could not forgive people who fail to follow the rules, sinners who repent, without the sacrifice of Jesus' death. Jesus' resurrection goes on to prove his significance and that God has the power to restore people to life after their deaths.

In early Christianity there was an immense and lengthy – and violent – set of arguments about the theological relationship of Jesus to the Creator/Judge God. For a period, whether Jesus could be the same as God or was a deeply holy prophet was argued about or, as some Christians still hold (the Nestorians), that Jesus had two 'natures', one human, one divine. The relationship is officially a 'mystery' and can nowadays be defined to suit the needs of the person asking.

The idea of a God who is killed and then rises to life again, in the process giving hope of life after death to others, was well known in many of the polytheistic Beliefs around the Roman Empire. It had a strong connection with the idea of the seasons: death in the winter, life returning in the spring. The oldest recorded example of the reincarnation of a godlet as a central religious idea is the story of Osiris, dating from at least

3000BCE. Osiris was an important Egyptian godlet, the hero of a number of legends (or versions of the same legend) that involve his death and resurrection. So Christian thinking about a godlet being killed and returning to life chimed in with some long-established ideas.

The idea of getting rid of sins by passing them on to an animal and then killing it or letting it escape was also well known and described in the Old Testament[xxx]. This is the origin of the term 'scapegoat' (short for 'escaped goat'): sins are ceremonially transferred to a goat that is allowed to escape, taking the sins with it. The Jewish ceremony of the Passover (Pesach) is linked to these ideas. It celebrates the legend in the Biblical Book of Exodus when Moses (Moshe) wanted Pharaoh to let the Children of Israel leave Egypt. Pharaoh was resisting giving permission, so to force him to agree, Yahweh sent the angel of death to kill the first-born son in every house in Egypt, but to 'pass over' those whose doors had been daubed with the blood of a lamb. The Israelites had been warned in advance to do this and so killed a lamb, using its blood to prevent the death of their child. So their children's lives were saved by the sacrifice of innocent lambs. In the Gospels, Jesus' death is set at the time of the feast of the Passover, linking Jesus' death to the death of the Passover lambs. Both are killed to save others. Terms like the 'Lamb of God' are sometimes used in place of Jesus' name in Christian liturgy in reference to this.

The death of Jesus also had resonance with the old, polytheistic belief that the bigger the sacrifice made to a godlet, the more likely the godlet was to listen to the request and grant it. So the sacrifice of a child, especially an only boy-child, was the greatest sacrifice one could make. The key legend is the story of Yahweh testing Abraham's faith by demanding that Abraham murder and burn his only legitimate son[27]. His willingness to do this pleased Yahweh so much that he promised the future prosperity of Abraham's descendants forever and that he would make them his special people. (Abraham had descendants because God let him off killing his son at the last moment.) This ancient tale of a godlet as a psychotic prankster has had great resonance. Christians see it as one of the key promises (Covenants) between God and mankind, with the human sacrifice of Jesus completing the process.

So there was a memory in Judaism and other religions that a human sacrifice could get a serious reward from a godlet, although it was rarely used in Roman times. God's desire for everyone's sins to be forgiven – a 'serious reward' indeed – was so strong that he needed to, and was prepared to, sacrifice his only son, Jesus. Paul's letters explain that is why Jesus had to die, although it is not clear why God could not forgive mankind without going through the process of a hideous killing.

The Holy Spirit (or in the King James Bible, the Holy Ghost) is the third, somewhat mysterious, aspect

---

[27] Abraham had only one son by his wife, Sarah: Isaac, who is seen as the forefather of the Israelites and Judeans. He had another, Ishmael, by his slave-girl, Hagar, the forefather of the Arabs.

of the Christian God. The 'Trinity' of Father, Son and Holy Ghost means that the Son is not just the junior partner to the Father, as he would have been in a purely Father/Son perception of God. The explanation of the relationship between these three is mysterious and was, for many years after Christianity became legal, another source of deep controversy and some violence. Since then it has been satisfactorily left as a mystery.

Absolute intolerance of other religions

Christianity largely invented religious intolerance and persecution. It is the only religion to be intolerant of all other religions and sects. The idea that you should, or can, physically force people to believe something is an odd one, but it is central to Christian history. Apart from a brief attempt by the Magi in Persia under the Sassanids, just before Christianity came to power in the Roman Empire, it was the first attempt to create a single Belief by force. This intolerance has faded over the last 200 years and is now very much a thing of the past for most Christian sects.

The Christian Belief has traditionally held that those with a creed that differs in any way, even if they call themselves Christians, are a danger to the Belief and should be converted or killed. This intolerance started as an adaptation of Jewish intolerance. Jews were intolerant, but only of other Jews who strayed. The Jews probably invented the concept of a 'sectarian' war, a war between people of the same overall Belief but different sects, seeking to force everyone to follow exactly the same creed. One sect attacking another in order to remove religious differences was certainly a flourishing practice during the Jewish revolt of 66–73CE. The Christian adaptation of this idea, following Paul's announcement of the concept of One God, was that everyone everywhere must worship the One God and must do so in the proper manner. The first full-blown Christian sectarian war, as opposed to the many earlier (and sometimes violent) sectarian quarrels, started just 200 years after Christianity was adopted as an official religion of the Roman Empire. The cause of the war was disagreement about the correct use of 'Holy, Holy, Holy' in the liturgy. The war was concluded in Constantinople in 518CE with a forced agreement and a death toll of around 65,000 Christians. Thereafter religious wars within (Romano/European) Christianity and between Christianity and other Beliefs were more or less continuous until around 1700CE.

Flexibility of belief and practice

The four different foundation sources of Christianity, the Gospels, the Epistles, Greek Philosophy and the Old Testament, could hardly be more different in their content or theology. This range of authorities has allowed a very wide range of beliefs and practices to come under the banner of Christianity. Indeed, it is difficult to think of any belief or (non-sexual) practice that has not been approved of as Christian at one time or another.

It would be impossible to list the many surprising

views that have been held in the name of Christianity. A couple of examples can show how wide the Belief could be stretched and still be seen as mainstream Christianity. For a long period, dirt – that is, not washing – was seen as a sign of holiness. Saint Jerome (Eusebius Sophronius Hieronymus, 347–420CE) so liked dirt that he encouraged Christians to tiptoe through puddles so as to prevent their feet being washed. Simon the Stylite, the epitome of this movement, gained a reputation for Christian holiness that spanned the Roman Empire by living on a small platform on top of a pillar for more than thirty years, refusing to wash or pick the lice off his body. He was much copied.

A second example: for centuries, owning a Bible in any form, including the official Church Latin version, was banned in many parts of Europe[xxxi]. People were sent to jail for owning or smuggling Bibles into many Catholic countries as late as the nineteenth century.

Some forms of Christianity have sought the richest, most elaborate music, art and architecture. Other forms require the most austere simplicity, banning music and 'frivolous' decoration. At one time, charity and self-sacrifice have been the sovereign Christian virtues. At another time, killing Christians with different views has been the sign of great Christian devotion. Some branches of Christianity require strict adherence to the exact words and movements in a service; Russia had a long-lasting civil insurrection over whether two or three fingers were to be used in the gesture of crossing, while other forms of Christianity believe in free expression as the Holy Spirit moves people.

Christianity was also very flexible in taking over and adapting traditions and festivities. Christmas took over from the old Roman mid-winter festival. It celebrated the return of the sun after the mid-winter solstice, heavy with candles. There is no Biblical reason for thinking Jesus' birth was at this time of year, which led the Scots Presbyterians (amongst others) to see Christmas as a Popish plot and to celebrate New Year's Day instead. It is said that the later Roman mid-winter festival lasted seven days, which is why New Year's Day is a week after Christmas.

The festival of Easter celebrates Jesus' return to life after his execution and is linked to the return of life after the winter. The Gospels say that Jesus' crucifixion was at the time of the Jewish festival of the Passover (Pesach), but the day of Passover is determined by the ancient lunar calendar and its date varies every year. Unfortunately, no one knows which year Jesus was crucified, although 30CE and 33CE are the best candidates, and, as a result, we don't know the date of his crucifixion. So the 'anniversary' of the event is linked to the variable date of the Passover, which is why the date of Easter varies every year.

In some cases, Christianity became so flexible it was in danger of losing its character altogether. When Augustine of Canterbury 'converted' the southern English to Christianity, so many compromises were made with the previous Polytheism – godlets turned into saints, etc. – that people couldn't tell the Christians apart from the pagans. The very name 'Easter' comes from the old Goddess of Spring, Eostre. So Augustine ruled that

Christians would not eat horsemeat. The Anglo-Saxon traditions still avoid horsemeat, happily eaten elsewhere in 'Christendom', to this day.

Life and judgement after death

Despite all the variations in Christian doctrine and practice, all Christians have always accepted that every person has a soul that continues after death. Most Christians have believed that the soul is judged after death, a judgement based on a person's obedience to the rules set by their Church. Judged on these, everyone's soul will be rewarded or punished, forever.

This belief came from Pharisaic Judaism, which was Paul's original faith and which believed in an afterlife. As the Pharisees were guided by Diaspora thinking in Babylon, which is close to the Zoroastrian homeland, they may, in turn, have got the idea from Zoroastrianism, which believed in an afterlife in which people would be judged. There are also passages in the Gospels about the future coming of the 'Son of Man', when he will judge the dead as well as the living, which can support the idea of a soul after death, although these passages refer to the end of the world. It is certainly a useful concept to explain the frequently observed disconnect between religious virtue and worldly success. It is a comforting thought that the rewards of virtue or the penalties of wickedness, although often unseen in this world, will be rebalanced – and more than rebalanced – after death. The wicked will eternally regret their errors as they are tortured forever, a sight, many preachers have asserted, that will add greatly to the refreshment of the virtuous as they look down on them from paradise.

What an individual has to do for their soul to go to heaven, rather than the eternal torment in Hell, has varied greatly. For many current Christians, it is self-evident that the key to approval in the afterlife is broadly ethical behaviour, aspiring to the ideal of treating others as you would, yourself, like to be treated. Technically, most Protestant theology disagrees with this. For Martin Luther, the original Protestant leader, man was saved by faith alone (Paul says this unequivocally in the letter to the Romans). So long as you truly believed the Trinity of God exists, you would go to heaven, regardless of your sins. For the Reform Protestant leader, John Calvin, whether you were saved or not was pre-determined: God is all knowing, so must already know whether you will be saved or damned to eternal torment. Nothing you could do would change your destiny and, in Calvin's opinion, not many of us are going to make it to heaven. Many Protestant sects, including the Pilgrim Fathers who sailed to America on the *Mayflower*, saw wealth as a sure sign that the wealthy person was one of the saved.

For the soul to go to heaven, Churches agree that good deeds alone are not enough; belief in the existence of the Christian Trinity and church attendance are also required. But it must be the right church: participating in the activities of other churches could lead to eternal damnation, regardless of good deeds. In the Medieval period, people deemed to be 'heretics', that is, people whose beliefs were different to those approved by the Church, were burned alive in Europe[28]. This was presented as a kindly act because, by destroying their bodies utterly, the fire would stop them having an afterlife and, hence, stop them being tortured for all eternity. It is said that the Inquisition took especial care to use green wood for burning heretics, since the slower burn gave the heretic longer to repent before they died.

Regular religious meetings in a special building, led by a special person

Early Christians did not have a temple where they could sacrifice and to act as a symbolic centre, so group meetings were held in the individual homes of the congregation. Gradually special buildings were created for religious events, following the same path as the Diaspora Jews 600 years earlier when they lost their temple. Christianity also copied the idea of religious services from the Jews and added a weekly community religious supper, re-enacting Jesus' last meal before his trial and execution. These two ceremonies merged into what is called Holy Communion, the Eucharist or the Mass in Christian churches, normally conducted on the weekly holy day – another Jewish invention. The need to conduct the weekly ceremonies and the existence of a special building gradually led to the development of a

---

[28] 'Heresy' came to mean 'wickedly wrong belief' in the language of the Church. It derives from the Greek word for 'choice'.

professional Church leadership and a priesthood – and hierarchy – developed.

For the vast majority of Christians (and Muslims and Jews), for most of their history, their religion has been about the Holy building, the Holy day and the Holy ceremony. It is a day when ordinary people stop working and come together as a community in a special and distinctive place. There they can touch something transcendent, something great and uplifting, something beyond the hard, humdrum lives they lead for the rest of the week. Although the message was sometimes muffled, they would be reassured that the God who created the universe loved them personally, that their sins would be forgiven and that they would, in the end, live forever in paradise. To get to paradise, all they had to do was avoid too much wickedness and come regularly to church, both of which they could realistically achieve. For many this was a great comfort in an often comfortless world and they cared greatly to keep it as it was.

This then was the complex Belief that emerged from its 300 or so years of illegality. The wilder variations of belief had been removed, the scriptures were agreed and the liturgy, the prayers and words of the services seem to have been similar across the Roman Empire. Sadly, as time was to show, there remained many different ideas about the nature of the Christian God and Trinity. But, despite persecution intermittently strengthening in the period after 250CE, there were many Christians in the Roman Empire, quite a few churches and a full hierarchy of priests, bishops and metropolitans (archbishops).

In 313CE the Roman Emperor Constantine endorsed Christianity after (it is said) a Christian vision had led him to victory. Following this, and with a few setbacks and internal arguments, Christianity, much as we know it today in its Catholic and Orthodox forms, gradually took over all the levers of religious power in the Roman Empire. In all, it took around a century for Christianity to officially displace most other religions in the Roman Empire. The replacement of Polytheism, Greek Philosophy and various cults by Christianity was accompanied by changes that made Christianity resemble Polytheism more closely, among the common people at least. Past heroes of Christianity and mythical figures, such as Saint Christopher, were raised to the status of godlets[29]. You could pray to them and they had their own areas of influence as patron saints of professions, of towns, of activities such as travel and so on. Pictures of saints, known in Orthodoxy as 'Icons', and relics, such as bits of saintly skeleton, developed magical powers and attracted the veneration of individuals and cults.

As Christianity became the dominant religion in the Roman Empire, in name at least, politics quickly divided it into three traditions.

Outside the Roman Empire, Christianity remained a minority religion, except in Ethiopia. These Christians had large congregations for many centuries, from Basra

---

[29] For the Greeks, the Old Testament prophet Elijah, under the name 'Elias' was made a saint. There are still many small shrines in Greece to St Elias where the sun, Elios, used to be worshipped.

on the Persian Gulf to Chang An in China. They seem to have quietly got on with growing their congregations until the whirlwind arrival of Islam. After that Christianity persisted in the east, sticking closely to its practices and core beliefs with gradually shrinking numbers caused both by periodic persecution and from just being in a minority.

The eastern Roman Empire, also known as the Byzantine Empire, survived another 1,000 years until 1453. The emperor was head of the Church in all but official name and ruled it through its hierarchy of patriarchs and bishops. The early centuries, however, were far from smooth, especially in the capital, Constantinople/Byzantium. This city became by far the largest in the empire and was known for its factional politics and rioting. With the coming of Christianity, faction fighting switched from different chariot-team supporters to different religious groups. The eastern Roman Empire was a region with a high degree of literacy, which enabled some people to form independent religious opinions within the overall name of Orthodox Christianity. The worst of the resulting riots came with the 'Iconoclastic' (Holy-picture-destroying) movement. The Iconoclasts argued that pictures of saints, together with a collection of 'high Church' practices, led to the worship of the pictures themselves and that this was a perversion of Christianity. They wanted the Church to move to plainer decoration and practices based more clearly on (their view of) the Bible. The Iconoclastic argument is similar to what Protestants said in the

Western European reformation 800 years later. It gained much of its strength from the huge military success of the Islamic armies at the time. Islam rejected any pictures of humans or animals and had inflicted a series of crushing defeats on the Byzantines. For a brief period the emperors followed Iconoclastic rules, but they returned to the ornamentation of churches, the veneration of saints and the domination of the Church by government power as soon as they could. This government-controlled version of Christianity became known as 'Orthodox' (Greek for 'straight thought'). It was later adopted by Vladimir of Kiev, ruler of the country that later became Russia, defining Russia's national religion to the present day. Despite the fact that literacy levels remained high in the Byzantine Empire, the Church gradually managed to build up a tight control of religious opinion. This was achieved in part by making the religion mysterious. Services were largely hidden behind screens covered in holy paintings and made deliberately inaudible to the congregation. Priests kept a tight rein on holy literature and the Belief became, in practice, a state-controlled Polytheism.

Religiously, little changed thereafter in the Byzantine Empire. The Byzantine patriarchs, as the top of the Church hierarchy was known, saw no reason why the Bishop of Rome, the Pope, should be particularly respected. Nor was there any reason to adopt the theology or practices of the Western Christians, whom they saw as uncouth at best. This disrespect was thoroughly reinforced by the arrival of the brutal, unhygienic

Frankish mob of the First Crusade in 1096, passing through Byzantium on their way to the 'Holy Land'. They were quickly helped on their way towards Jerusalem. In 1204, the Knights of the Fourth Crusade topped this. They were again, in theory, on their way to 'liberate' the Holy Land, but they 'accidentally' sacked and occupied the immensely wealthy city of Constantinople/Byzantium instead. This experience convinced many Orthodox Christians that Islamic rule would be better for their religion than Catholic rule.

After the final conquest of the Byzantine Empire by the Turkish sultan, Mehmet, in 1453, this expectation turned out to be true and the Orthodox Church continued, with no direct interference from the Islamic beliefs of the sultan. The Christian patriarch simply reported to the sultan rather than the emperor. The Greek Orthodox Church continued to act as an instrument of government for the Christian population of the Ottoman Empire until the influence of Nationalism after 1821 destroyed the centuries of religious co-existence. Despite this, the Patriarch of Istanbul (in Turkey) is still head of the Greek Orthodox Church.

While the Byzantine Empire lasted over a thousand years after conversion to Christianity, the Roman Empire in the west soon fell to bits. From around 400CE pagan tribes from the north assailed it and all central authority was lost. Large areas of Western Europe reverted to simple, illiterate peasant living with intermittent primitive warfare, a lifestyle that continued for hundreds of years. But, while Rome, the former imperial capital, was repeatedly sacked, Christianity hung on and the patriarch of Rome, known as the Pope (it simply means 'Father'), was, generally, free of a dominating emperor. At first, the northern part of the empire largely forgot about Christianity, but missionary efforts by Christians from Italy, England and Ireland, supported later by massive forced conversion and the slaughter of thousands of recalcitrant heathens by Charlemagne and others, resulted in the conversion or re-conversion of most of Western Europe to Christianity, in name at least.

We can pick up the story around 1000CE. Western Europe was recovering from its decline and warfare was becoming a little less frequent as the development of the castle consolidated the authority of leading families. The Church in Western Europe had become a separate and important power in itself and virtually the whole of the area called itself Christian. The Papacy in Rome was regaining some esteem after a period when it had sunk to startling levels of debasement. Self-sustaining monasteries, a crucial development of the earlier period of turbulence, embodied civilised values and preserved what little literacy there was. To avoid obedience to local bishops, who at this date were mostly appointed by kings, monasteries often arranged that they owed obedience only to the Pope. Over the next hundred years or so this was to enable the Pope to develop the authority to gain a great deal of control over the Church in Western Europe. It was also at this period that priestly celibacy became a requirement.

Medieval Christianity in Western Europe produced the most technically accomplished and beautiful buildings anywhere before the industrial age. But Christianity itself fell into the pattern of a standard Polytheism. Church services were in Latin, incomprehensible to all but churchmen – and only a few of them understood it well. There were a very limited number of copies of the Bible or other books and, because only churchmen were literate and could understand Latin, the books were accessible to only a tiny number of people, pretty much all of them committed to supporting the Belief as it stood. Only a few popularised stories from the Bible and other religious sources, such as the lives of the saints, the equivalent of polytheistic legends, were widely known, even to most churchmen. In the absence of any depth to faith, relics – magic objects – became consumingly important; bones of saints, fragments of the true cross and odd items associated with holy people were seen to have great importance and magic powers. There was a generalised understanding that there was a God who was the Creator and Judge and that there was an afterlife with heaven and Hell and that your sins could be forgiven, perhaps by getting the saints or the Virgin Mary to plead with Jesus/God on your behalf. Merit could be gained through pilgrimages to certain holy places and assorted holy activities. Finally, the prayers of the living could help the fortunes of the dead, waiting in the afterlife for their sins to be purged away before they could ascend to heaven.

The crusades (taking up the cross) were a defining factor for Western European Christianity in this period. The First Crusade, a mission to recapture the Holy Land from 'infidels' who were preventing Christian pilgrims from visiting Jerusalem, was announced in 1095 and immediately caught the imagination of Western Europe. In fact, Christians at the time had perfectly easy access to anywhere they wanted in Jerusalem. Fifty years earlier it had been closed to Christians for a short period under Al-Hakim, the Imam of Egypt, who came to believe he was a god himself[30]. After his death in 1021, access to Jerusalem had been reopened to all as it had been before.

The First Crusade succeeded in capturing Jerusalem and several Catholic mini-kingdoms were set up (for more detail see the chapter on Islam). These kingdoms lasted for around a hundred years, largely dependent on continuing help from the west. There were several later military missions, also called crusades, to the area. The crusades gave Catholic, Western European Christianity a unity that little else could, a unity that strengthened the moral power of its head, the Pope. They also went a long way to defining Islam as a separate religion. Before the crusades it was not fully agreed by Islamic scholars whether Christianity, Judaism and Islam were different schools of the one true religion or different religions. The crusades clinched the argument in favour of the different religion opinion.

While there were several waves of crusades directed at Jerusalem, there were on-going crusades in Iberia,

[30] An opinion apparently shared to this day by the Druze, a tribe/group based in Syria/Lebanon.

where the Christian kingdoms of the north saw their battle with the Muslim south as part of the same struggle, and on the Baltic coast, where, for many years, the Teutonic Knights offered a summer season of heretic killing for knights from across Europe[31]. The Medieval Church in Western Europe united itself and extended its reach by arms ruthlessly wielded.

The idea of a single, monolithic Medieval Catholic Church in Western Europe is both right and wrong. Wrong because both faith and practice varied enormously. But as far as being a Belief with a unified system of higher education, access to reading, the holy language of Latin and the power to save the souls, it was one organisation from Oslo in Norway to Naples in southern Italy.

The treatment of a group of heretics in the south of France illustrates both the Belief's power and its limits in the Middle Ages. They were known as the Cathars, from the Greek word meaning 'pure', or Albigensians, after the regional town, Albi. The Cathar Belief was extremely anti-Catholic. Cathars saw the world, as the Manicheans and Gnostics had done, as a battleground between a good, spiritual godlet and an evil, material godlet. To add to that, they believed that the godlet the Catholics worshipped was the evil one. In practice, however, their appeal stemmed from the transparent

---

[31] The heretics in question were called the 'Prusai' and their country 'Prussia'. At the reformation, the Grand Master of the Teutonic Knights changed into the Count of Prussia. Later his family became the kings of Prussia and, later still, emperors of Germany.

spirituality of many of their leaders. This was in stark contrast to the worldliness and greed of much of the Catholic hierarchy. Despite their extreme position, they were ignored for at least fifty years before the Church reacted. This period enabled the Cathars to establish a strong position with eleven of their own bishops. The Pope finally declared a crusade against them in 1209. Even then, it was largely the Pope's promise that knights could keep any land they seized from the Cathars' protector, Count Raymond of Toulouse, that drove the crusaders to attack. Frankish barons at the Church's behest exterminated the Cathars in an intermittent twenty-year campaign. The various sieges often ended in mass killing of Cathars who refused to accept the Church at sword-point. The Catholic Inquisition was originally set up in 1229 to prevent a repetition of such heresy. It lasted until 1908.

The elements of civilisation improved during the Middle Ages. By 1250 the authority of the Pope had become so effective throughout much of Western Europe that he was largely able to select the bishops and abbots he wanted. The Church on the ground was improving its religious teaching, with relatively well-taught travelling friars helping local priests, who were often near-illiterate, to communicate the elements of Christianity. Some of the more dubious local practices were abolished and there was widespread building of churches and the start of universities. There was a flowering of philosophical thinking about Christianity, most notably in the writing of Thomas Aquinas.

Education and literacy were beginning to be found among some non-priests, as well as in Church life. The development of independent approaches to the Bible shows the growing literacy. The Valdensians, for example, founded around 1170 and declared heretical in 1184, translated the Bible into the Provençale language. The Lollards in England started to rethink belief based on the Bible and had a brief period of success in the late 1300s. Each movement we know about probably represents a much larger number of less organised independent thinkers and quiet critics of the Church.

But the revival of literacy and philosophy in the Church seems to have slowed in the century after 1300. This might have been because of the endemic and worsening corruption of the Church, or because of the effect of the Pope moving to Avignon in 1309 and the later splitting of the Church, with two competing popes from 1378 to 1415. The main reason was probably distraction caused by the slaughter of one-third to half the population in the Black Death, which started in 1348 and returned a number of times.

The growth in literacy seems to have returned gradually after 1400 in Western Europe and, with it, the development of the printing industry (moveable type printing had already been used in China for 700 years). From around 1450 printed leaflets, pamphlets, newsletters, small tracts and scripture excerpts came out in huge and profitable profusion, sold for pennies at street corners to an increasingly involved public. People's willingness to pay for pamphlets shows the extent of literacy and the availability of interesting written material in the everyday languages led to further improving literacy. This set off the bomb that lay at the heart of the Medieval Christian Belief: that there was no link between the Belief as practised and its founding documents. Literacy and printing meant that, over the following century, the Bible, sold in parts as cheap pamphlets, became widely available in the ordinary languages people spoke. Effectively, a new Belief became possible, one that shared only the name, Christianity, with the Polytheism of the Middle Ages. A process started that had strong similarities to the impact of the Qur'an on the moderately literate population of the eighth-century Middle East: a new religion arose where a book, not the Church, was the fundamental link between man and God.

The (Roman Catholic) Church simultaneously reached new levels of disgrace. It was led from 1492 to 1521 by three successive popes of varied, obvious and outstanding wickedness. These were: Alexander VI, the Borgia Pope. He was famous for the orgies he organised and the lengths he went to promote the interests of his children. He was followed by Julius II, from the Della Rovere family, who donned armour to fight in battle, and Urban IV, the first Medici family Pope, who was not even a priest when he became Pope and who promoted the mass sale of indulgences to fund his lifestyle (and, to be fair, the rebuilding of St Peter's in Rome). All achieved their high office through bribery. Their biographies make stimulating, but not improving, reading.

This catalysed the split in Western European Christianity, starting in 1517, between peoples who followed the authority of the Church, who remained Catholics, and those who gave primacy to their own understanding of the sacred texts, who became known as Protestants. There had been earlier splits, such as the Lollards in England and the Hussites in Bohemia, but the Church and its royal supporters had contained them. This, later, explosive break was fuelled by widespread literacy, inflamed by printed leaflets, fired by the profound corruption at the top of the old Church and could not be damped down.

The Reformation of the Church is normally seen as starting when a German teaching monk, Martin Luther, put forward a list of objections to Church practices. He particularly objected to the Church selling 'indulgences', certificates that reduced the time the soul would have to wait in purgatory before it could go to heaven. Once he translated his list into German (from its original Latin), the criticisms went viral. Within a month Luther's 'Ninety-Five Theses', printed as leaflets, were on sale all over Western Europe.

Disgust with the established – and Mediterranean-dominated – Church meant that much of Northern Europe needed no more than this spark for change to catch fire. Informal Protestantism spread rapidly. Almost immediately it included several of the leading princes of the Holy Roman Empire, a rambling relic of medieval feudalism that covered much of central Western Europe. Such was the desire for change that the lands of the empire were seized by a widespread peasants' revolt in 1524/5. This appalled Luther and put him firmly on the side of the existing powers of the aristocracy. Ever after, Luther was a solid supporter of princely authority and, since then, Lutheran Churches have remained supportive of secular authority and have adopted a top-down structure of authority themselves.

Very shortly after Luther's leaflet, the anti-Catholic movement spread to districts that did not have a prince but were ruled by committees of leading citizens. These, led by the towns of Zurich, Geneva and Strasbourg, adopted Protestantism, but, not having princes, their approach was different to Lutheranism, emphasising the puritanical values of their ruling bodies. This strand is generally known as 'Reform Protestants' or Calvinists, after John Calvin, the leader of the Geneva Church, to distinguish them from the Lutherans.

Protestantism in all its varieties rests on the belief that Christianity is best understood from the Bible. This inevitably means that different people draw different guidance and that some of their takes will be different enough to form different Churches. So Protestantism naturally splits into differing sects. Some of these sects became so different as to be considered outside Christianity altogether. During the reformation these extreme groups were often lumped together as 'Anabaptists' (believers in being re-baptised).

The response of the Catholic Church to the criticisms of Protestantism and to its loss of control over large areas of Northern Europe was to react back. A full council of the Church was called in Trento in northern Italy to respond to the development of Protestantism. The Council of Trent, as it is known in English, redefined the Catholic Church; the supreme authority of the Church on belief was reasserted: services, prayer and the Bible were to remain in Latin. Catholic practice was put under much tighter regulation than previously. On a more visceral level, the Catholic Church redoubled its efforts to impress with art, magniloquent church architecture and music to battle against the, sometimes dour, protestant practices and churches.

This set the stage for the subsequent bloodbath, a struggle for dominance between the Catholic Belief of the Church and the Protestant Belief of the Book. What caused the change from the earlier, less bloody period was not the changes in the faith, nor even the many changes in the Belief itself, but the circumstances the Belief found itself in. Before the reformation, Christianity seems to have believed in killing those who disagreed with it just as vigorously as afterwards, but it had fewer targets and a looser definition of its Belief. Few European heretics or schismatics ('splitters') were killed before 1517 because (Western European) Christian Belief encountered few of them. As soon as the Belief encountered a large number of non-Christians, the Cathars, for example, or in the newly discovered continent of America, the 'convert or kill' pattern was adopted the minute it became practicable. Before the reformation, the Castilians had already applied this to Granada, the last remnant of the Arabic Empire in Iberia, which they finally conquered in the same years that Columbus 'discovered' America. What changed with the reformation was not the pathology (pattern of disease) of the Belief but its environment. Suddenly it found people it disagreed with in large numbers as Europe split into two opposed camps, albeit within the same overall Belief. All sides were equally vile to each other in the religious wars that followed.

The conflict between the two branches of Christianity started with insults but rapidly became violent. Religious differences were added into existing political conflicts, compounding the horrors of war, embittering already difficult situations and adding another source of discord. When a political problem was solved, the religious divide kept the conflict alive. When a religious dispute was settled, a political one reignited the struggle. One by one, the different regions of Western Europe fought sustained wars, wars that only came to an end after years of barbarity, slaughter and atrocity, with the complete exhaustion of all involved. This mixed religious/political struggle across the whole of Western Europe was complicated, but its long-term impact on the Belief was minimal, apart from the exhaustion. It is a period when the Christian Belief demonstrated that it had the flexibility to endorse and encourage the worst in human behaviour.

The Holy Roman Empire, the area roughly of modern Germany, suffered particularly badly, as the religious conflict was linked to the political conflict between the power of the emperor and the independent power of the princes. While the emperor was, in theory, elected by a very small group of individual electors, at this period, the Hapsburg King of Austria was always elected. The title of emperor led the Austrian kings to assert authority over the princes of the 'Holy Roman Empire', against their determination to remain independent in practice. The independence they treasured was both political and religious – hence the endless confusion as these issues became muddled. The emperor attempted to enforce Catholicism within the empire but faced strong resistance from Protestant princes, often supported by (Catholic) France, keen to prevent the emperor gaining real control in the areas bordering France. The kings of Poland and Denmark were also involved because they also had principalities within the empire, so they and their friends, notably the King of Sweden, joined the fight and added to the misery. The early wars of religion 1531–48 were followed by a restless peace before the same basic set of conflicts restarted as the Thirty Years' War of 1618–48. Both wars were devastating. The Thirty Years' War alone is said to have reduced the population by one-third. At the end, the various states that make up roughly what we now call Germany were still split between Catholics and Protestants and the issues of the emperor's real power over the kings and princes was just as unresolved as it was at the start of the wars.

For two centuries, Europe seemed to be playing tag with anarchy and mayhem, with different areas dissolving into war in turn. The French Civil War 1562–98, the

Dutch Wars of Independence 1556–1609, and the English, Scottish and Irish Civil Wars of 1642–51/3 were all rendered longer and grimmer by the toxic mixture of religious and political issues. Only Italy's endemic anarchy and Spain's ferocious monarchy avoided religious complications in their wars.

As the religious wars finally ground to a halt, the position of the two groups in Europe was largely unchanged. Italy, Spain and Portugal remained Catholic; France and the empire stayed split between Catholics and Protestants, although France expelled or forced conversion of most Protestants later. The Scandinavian countries, England and Scotland remained predominantly Protestant and Ireland predominantly Catholic (but ruled by Protestants) as they all had been before the wars. The northern Netherlands remained Protestant (and got independence from the Spanish king), the southern Netherlands remained Catholic. Even Bohemia (the Czech lands), most of whose people had been effectively Protestant since Jan Hus in 1420, was forced, as a kingdom, to stay officially Catholic, as it had been from the start of the wars. The exception was Poland, which became Catholic after several options were considered.

Despite being forced by necessity into groupings, the many different Christian sects that arose covered a wide spectrum of religious belief and practice. On one extreme was Catholic Spain, where unauthorised possession of a Bible – even in Latin – remained a crime punishable by prison. At the other extreme there were black-dressed Puritans who read the Bible three times a day. Some of these recorded their attempts to lessen their love for their children in order that they could beat them harder and so force God's way into them better. All that these diverse Beliefs seem to have shared is the name of their religion, the idea of one God/three aspects and a deep intolerance of anyone with different religious views. It is difficult to exaggerate how odd some of these groups were in both their theology and practices. Although the Catholics were always theoretically united, some quite divergent strands developed, going from the intellectualism of the Jesuits to the mysticism of the Discalced Carmelites (don't ask). Some Protestants went through many vicissitudes to become the eccentric Mennonites and Amish of Pennsylvania. Others formed a totalitarian commune in the town of Munster that perished after a ghastly siege and defeat. Some followed the mystery of the Rose Cross, even after its founder was exposed as a fraud. And so on. The Netherlands stands out as the only area that practised a toleration of diverse religious opinion. Elsewhere Protestant majority and Catholic majority areas were in complete agreement on only one matter: that persecution of other forms of Belief was righteous.

During the 1700s the political passion for religion in Western Europe that had fuelled the earlier wars somehow drained away. The last battle where the sides were principally defined by being Protestant and Catholic was the Battle of Aughrim, 1691, in central Ireland, between forces representing the Dutch Protestant interest under General Godert de Ginkell and the French Catholic interest under the Marquis de St Ruth. (In

Ireland it is often creatively described as a battle between the English and the Irish – see Nationalism.) Somehow, after all this slaughter, moderation and some level of tolerance became the norm. Disagreements that had fuelled murderously strong passions in 1640 had become a matter of mild reproach by 1740. It came to be seen as a largely private matter which sect of Christianity someone belonged to; a personal choice, although minority sect followers were generally debarred from public office. Even overt and public disbelievers, like Voltaire, Gibbon, Benjamin Franklin or Goethe, were quietly tolerated where once they would have been tried or lynched. Unorthodox associations and Churches were officially accepted with little more than disapproving comment, even when, like the Quakers, Freemasons, Unitarians or Mormons, their beliefs were very different to the majority – although local hotheads continued to stir up trouble for unusual believers at times. It seems that, once every form of murder and cruelty had been tried, tried again, and still failed, attempts to force a particular Belief on people were simply abandoned, albeit only after decades of murder, cruelty, etc.

The history of the North American colonies reflects this extraordinary change in the tolerance of the Christian Belief. Before about 1700 many of the colonists had, famously, fled to America to escape persecution of their particular Beliefs. However, and with some honourable exceptions, as soon as they arrived and settled, they started to persecute individuals whose views or religious practices diverged from theirs. Yet, they too seem to have found religious tolerance after 1700. So much so that, during the 1800s, the USA became a fertile source of very divergent sects, all living together at peace with each other. European empire building after 1700 was completely disconnected from religious belief. The Christian missionaries that did come to the lands of the empires were mostly resented by the colonial authorities as troublemakers, rather than welcomed for converting the heathens.

New European Christian movements after 1700, such as Methodism, concentrated on practical issues, such as making access to Christianity physically available to all, by preaching outdoors and by building new churches for the growing population. For many, religion became just something people did on a Sunday and the Church became part of the social structure, abandoning political activity. Although non-conformists at the start of this period still faced discriminatory laws in much of Europe, the discrimination was more a limitation in the role they were allowed to play in government and society, rather than the daily persecution they would have faced in the previous century. After a quiet century or so the new Belief of Nationalism took over the role of stirring turbulent political passions among the Europeans from 1792. It seems as though the Christian Belief was settling down to a period of political quiescence again, as Judaism did after 500CE and Islam after 900CE.

An exception to this quiescence was China. Here circumstances were such that, when a mutant variety of Christianity arose, a bloodbath ensued. Around 1850

Hong Xiuquan announced that he had discovered in a vision that he was the younger brother of Jesus. Before it was suppressed, the ensuing Taiping rebellion cost the lives of some 20 million people, probably the largest death toll from any single war before the twentieth century.

For the vast majority of Christians today the original six key ideas of Christianity remain. Paul's idea of a universal Creator/Lawgiver God is completely entrenched, Christians agree that Jesus is the human aspect of a tripartite God (with the God the Father and Holy Spirit) and few worry about the exact nature of this identity. The eternal life of the soul is accepted, although the population of Hell is now thought to be smaller than it was – most Christians now think God's judgement will be more forgiving than they used to. (But not all Christians have so generous a view: Jehovah's Witnesses believe that only 144,000 people will be saved.) The intolerance has faded and there remains a huge variety of practice and belief: from rocking Pentecostals to chanting Monks, from devotees of the Virgin Mary to those Christians who see all religions as different views of the same truth.

Like Buddhism, Christianity had become a path for a personal journey to enlightenment or salvation. Each individual chooses his or her own path – or, more generally, inherits the choice from their parents – and selects the Church they see as best able to help them. Over the last 100–200 years this has become largely accepted as an individual's right to choose. The results of

Christian faith are now most often seen as personal: a better, happier acceptance of this world through understanding each person's importance to God and the prospect of happiness in the life after death.

Over the last 200 years the newer, secular Beliefs have dominated politics. There are, however, signs that the Christian Belief in some areas is beginning to revert to the political and intolerant position it has had for most of its history. In the USA and in parts of Latin America, Asia and Africa, a unified political stance of the Christian Belief is emerging.

In America, starting with abortion, there are an increasing number of areas where the Christian Belief is moving to a position where it is seeking ways to compel everyone to behave in certain ways. As the divisions in American political society continue to build between the 'Liberal' and 'Conservative' groupings, a united political Belief may emerge again under the Conservative-Christian banner. There have been several attempts to set up such a united front already. If it succeeds, there is no reason to expect it to be any kinder than the Christian Belief was when it was previously politically powerful.

Some form of mutation of the Belief in a country new to the Christian Belief cannot be ruled out either. Many developing areas have dissatisfactions that are not unlike those of the Chinese at the start of the Taiping rebellion. There are many charismatic preachers developing powerful followings in parts of Africa and it is entirely possible that some might follow a charismatic leader with claims of Christianity into political and violent action as the Chinese followed Hong Xiuquan.

On balance, though, it looks as though the Christian Belief will keep its position as a mainly personal religion and not reprise its violent history. But this is by no means assured and we must be careful to identify and address pathological mutations at an early stage.

Postscript: The Old Testament

The Old Testament of the Christian Bible, and the very similar (but much later) Jewish Tanakah, has a complex origin. It is most of the literature of the Jews before the year 1, but all bound into one book and with some other stuff added: thirty-nine completely separate Hebrew scrolls with an additional seven later scrolls (or some say nine) that seem to have been originally written in Greek and some of which were, in part or all, written in Aramaic. Doing the same thing for the Greeks would have put together the *Iliad* and *Odyssey* with the plays of Aristophanes, some old folk-legends, the histories of Xenophon and Herodotus, the writing of Plato, the poetry of Sappho and the odd Latin piece as well. So the Old Testament is a fairly mixed bag.

The writings were selected because of a legend that the Jewish Scholars of Alexandria, who translated Jewish literature into Greek, were divinely guided. They were, according to legend, seventy-two scholars, called the 'Septuagint' (from the Latin for 'Seventy'). Septuagint also became the title of any writings that were thought to be translated by them.

Most Jewish literature had been translated into Greek by the time of the early Christians. The first five books of the Bible, known as the Torah to the Jews and their core holy texts, had been available in Greek for around 300 years. More Hebrew writing was being translated up to about 100CE. Many early Christians – and probably most Jews in the Roman Empire at the time – spoke Greek and very few of them spoke Hebrew, so the Septuagint provided them with access to this huge and long-established body of writing.

We don't know directly what the Septuagint included. Only the Torah, the first five books, had been held together as the Jewish holy book before. The book we now call the Old Testament consists of what were, originally, forty-six completely separate scrolls that the early Christian scholar, Origen (200CE), decided were in the Septuagint.

Origen left quite a lot of old Jewish material out of the Old Testament, including some that is mentioned in the New Testament, such as the Book of Enoch. Perhaps it is as well that Enoch's tales were left out. The story of angels coming down to earth to seek earth women and the resultant race of giants called the Nephrim that were wiped out in Noah's flood – and much else contained in it – is not very elevated. On the other hand, Origen included some very odd material, such as the 'Song of Songs' or 'Song of Solomon', an erotic poem with no apparent spiritual content. But Origen was a great believer in allegorical interpretation of scripture: the less obvious the straightforward meaning of a text, the more he saw it as holy. The Song of Songs was a particular favourite of his. He interpreted lines such as *'Thy two breasts are like two young roes that are twins that feed amongst the lilies'* as showing God's love for his Church. But then Origen was more than a little odd. He decided that

Christianity was opposed to sex and so, in order to, as he put it, 'disarm the tempter', he castrated himself.

How the forty-six scrolls became one book is even odder. It happened that the early Christians mostly kept their writings in the then-unusual format of codices (singular, a codex). This format is the same as the books we have now, with separate pages and a binding. The codex format was uncommon at the time, except for use as personal notebooks, and scrolls were the universal format for 'proper' books. We don't know why the Christians preferred the codex form, but it may have been because, for an illegal religion, it is easier to hide. By the time Origen was considering the Septuagint, it was accepted that Christian writing was never in scrolls but always bound as a codex.

As a result, all the different Jewish scrolls in Origen's Septuagint were united between one set of covers in Christian usage. Also as a consequence of this preferred style of bookbinding, they were given one name, the Old Testament (meaning 'witness'), rather than being in forty-six different scrolls. This gave all the scrolls some sort of equality of authority and venerability, although they include material of many different types, ages and qualities in two main languages. Some of it is Jewish law, some history, some prophecy, some family lists, some poetry or songs, some priestly rules of the old polytheistic religion before the Exile. Many old legends are included, and some improving plays, such as the book of Job, as well as the lustful Song of Songs. So, while much of the Bible was translated later into Latin direct from Hebrew sources, rather than from the Greek translation, the decision as to what was included was never questioned.

There is more dispute about the basic contents of the Old Testament than you might imagine. Churches of the East have some books that the West does not have and exclude some the West includes – but none of these are very central texts. Martin Luther excluded the later books from the Old Testament and called them the 'Apocrypha', meaning 'hidden' in Greek. Most Protestant Churches follow Luther's lead, but Catholics keep them in, as they have done since the earliest period of Christianity.

Protestant and Catholic Churches even have noticeably different versions of the Ten Commandments. The first three Catholic Commandments read:

1. *I, the Lord, am your God. You shall not have other gods besides me.*
2. *You shall not take the name of the Lord God in vain.*
3. *Remember to keep holy the Lord's Day.*

The Protestant ones read:

1. *You shall have no other God but me.*
2. *You shall not make unto you any graven images*
3. *You shall not take the name of the Lord your God in vain.*

Jesus is reported in the Gospels as saying that he came to fulfil the law and the prophets, while St Paul said that Jesus brought a new covenant (agreement with God) to replace the old one. This allows Christians to use the enormous range of writings of the Old Testament, a rich and, even at the time of the early Christians, prestigiously ancient group of scriptures, without requiring that they accept it all.

The Jews call the Old Testament writings the 'Tanakah' but only agreed the final version around the ninth century CE when the so-called Masoretic text was finalised by members of the Masorite part of the Karaite Jewish sect. The term Tanakah is a compound word derived from the Jewish view that it is formed of three different kinds of books: 'Ta' from the 'Torah', meaning 'teaching', the first five holy books; 'Na' from 'Nevi'im', meaning prophets; and 'Kah' from 'Ketuvim', meaning 'writings'.

Rabbinic Judaism uses only the teaching of the Torah (the first five books of the Bible) and the Talmud, which is not included in the Tanakah, as the Karaite Jews did not follow it. Conventional Judaism regards the rest of the Tanakah, the Nevi'im and Ketuvim, as mainly of historic interest. The decision by the Masorites to put all this mixed material together into one book – but excluding the Talmud – was surely taken in imitation of the Christian Bible.

.5.

ISLAM:
THE PATH THAT
LOST ITS WAY

slam is the name of the religion founded by the
Prophet Mohammad in 622CE. It means 'submission'
(to the will of God) in Arabic, the language of
Mohammad. All the early Muslims, as the followers of
Islam are known, spoke Arabic.

Islam is proud of its simplicity. One God, one
Prophet, one Book and five simple rules make someone
a Muslim. Every Islamic revival has been presented as an
attempt to regain this simplicity and re-live the life of the
early companions of Mohammad.

Islam is the product of one man's experience and life.
Mohammad ibn (son of) Abdul Muttalib was a happily
married family man and a prosperous trader in the
Arabian city of Mecca when, in 612CE, at around the
mature age of forty, he started to have visions, messages
sent to him by God. Ten years later, Mohammad fled
from Mecca, just escaping a plan to murder him. Another
eight years later and he returned to Mecca as a conqueror.

Within thirty years the Arabs, who had previously been a no-account collection of feuding desert tribes, had conquered most of the world he knew and, fired by their new Belief, were going into lands Mohammad himself had barely heard of. For 300 years, Islam progressed forwards: powerful, tolerant, enlightened, sophisticated and successful.

Then it stopped: somewhere around 1000CE and, it is said, the doors of '*itjihad*', that is independent or progressive decision-making, were closed. Religious intolerance started to develop together with polytheistic-style collections of godlets and legends. The few reform movements of the next 1,000 years were backward looking and puritanical, until we arrive at the conflicted pattern of contemporary political Islam.

For many young Muslims and for as many outsiders, the image of Islam today is of an apparently ignorant old man with a huge beard and desert clothes, harshly claiming absolute religious authority to lock everyone into a nightmarish world of bigotry and poverty – a world from which so many Muslims have fled and so many more would flee if they could. What was a Belief of clarity and scholarship seems to have become a vehicle for bigots and bullies. What was the unifying, progressive force of Arabia has become a medieval-style set of kingdoms and dictatorships, spiced with RPG (Rocket Propelled Grenade)-toting fanatics. These keep their people in dirt poverty and ignorance, unless they are fed free money because they sit on land with oil under it. Then they seem to want to keep their people in pampered prisons:

plenty of material goods but little freedom to travel, discuss politics or meet persons of the opposite sex.

But let us start with the good bit at the beginning.

As the young Mohammad was growing up, Mecca's wealth as a trading town was growing rapidly, its success largely connected to having in the town Arabia's holiest polytheistic shrine called the Ka'aba ('the Cube'). Every year, during their holy month of Ramadan, all the Arab tribes observed a truce in their otherwise never-ending raiding and blood feuds and came to Mecca from throughout the huge peninsular of Arabia to worship their godlets, headed by their principal godlet, Allah[32], at the Ka'aba. This gathering of peoples and the truce around it helped the people of Mecca to build successful trading businesses, including those of both Mohammad's uncle and his wife.

Mohammad was an orphan and had been brought up by his uncle, Abu Talib, and had first started working for him on his camel caravans, carrying goods far across the Middle East. Later he moved to work for a widow called Khadija who needed a man to operate her caravan business. Despite being fifteen years younger, Mohammad married her and they remained devoted to each other until her death. On a personal spiritual retreat one year, when he was already in his forties, Mohammad

---

[32] 'Allah' is simply the Arabic word for 'The God'. Arabic-speaking Christians, as well as Muslims, use the word Allah for God. It is a condensed form of 'Al Ilah' (The God). 'Ilah' is a variation of the word 'El', the old polytheistic supreme godlet of the tribes of the Middle East.

had a vision of an angel, who told him to prophesy. Mohammad was not at all pleased by this turn of events and initially assumed he must be going mad or that a Jinn, a desert spirit, was deceiving him. However, with the encouragement of Khadija, he started to take the revelations seriously and continued to have periodic visions. As his early visions coalesced into a doctrine, Mohammad started to build up a small following, starting with his young cousin, Ali ibn Abu Talib. But Mohammad's fellow merchants initially laughed at his revelations, asking who he was that God should have selected him. Then, as time went by, many Meccan merchant families became concerned that Mohammad's revelation threatened the town's prosperity. They feared it would destroy existing religious practice, alienate customers and end the peace of the month of Ramadan that so helped their trade and gave them the huge pilgrimage business. Hostility to him and his followers built up, getting worse as Mohammad's following grew, until it became an intense campaign against them.

At this point, in 619CE, Mohammad's uncle, Abu Talib, and his wife, Khadija, both died in what Mohammad called his 'Year of Sorrow'. Abu Talib was Mohammad's clan head and his death removed his vital protection from Mohammad. Earlier, some of the tribal leaders from Yathrib, an oasis some 200 miles away, had asked him to come to their region to act as a judge. A traditional way to try to end repeated blood-feuding amongst tribes was to find an impartial outside judge and Mohammad's reputation for fairness, and an appalling cycle of killings in the oasis, had led to the request for Mohammad to take this role. (Yathrib is now known as Medina, a shortening of the Arabic for 'City of the Prophet' – '*madinat al-nabi*'.) With the heat on him, Mohammad sent his family and many of his supporters there and, in September 622CE, warned of a plot to murder him, he slipped out of Mecca with only the company of his old friend, Abu Bakr, to follow them. The Muslim calendar starts with this journey (Hegira).

After Mohammad arrived in Yathrib/Medina he continued to have revelations and became the dominant force in the oasis. The need to find occupation and revenue, to defend his followers against attack from his Meccan opponents and the complex tribal politics of Yathrib itself, turned Mohammad into a war leader. Several desperate battles were fought. In one Mohammad was wounded and, for a short period, presumed dead. One tribe (of Jewish Belief), having betrayed Mohammad twice, was condemned to be destroyed by his troops, the men killed and the women and children sold into slavery. It was, at times, a desperately close-run thing. All the time his visions continued and he set up the practices of the religion of Islam.

Eleven years later, at his death in 632CE, Mohammad and his followers commanded the allegiance of all the Arabian Peninsula, including Mecca, and many Arabs had accepted the religion of Islam. His revelations were collected together from memories and notes made at the time and written down after his death as the Holy Qur'an (Recitation).

Less than thirty years later his followers had conquered most of the Middle East. They took over the (Sassanid) empire in Iran and Iraq and halved the size of the Byzantine (Eastern Roman) Empire, taking Egypt, Syria, Jerusalem and Libya. At this period, Islam was seen as appropriate only for the Arab followers of Mohammad and no attempt was made to convert people of the Book – Christians, Jews and Zoroastrians – for many years after the Arab conquest. Over the next 100 years further conquests were added, including the whole of North Africa and almost all the Iberian Peninsula (now Spain and Portugal).

For Mohammad there is only one true religion. Judaism, Christianity and his own revelation are the same religion of the one God, the creator of the world and the judge of mankind. As Moses was chosen to reveal the religion to the Jews, and Jesus the messenger of the true religion to the Christians, so Mohammad is God's messenger to the Arab people. He is the latest and last in the long line of prophets – all those mentioned in the Bible. All proclaim the same message: God's care for his people, his hatred of the worship of bogus godlets, his rules for behaviour and for proper living. God's message to the Arabs through Mohammad was clear and unmuddled because it was direct to them in Arabic, not confused through translation and disputed interpretations. The Angel Gabriel gave the message directly to Mohammad in his visions. He received this message in a trance-like state, reciting it as he heard it, with his words being memorised and sometimes written down by those who were with him. Over twenty years or so, both in Mecca and in

Medina, Mohammad had some 114 such trances, each of which is recorded as a chapter ('surah') in the Qur'an. Muslims believe that these are the direct words of God.

Mohammad was illiterate and gained much of his worldly understanding of monotheism from the many local Arabs who had adopted Christian and Jewish Beliefs. Islam started with a proud record of tolerance and respect for both Jews and Christians. Mohammad was less familiar with the variations of Christianity. The dominant form of Christianity in Arabia viewed God as a single entity and when Mohammad learned of the Western view of God as a Trinity, he saw it as verging on Polytheism and as deeply wrong. It seems likely that Mohammad thought the Catholic/Orthodox Trinity was made up of Father, Son and Virgin Mary.

Abraham, Joseph, John the Baptist and Jesus are important prophets in Islam. Mary (Maryam or Miriam in Arabic and Hebrew), the mother of Jesus, is praised 'above all women' and a chapter of the Qur'an is called 'Mary' after her. Arabs are seen as descendants of Abraham through his son Ishmael, and legend has it that Ishmael and Abraham built the Ka'aba in Mecca together. The second biggest celebration of the Islamic year after Ramadan, the Eid al-Adha, commemorates Abraham's obedience to God in planning to kill his other (and only legitimate) son at God's request. Tradition has it that the altar for the planned sacrifice is in Jerusalem and is the rock inside Islam's first specially commissioned holy building, the Dome of the Rock.

In general, the historical references in the Qur'an

agree with those in the first books of the Bible, the Torah, although there are telling variations, where the Qur'anic God is more forgiving than the Old Testament God. The Old Testament has Eve being cursed with birth pains by God for leading Adam astray and both are exiled in punishment. In the Qur'an, God forgives them.

To be a Muslim you have only to follow five rules: you must be able to say the basic confession of faith 'There is no god but God and Mohammad is his messenger', *'La ilaha ila I-Lah, Mohammad rasulu I-Lah'* in Arabic; you must say prayers five times a day (originally three); you must fast during the hours of daylight during Ramadan; you must give a tenth of your income to the poor; and you must, if you can, make the pilgrimage to Mecca.

The most important connection between God and mankind is the revelation Mohammad was given, now held in the book called the Holy Qur'an (it means 'recitation'). This is the principal guide for Muslims. They also have the example of Mohammad's life. These are the practices he started for Muslims, the 'sunnah', plural 'sunnan', and his reported sayings, the 'hadith', plural 'ahadith'. For example, practices such as washing hands and feet before prayer and touching the head to the ground during prayer are sunnan taught by Mohammad, not given in the Qur'an. (In both of these Mohammad was being practical as well as religious: he was keen that his followers should wash more regularly and get more exercise, as well as improving their spirituality.)

The Qur'an is primarily a book of worship and is full of praise for God. The book we have now was a 'final version' collected together under Mohammad's third successor, Uthman, from material that was memorised or written down during Mohammad's life and shortly after his death. Uthman wanted to create a definitive Qur'an and remove the differing versions that were beginning to be spread around. Because there was little or no written Arabic, a new script, derived from a closely related language, had to be used.

While there are scholarly debates about detail, no one seriously doubts that the Qur'an reflects the principal content of Mohammad's recitations. There are a few who claim that the Qur'an was written later than tradition has it, but their only evidence is the lack of references to it in other writing. It seems unlikely that the faithful delayed longer than they could to produce the central document of their religion. The Qur'an is also free of the kind of 'predictions' that one might expect if it had elements added later. Each of the 114 recitations is a separate chapter (surah) and overall the book is similar in length (77,701 words) to the Jewish Torah (79,847 words) and shorter than the Christian New Testament (138,020 words).

With the exception of the first surah, also the basic prayer of Islam, surahs are given with the longest first and the shortest last.

The first surah itself translates roughly as:

In the name of God, most forgiving, most merciful.
All praise to God, Lord of worlds,

Most generous and most merciful,
Lord of the day of Judgement,
You alone we worship and from you alone we seek help.
Guide us onto the right path,
The path of the righteous, not of the cursed,
nor of those who stray.

Scholars distinguish between those surahs given in Mecca, when Mohammad was a persecuted leader of a sect, and the stronger and more confidently worded surahs given in Medina, when he was an increasingly powerful religious and political leader. Each surah (bar one) starts with the words *'In the name of God, most forgiving, most merciful' – 'Bismillah Ir-rahman Ir-rahim'*. The one surah that does not start with the Bismillah can probably be explained by the suggestion that it is, in fact, a continuation of the previous surah. The language used in the Qur'an has a poetic quality that is seen as beautiful by many Arabic speakers. The book covers many subjects and much material is repeated in many surahs. Although some have objected to the amount of repetition, it seems that the many verses requiring tolerance and moderation, for example, could have done with even more repetition.

The meaning of the language of the Qur'an is not altogether without difficulties. Some argue that Arabic as spoken today is, in reality, a family of different languages. It is said that there is more variation between some different 'forms of Arabic' than the differences between the separate Slavic languages of Russian, Czech and Polish or that Moroccan Arabic, Egyptian Arabic and

Iraqi Arabic are no more similar than Spanish, Portuguese and Italian. So the exact meanings of words in the Classical Arabic of the Qur'an often pose problems today. For example: when there is an argument, is the other person to be 'left in peace' or to be 'abandoned'? We don't know which better expresses the classical Arabic term used in the Qur'anic verse.

However, the Belief revealed in the book is simple and clear. God, Creator and Judge, has rules he wishes to be obeyed: some are dietary rules, very similar to the Jewish rules; some ceremonial rules, especially regarding prayer; some lifestyle rules, for example, the bans on gambling and alcohol. The stress is on following these rules sensibly and realising that God is not pedantic. But the key elements are to behave well: firstly, to your fellow Muslims, then to all men and women; to worship the one God alone and to respect his laws and his Prophet. This will be rewarded by a good life here and paradise in the afterlife. There is much other guidance and many Muslims read the Qur'an or listen to readings from it for help at difficult times. For the period, the Qur'an has notably liberal rules about the rights of women and is especially forceful on the rights of orphans. But it is important that the Qur'an is not seen as a book of rules. It is far more a book of praise, of prayer, of joy, of poetry and of rapture at the goodness of God and his gifts. The rules are almost incidental to the sense of worship and of understanding through story.

But Islam is not only a personal Belief. It was of critical importance to Mohammad to remove the continuous inter-tribal feuding that debilitated the Arabs. In Islam the community of believers, the Ummah, replaces tribe and there are different rules for Muslims when in the area ruled by Islam and when they are in the area ruled by others. All Muslims are one community to Mohammad, required to support each other and hold together. The early history of Islam, first as a persecuted group in Mecca and then as a struggling new religion in Medina, did indeed weld a strong, mutually supporting Belief – a unity of faith and purpose that has been the aspiration of Muslims ever since.

Eight years after his flight, Mohammad conquered Mecca with hardly a fight and the whole of the Arabian Peninsula allied with him. He died in Medina two years later in 632CE. The historian Edward Gibbon, no lover of religion, summed up his effect: '*The most bitter or bigoted of his Christian or Jewish foes will surely allow that he… inculcated a salutary doctrine… The idols of Arabia were broken before the throne of God… he breathed among the faithful a spirit of charity and friendship; recommended the practice of social virtues; and checked, by his laws and precepts, the thirst for revenge, and the oppression of widows and orphans. The hostile tribes were united in faith and obedience and the valour which had been idly spent in domestic quarrels was vigorously directed against a foreign enemy.*'[xxxii] Mohammad ibn Abdul Muttalib certainly had an impact.

After his death he was succeeded, in turn, by four of his companions: Abu Bakr, Umar, Uthman and, finally, his cousin Ali, who had also married one of his daughters, Fatima. These first four successors (caliphs) are known as the Rightly Guided (Rashidun). During this period, the Arabs conquered the whole of the Middle East under the flag of Islam.

This bland sentence obviously covers a dramatic story of conquest. This started with the need to regain Arabia, after the death of the Prophet had led to considerable backsliding amongst previously allied Arab tribes. Then the Arab troops, marshalled by the caliphs and under their formidable general, Khalid, known as the 'Sword of God', defeated the Iranian Sassanid Empire completely. The Arab armies, again under Khalid, inflicted a series of catastrophic defeats on the Byzantine Empire, leading to the Arab conquest of Syria, Egypt and the surrounding region. As is the way of these things, the caliph Umar, Khalid's cousin, who disliked the reverence he was being given, dismissed him at the peak of his success. He died in bed four years later, furious at not being killed in battle.

The third successor to Mohammad was Uthman, who came from the Umayyad family. The Umayyads had been, with the exception of Uthman himself, particular enemies of Islam, until Mecca fell to Mohammad. Then, to everyone's astonishment, Mohammad forgave the Umayyads for their previous attempts to kill him and his followers. He allowed them all to live and to convert to Islam. When Uthman became caliph he became not only a religious leader but also head of a vast empire, held together by little more than the new Belief of the conquering Arabs and appointed members of his, Umayyad, family to many of the key posts that arose, notably as governors of Egypt and Syria. After years of rule, Uthman was murdered by a madman and Ali was accepted as caliph.

There is something very odd about the story of Ali. He would appear to have been the natural successor to Mohammad: he was Mohammad's cousin and close companion from the first, he was the first Muslim after Khadija, and he was Mohammad's son-in-law and the father of his grandchildren. He was strong, tall and notably brave in battle. But Mohammad did not name Ali as his successor, despite ample opportunity to do so when he knew he was dying. After Mohammad's death, the powerful Umar (who later became second caliph) was determined to prevent Ali succeeding Mohammad and shoved the mild Abu Bakr in as first caliph instead. Ayesha, the Prophet's (self-proclaimed) 'favourite' wife, could not abide Ali and, when Ali's turn came to be caliph, largely in the absence of any realistic alternative candidates, Ayesha raised an army and fought, literally, to prevent his succession. His caliphate, when it finally came, was a catastrophe, so maybe they all saw something in him that led them to fear this. Possibly he was a bit thick.

The Umayyad brothers who had been appointed governors of Syria and Egypt by the previous caliph, Uthman, ignored the fact that Ali had become caliph and ruled their provinces independently. Eventually, Ali came to battle with them, which ended bizarrely, but with the same effect as a defeat for Ali. The story is that, after weeks of negotiation, skirmishing and battle, Umayyad troops put copies of Qur'anic verses on their spears, which meant that Ali's army lost the will to fight them.

Ali then agreed to arbitration but had lost the respect and support of his troops and had to retreat. He retired to his capital, Kufa in Iraq, where he was assassinated by extremists who appeared to think that Ali had not supported himself with sufficient vigour. The Umayyad brothers smoothly took over the whole empire, with one taking on the title of caliph from Ali at his death.

The Middle East was at a high level of literacy and development when the conquering Arabs exploded out of the desert. This degree of literacy enabled some people to read the Qur'an themselves, as their personal link to God. Even more people had access to a teacher with a copy of the Qur'an and the full ability to read the book and use it as the direct link to God for their congregation. This led to the development of a local and personal approach to their religion. The Sunni (from Sunna, the practices of the Prophet) Islam Belief that resulted was a bottom-up, intellectual but fissiparous (splitting) religion. Each group of local elders and the leader of prayer, the imam, could decide which school of Sunni Islam their group would associate with. This local independence was helped by the fact that leadership of the Arab Empire had been taken over by the Umayyad family. Their support for Islam was widely believed to be completely cynical, so they could never use their political power to direct the religion.

At the same time, a branch of Islam developed that looked to the authority of Mohammad's descendants to help mediate the relationship with God. These were the 'Party of Ali', the Shi'Ali or Shi'a. The Shi'a believe the direct descendants of Mohammad via Ali and his wife, Mohammad's daughter Fatima, possess a special degree of God-given authority. They give direct descendants in the male line the title of 'Imam'[33]. From its foundation, the Shi'a have deferred to living authority much more than the Sunni and they are structured as a top-down, Church-like organisation. The tragic story of the death of Mohammad's grandson, Husayn (the third Imam of the Shi'a, after Muhammad and Ali) at the hands of the Umayyads is a strong theme in Shi'a religion. Husayn crossed the desert from Mecca with his family and a small band of supporters to Iraq, where he had been promised the support of the people. When he got there, an overwhelming number of Umayyad troops were waiting for him. In circumstances of great pathos he, his family and his small band fought to the death. His head was taken to Damascus and shown to the Umayyad caliph. For the Shi'a, this tragic death is at the centre of their religion. The often sad history of later Shi'a imams adds a mournful tone to many Shi'a ceremonies, especially on Ashura, the day the death of Husayn is specifically remembered.

The Shi'a split later into two main groups: those who believe that the line of imams descended from Mohammad stopped at seven and another group who believe there were twelve imams. The last of the twelve

---

[33] Not to be confused with the same title used in Sunni Islam for the leader of a mosque.

imams disappeared, but Shi'as believe that he is not dead but concealed from us – he is in 'Occlusion', and will reappear. This larger group of 'Twelvers' is normally the only one now referred to as Shi'a. Most 'Seveners' are now in the Ismaili sect, led by the Aga Khan, the head of their hereditary priesthood. In the past 'Sevener' sects have included the Assassins and there are still other small groups based on Sevener ideas. 'Twelver' Shi'a Islam is the principal religion of Iran and parts of Iraq. It has a hierarchy of clergy including ayatollahs and grand ayatollahs, similar in position to bishops and archbishops in Christianity.

The Umayyads were thrown out as rulers of the Islamic world (except in the very west of their empire, Spain) and replaced by the Abbasids in 750CE. A key part of the appeal of the Abbasids – descendants of Mohammad's uncle, Abbas – was their promise to represent Islam better.

They moved the capital to their purpose-built new town of Baghdad in Iraq, some fifty miles away from the site of Babylon. The next 200 years are seen as the Golden Age of Islam. The Abbasids had been put in power by a broad coalition of support, including many non-Arabs. As a result, they saw Islam as being for everyone, not just native Arabs, and the religion expanded greatly. At the same time, the Arabic language became much more widely spoken and became a unifying force across the empire (outside Iran, which continued to speak Persian). The religion progressed in learning; many of the classical writings of the Greeks that would otherwise have been lost were translated and copied. Mathematics, science, medicine, technology and literature all advanced. The so-called 'Arabic numbers', which were originally from India, were transmitted to the west by this civilisation and it is significant that the mathematical terms 'algebra' and 'algorithm' are both Arabic words, as well as many of the fundamental terms of science such as 'chemistry'.

From the point of view of Islam, the early Abbasid period of comparative peace and wealth defined much of the religion. It was an intensely scholarly period, with effort put into ensuring the religion of Islam was as thoroughly thought through as possible. There was extensive debate about aspects of the religion and several schools formed, of which the Sufi, mystic tradition and the Falsafa tradition, based on Greek Philosophy, are the most notable. The law was developed through careful legal processes and debate into sophisticated schools of jurisprudence based on the Qur'an and the life of the Prophet. Around 850CE, the caliph Al Mutawakkit made a serious attempt to force all the different groups of Sunni Islam to accept a unified view, persecuting opponents of his favoured Mu'tazili School. The Mu'tazili were involved in a fierce debate, reminiscent of the Arian arguments in Christianity, about whether the Qur'an was co-eternal with Allah or produced by him. Al Mutawakkit failed completely and Islam continued to form separate schools and factions with vigour. More generally under the Abbasids, Islam saw itself as a religion strong enough to allow debate and, for different opinions to be held, a religion that was highly successful in both arms and argument.

The Umayyads had continued to rule in Spain, known to them as Al Andalus, and developed a rich and sophisticated society of Muslims, Christians and Jews that was not finally driven out (by Ferdinand of Aragon and Isabella of Castile) until 1492. Much of the learning of Western Europe in the Middle Ages and Renaissance came from the scholars and libraries of Al Andalus.

The early Abbasid caliphs had come into conflict with the Shiites. After a number of uprisings and wars, the Shi'a imam was killed and the remaining Shiites fled to the Maghreb (now Morocco) where they set up an independent kingdom. From this base the Fatimids, a family claiming descent from Fatima, the Prophet Mohammad's daughter, expanded out again to rule in Egypt by 969 and, at their peak, ruled much of the western half of the Middle East. But within a hundred years they were removed and Sunni practice dominated Egypt again. Shi'a remained low profile until the Safavid Dynasty took over Iran in 1501CE. The first Safavid shah, Ishmael, made Shi'a the state religion and put the full power of the state behind forced conversions, excluding Sunni clergy and giving authority to the Shi'a council[34]. The Shi'a saw him and his successors as

---

[34] There is a striking parallel between the Shi'a religious enforcement of the first Safavid shah in 1501CE and the earlier Zoroastrian religious enforcement of the first Sassanid shah in 224CE.

divinely ordained rulers. This link between a strongly organised Shi'a priesthood and government continues today in Iran.

A Muslim view of Christianity and Islam in the Middle Ages can be seen by the way each religion captured Jerusalem from the other. In 636CE the Arab Army under the second caliph, Umar, laid siege to Jerusalem. After four months the Patriarch (Christian Archbishop) of Jerusalem agreed to surrender, but only if he could do so to Umar in person. Umar accepted this and the surrender was made peacefully, with Umar placing a guard to prevent any desecration of the Church of the Holy Sepulchre. The Jews, who had been banned from the city by the Romans and Byzantines since 120CE, were allowed back in.

In 1099, the First Crusade captured the city after a brief siege and assault. There was huge, uncontrolled slaughter and the Jews who took sanctuary in the synagogue were all killed when it was burned down. There is debate about the exact level of horror involved, with the boastings of the crusaders and later Muslim polemics probably exaggerating what was undoubtedly a slaughter. The crusaders used Jerusalem's Al-Aqsa mosque, the third holiest in Islam, to stable their horses, deliberately to defile it.

In 1187 Islamic forces under Saladin recaptured the city. Before the siege he offered generous terms for surrender, which were rejected. After the siege was underway, the Franks (the heirs of the crusaders) sued for terms and Saladin allowed them to leave peacefully on the promise of ransoms. It was not all reason and light, though – the common soldiery were sold into slavery. The Jews, who had been, once again, excluded under Christian rule, were, once again, allowed to return.

The Abbasid caliphate declined drastically after 1000. Provinces became, in practice, separate kingdoms, paying nothing but lip service to the power of the caliph at Baghdad. Internally, the Turkish generals, who came from central Asian tribes, gained effective control of the provinces. An extreme sense of decay and decline was noted at the time. The essential irrigation channels of Iraq fell into disrepair for only the third time in all history, the previous occasion being more than 2,000 years earlier. It was agreed that the 'Doors of Itjihad' had closed, that no further change or development could happen. The remnants of the Abbasid system struggled on until the Mongol invasions of 1258 when the last caliph, by then a holy cypher, was killed. By this time, the Islamic Belief itself had entered its long period of stagnation and slump. There is much political history in the Islamic world after the Abbasid Empire, but the Belief itself and all its variations degraded and stagnated for the next 1,000 years.

Politically, the Islamic world splintered and the Middle East returned to a familiar pattern of rising and declining kingdoms, extending out and falling back. In terms of Belief, however, it was one-way traffic away from the simplicity of early Islam: Sufi mysticism added complexity and paradox, reversion to simple polytheistic thinking led to the multiplication of 'wali', saints, and the full panoply of shrines and holy relics. Persecution of other Beliefs began in earnest. The crusades had clearly positioned (Latin) Christians as an aggressive force to Muslims. But, going further, the Mongol invaders who destroyed Baghdad in 1258 had, initially, Christian associations, coming from areas where (Nestorian) Christianity was strong. They were cheered on by local Christian rulers. Once they had conquered the Muslim heartland of Syria, Iran and Iraq, the Mongols appointed many Christians to power under their overall rule, in line with their principle of using non-locals' assistance. Some of these took the opportunity to oppress Muslims, ensuring that any doubt about the opposition of Christianity to Islam was removed. Then, when the Mongols ruling the area converted to Islam, Muslims copied Christian-style 'convert or kill' levels of persecution in reverse. Christianity was all but wiped out in many Muslim areas by 1450. Ever afterwards, relations between the two religions in the Middle East were problematic and religious killing by whichever side had the power was always a possibility.

There was a strong military revival of Islamic rulers under the Ottoman Turks in the Middle East and Southeast Europe and under the Mughal emperors of India from the sixteenth century CE, and Islam was spread further, especially into India, Bengal, Malaya and Sumatra, but with no change in its structure. The informing characteristic of Islam in this long period is conservatism. Little changed and most Muslim life was as close to Polytheism as Medieval Christianity until the backward-looking reform movements that sprang up under European pressure in the 1700s.

Muhammad ibn Abd al-Wahhab (1703–1792CE) started such a movement to purge Islam of what he saw as its many un-Islamic accretions and return to his vision of early Islam. Al-Wahhab's vision of Islam was ferociously puritanical; to be enforced with whatever violence seemed necessary. This approach 'cleaned up' many of the dubious additions to everyday Islamic practice that had arisen by the eighteenth century, notably shrines to 'saints' (wali). At the same time, its insistence on a Puritan approach to life is at odds with conventional Islam, especially in regard to the role of women and the bullying enforcement of petty rules, so different to the ease and openness of the Prophet's approach to Belief. Al-Wahhab's followers believed in and acted with violence and intolerance towards non-Wahhabi fellow Muslims. Al-Wahhab formed a strong alliance with the tribal leader, Muhammad ibn Saud and their families intermarried. Descendants of al-Wahhab and ibn Saud form the current ruling royal family in Arabia and have made Wahhabism the official version of Islam in that country. The act that first drew the wider world's attention to modern Wahhabism was the destruction of the tombs of Mohammad's family after the Wahhabis conquered Medina in 1925[35]. They also planned the

---

[35] Many of these had been destroyed by the Wahhabis in an earlier conquest and had been re-built.

destruction of Mohammad's tomb itself, but this was abandoned under pressure from many distressed Muslims. The guards at the tomb are still known for hitting anyone who shows any physical sign of reverence while visiting the Prophet's tomb, for example, by bowing their head.

In the nineteenth century CE, faced with the surging military and cultural challenge of Europe, the Islamic powers were swatted away almost carelessly. The Turkish Ottoman Empire clung on until 1918, only because rivalry amongst the European powers prevented any one of them from seizing it. Islamic religion, the Arabic peoples, Turks, Iranians and Muslims of India were all seen as second-class peoples by the dominant Europeans of the Victorian era. The blow to Islam's self-esteem was huge, painful and continues today. Many sought reform, but all the dominant Islamic reform movements were backwards looking to the time of the Prophet, or perhaps to the Abbasid caliphate of the 800s, not forward-looking to handle the challenge of Europe. Because Mohammad started with religion but ended with political power as well, Islamic Belief has, from its origin, combined the two aspects: the personal relationship with God through the Qur'an, and the power wielded by the people of Islam. So outsiders having greater power than Islamic countries feels like an attack on the Islamic religion and the relative military and economic weakness of Islam is confused with weakness of faith.

One response to this challenge was the Deobandi movement of Islamic Reform, started in India by a group of Islamic thinkers in 1866 and named after the town where it started, Deoband. As ever, they were striving for a return to a purer form of Islam, close to the simplicity of the faith in Mohammad's time. They formed an influential school, often austere, intolerant and disapproving of modern developments of all kinds. They developed links to Wahhabism and built a strong base in religious teaching. Today Deobandi Madrassas (religious schools) are mainly in Pakistan, where their austerity and primitivism act as the background to the endless feuding in the tribal areas near the Afghan border. The majority of UK mosques are also currently associated with the Deobandi movement, despite its position in the turn-the-clock-back school of Islam.

In 1928 Hassan al-Banna and others founded the Muslim Brotherhood in opposition to Western ideas. It came to prominence after the Second World War as a political force in Egypt where, despite being repeatedly suppressed and having a brief period in power, it was and remains a leading vehicle for opposition to the various dictators who ruled the country.

After the Second World War the European powers retreated from their empires and the countries of the Islamic world returned to being ruled by Muslims. But while Muslims now ruled them, the form of rule reverted to medieval patterns through absolutist kings and dictators. Moreover, in practice, these princes, kings and 'strongmen' were often so dominated by Western influence as to be virtual puppets in their external affairs. At the same time, because much of the world's oil is found in the countries at the centre of the Islamic world, the money provided has enabled some of the same regimes to preserve their highly repressive internal rules.

There were several attempts to modernise rule in the Muslim world linked to largely anti-Islamic, socialist ideas, notably under Gamal Abdel Nasser in Egypt and the Baath parties of Syria and Iraq. But neither made an appreciable difference. In practice, they amounted to no more than a new name for a familiar dictatorship.

In contrast to these secular movements, there have been a number of religious revivals over the last fifty years. The Shi'a revolution in Iran in 1979 was the most spectacular, with a revolt against the increasingly oppressive regime of Mohammad Reza, the shah, in the name of a religious revival led by Ruhollah Khomeini. Khomeini seized government and created a constitution dominated by a religious controller, initially himself. The subsequent government appears to have followed the pattern, familiar from Iran and elsewhere, of decline from an idealistic/fanatical start into cronyism and corruption.

At the time of writing, the best-known Sunni revivalist groups still seek to return to the first glory days of Islam – although they vary on which aspects they see as crucial. They are collectively known as Salafis (meaning 'predecessors'), a term that, while it covers many different groups and views, refers mainly to people dressed in imitation of seventh-century Arabia and with harsh attitudes, ironically more reminiscent of Christian history than of the original Islamic tolerance. At the extreme, represented by Al Qaeda ('the Base') or 'ISIS', there is a nihilism (belief in destruction as good) reminiscent of the Anarchist movement in Russia in the nineteenth century, a movement that was also a response by young men trapped in a deeply conservative society.

The concept of 'Sharia law' encapsulates a problem within Islam. It is a powerful brand but has no agreed content. 'Sharia', meaning 'path', is a key word in the Qur'an and, hence, a resonant word in Islam. So the concept of a law based on Sharia, the true path of Islam, excites many who dream of the day Sharia law arrives as the day justice will arrive in their lives. But Sharia law does not exist. In principle, all Muslims agree that laws should be based on the Qur'an and Sunnan. But, as with all law, complexity crops up in applying simple principles to practical cases. This inevitable complexity was discussed and worked through with great thoroughness in the Golden Age but without agreeing conclusions and Islam is left still with four different schools of 'fiqh', philosophies of law. So, despite many yearning for its arrival, there is no agreed 'Sharia law' to arrive and the enthusiasts for Sharia are chasing a ghost or, worse, misrepresenting some primitive folk-justice as 'Sharia law'.

Today, we have in Islam a Belief suffering from a truly split personality:

Belief 1: The sophisticated, simple, scholarly and enlightened faith seen in the Golden Age of Abbasid rule and, later, in Al Andalus in Iberia. Based on the extraordinary visions and success of a kind and brilliant man, this is the Belief that maintained civilisation while Europe languished in muddy ignorance.

Belief 2: An intolerant, Puritan, destructive, negative, aggressive, terrorist, misogynistic, homophobic, anarchic, bullying, medieval-style opponent of freedom, liberality and progress. Fired by fury at the repeated humiliation of Muslims by the West and determined to hit back by any means. The names of Wahhabism, Deobandi, Salafi, Al Qaeda, the Taliban, Islamic State – ISIS or ISIL – and the Muslim Brotherhood come to mind, all associated with these attributes to a greater or lesser extent. Much of the violence of these movements is now being diverted towards sectarian wars.

Belief 3: Simple personal acceptance of the Qur'an and Muslim tradition, finding in them no contradiction with the modern world nor any need to wear specific garments. Irritation that the media should so often portray idiot throwbacks as the face of Islam but equal irritation with so many Muslim governments for allowing self-evidently medieval attitudes to persist.

The Belief of Islam is obviously at some form of turning point. Optimists suggest that the current extremists have made a contribution to the debate – that their efforts have made sure that a plan of nihilistic bombing back to the tenth century is discredited in the Islamic world. But, as the tenure of the dictators and the rule of the kings becomes more and more threadbare, where to go? The turmoil of the so-called 'Arab Spring' led nowhere at all. So desperate are some Muslims for guidance that they seize on the very modestly inspiring example of modern Turkey's first openly Muslim prime minister, Recep Tayyip Erdogan, as proof, if proof were needed, that rule by a Muslim does not have to be a disaster of one sort or another.

One dispiriting development is the increasing violence between Sunni and Shi'a sects. No suggestions for addressing this problem have been put forward that seem likely to work. Positions in Syria, Iraq, the Gulf, Iran and Pakistan give ever increasing sectarian conflict the appearance of grim inevitability. The mixture of religious and political conflicts and the occasional intervention of outsiders bears a disturbing resemblance to the Thirty Years' War (1618-1648, see above) that resulted in the destruction of much of the population and wealth of the areas where it raged.

Maybe Islamic Belief will retreat from politics, as most Christian sects have done, but, in its current pain, it seems unlikely. Many in Islam are desperate for a Martin Luther, a Ghandi, a Martin Luther King, a Nelson Mandela or, conceivably, a Mohammad to inspire, to reunify and to restore pride in their Belief and their tradition. Can such a person arise in an Islamic world that is so thoroughly split on every possible issue? What would be their lesson and plan? It seems sadly likely that the only way such a person might unite Islam is through war, war having the great ability to make people forget their differences.

We have to expect that the Belief will become more violent and that this violence will start with a steady move to war between Islamic sects across the Middle East.

Postscript: Sex, Homosexuality and Religion

Many Beliefs have no more to say about sexual matters than they have about cooking; to them both activities are earthy areas of life, reflecting the animal side of humankind. This animal aspect of our lives is seen as almost diametrically opposite to the matters of interest to Beliefs, which are the things of the mind, the spirit and soul, issues like freedom, fairness, purpose and meaning. Caring and relationships matter to these Beliefs; grubby, physical fumblings do not.

The link between the elevated things of the spirit, the business of many Beliefs, and the unhygienic process of rutting is desire, the word for the spiritual, or at any rate, mental, aspect of sex. Most Buddhist schools feel that the ability to escape from sexual desire is a necessary part of escaping all desire and, unless they are in Japan or Korea, where monks are allowed to marry, Buddhism requires chastity of its monks. But the real exceptions are Christianity and, in a few versions, Islam. Christianity is widely seen as having rules about sex at its core. Indeed, many Churches take firm positions on sex: generally, the less of it, the better. Sex is, as far as possible, forbidden, except as a regrettable necessity in the narrow space allowed for official procreative purposes.

All this opposition to sex comes despite there being remarkably little authority for sexual rules in the faith. For Christians, the only reference to sexual behaviour recorded in Jesus' sayings was when he was asked for an opinion on a woman who had been *'caught in adultery'*[xxxiii]. Jewish law was that she should be stoned to death and his enemies were trying to trap Jesus into either disagreeing with the law or becoming party to a murder. He skilfully avoided the trap, saying '*He that is without sin amongst you let him cast the first stone*'. Everyone drifted away, leaving Jesus with the woman and he said, '*Neither do I condemn thee. Go and sin no more.*' A message of moderation and toleration, one would have thought; certainly an example not to judge others in sexual matters. This message is, however, defiantly ignored by many Churches. To be fair, St Paul's first letter does require that Christians abstain from '*fornication*', that is, sexual incontinence.

The Qur'an is set against the background of relations between the sexes at the time: the presumption that men can and will get sex wherever they can, while complete fidelity is required of women. But, within the context of its age, the Qur'an and Mohammad asserted principles of women's rights much in advance of those of the Arab society – and any other well-known society – of the time. A man may have up to four wives, but he must treat them equally and must have the resources to do so. The Qur'an emphasises the importance of proper care and equality between wives and how difficult it is to achieve. Women have the right to divorce – unheard of before Islam. In theory, Islam follows the Jewish rule that women must be stoned to death for adultery; in practice, Islam requires four male eyewitnesses for female adultery to be proved. Mohammad set this impossible-to-achieve level of proof as a way of effectively removing the death sentence for adultery[36], while remaining consistent with established rules. Muslims of the Golden Age were proud of the liberty of Muslim women. They saw the complete legal subordination of women in Christian Europe at the time as an example of its backwardness.

The veiling of women in Islam is wholly without Qur'anic support, unless you desperately twist the meanings of the words of a few verses[xxxiv] further than can be justified. There is a Hadith (saying) that the Prophet was once shocked when Asma, the sister of one of his later wives, came in wearing a thin garment. He is reported to have said that *'it is not proper that anything should remain exposed except this and this'* (pointing to his head and hands). This story, said to have been told much later by Asma's sister, Ayesha, provides the only Islamic justification for continuing the female hair and face covering traditional in many societies that have adopted Islam. Most women in Yathrib at the time of the Prophet were not veiled and, although it is traditionally held that the Prophet's (later) wives wore veils as a particular mark of the Prophet's importance[37], the actual words of the Qur'an do not support this.

---

[36] Similarly, the sentence for theft in the Qur'an is, indeed, having the hand chopped off – but only if the thief is unrepentant.

[37] The verse in the Qur'an that states this (33.53) actually requires people to speak to the Prophet's wives 'before a screen', which is interpreted, questionably, as saying they wore the Niquab. In contrast, St Paul definitely says that it is a disgrace for a woman to have uncovered hair in church. I Corinthians 11.

Both Beliefs, Christianity and Islam, draw some hostility to sex from the ancient tale of Adam and Eve, included in the Jewish Torah. This story reflects everyone's experience and observation of puberty: innocence is lost with the mysterious arrival of sexual desire. In the Garden of Eden, the first man and woman, Adam and Eve, initially know nothing of sexual desire. Then, against Yahweh's specific instruction, they eat a fruit that gives them knowledge of sex. This disobedience causes Yahweh to ban them from the good life of the garden to a harsh existence wandering the earth. So, in the tale, all human misery was originally caused by sex.

St Augustine made the connection that, because of this 'original sin' by Adam and Eve, all humankind was damned for all time, until they were saved by Jesus' sacrifice. This huge sacrifice enabled God to forgive at least some members of humankind. Augustine's view, developed as he aged after a youth of notable debauchery, was that sex was a regrettable necessity and chastity was always more godly.

But all this pales in comparison with the hostility some Christians show to homosexuality. This is odd. Jesus said nothing about homosexuality. Christians who condemn homosexuality must believe that the Son of God forgot to mention this sin and that they know better. There are Christians who argue that Paul was against homosexuality. He is, the only time he mentions it, in the letter to the Romans, but he is sniffy, rather than hell-fire condemnatory. The word used in the King James Version, for men who *burned in their lust towards another [man]'* is *'unseemly'*[xxxv].

In the vast mass of writing that is the Old Testament, rules about homosexuality are given only in the book of Leviticus, which mentions it twice, in virtually identical passages. One of the passages in Leviticus, after condemning homosexuality, adds that the punishment is death, as it is for adultery. (For adultery, the death penalty is for both parties, although it seems only ever to have been applied to women.) Those who suggest that we take the rules of Leviticus seriously, and it is a primitive document indeed, must not only require us to reinstitute the death sentence for homosexual acts but also for adultery, which may be difficult to carry out in a world with high divorce rates. Leviticus also requires us to be much more diligent about the ways we sacrifice our sheep and goats. It spends much more time on methods of ritual animal killing and cares much more about them than it cares about homosexuality. We can conclude that anyone who has not sacrificed a goat recently and who has not ensured that its kidneys and kidney fat have been properly burned is not taking Leviticus seriously and their insisting that it has authority is hypocritical. In Deuteronomy, the actual basis for the Jewish law, there is no mention or condemnation of homosexuality, although there is a long passage of rules about other sexual relations.

Finally, we can go back to Genesis, the first book of the Bible/Torah, where the story of Lot, Abraham's brother, and the Cities of the Plain, has been used to condemn homosexuality.

This ancient and unattractive legend starts with Yahweh deciding to destroy the cities on the plain,

Sodom and Gomorrah, because they are so wicked
(wickedness unspecified). But Abraham persuades
Yahweh that, if he can find just ten virtuous people in the
cities Yahweh will spare them all (Abraham had to
negotiate Yahweh down from his initial start-point,
requiring there to be fifty virtuous people). To establish
whether there are such, Yahweh sends a couple of angels,
who arrive in Sodom and call on Abraham's brother (or
nephew), Lot. While they are there, a crowd arises and
demands to rape the angels – who the crowd certainly
think are men[38]. Anyway, Lot tries to fob the crowd off,
making them the civil offer of two of his daughters '*which
have not known man*' instead, but the crowd will not be
pacified. All is OK though, as the angels make the
attacking men blind, so they can't find the door. So Lot's
house proves impregnable and Lot and his family escape
with the angels early next morning. Naturally, Yahweh
has decided to go ahead with Plan A and destroy the
cities, giving Lot and his family just enough time to get
out but warning them not to look back. Lot's wife does
look back and is turned into a pillar of salt.

Primitive legends like this are often crude and cruel.
You have to have an agenda to take any specific lesson
from them; perhaps, more than condemnation of
homosexuality or the duty to protect guests, what we
should learn is that it is a virtue to pacify a sex-mad crowd

---

[38] For this reason, male homosexual sex has often been known as sodomy.
What it was they did in Gomorrah is not disclosed.

with the offer of virgin daughters for them to, in the words of Lot, *'do ye to them as is good in your eyes'*.

The story of Lot is mentioned several times in the Qur'an, with the focus being on the fate that awaits those people and towns who do not heed God's warning, who do not listen to the angels he sends[xxxvi]. That said, it is made clear in some of the surahs that tell the story of the Cities of the Plain that the men of Sodom, because they have sex with men, are 'transgressors'.

These are all the mentions of homosexuality in all the major texts of Holy Scripture, unless you include Plato's *Symposium* as some form of scripture. This is Plato's record of an extended series of speeches after a celebration dinner attended by a small crowd, including Socrates. The speeches they make are in praise of love, which they all take to mean a man's love for other men. They praise its many benefits that, various speakers agree, can sometimes also result when a man loves a woman.

.6.

NATIONALISM: THE INVISIBLE KILLER

Very few people initially see Nationalism as a Belief. Until the issue is drawn to their attention, most people vaguely assume that Nationalism is a word for a 'natural' set of feelings, an instinct that has always existed or an inevitable human drive. Yet among specialists and those who study it, Nationalism is seen as a Belief that was invented just over 200 years ago in Western Europe and one that has, since then, caused more untimely deaths than any other single cause, apart from plagues.

We have many types of 'belonging': we belong with our family, we belong in our locality, to our workplace or school, among our sports team's supporters, and so on. In exactly that sense, we belong in our country, and we support it exactly as we support our child's school soccer team or our city's baseball team. This sense of belonging is 'Patriotism'; the word for love of your country and its culture, for pride in its successes, fondness for its particular character and pleasure in its traditions. It is not the same as Nationalism. Nationalism is a Belief that people are divided into different types and that each of these types of people belongs to a different 'Nation'. The people of other Nations have a lower value, as human beings, to people of my Nation; they count for less. Nationalism says that these different Nations each have their own area of land to live in and rule, unmixed with people of other Nations: their Nation-State. Nationalists think that people of their Nation should fight to get this separate Nation-State and that, if necessary, they should be willing to kill others to achieve it. Charles de Gaulle put it slightly differently when he said, *'Patriotism is when love of your own people comes first; Nationalism, when hate for people other than your own comes first.'*[39] Nationalism is to Patriotism as the Mafia is to the Chamber of Commerce: a violent and extreme extension of the same basic urge.

Although the distinction between Patriotism and Nationalism is vital, they are always being muddled. Because many people feel Patriotic, but think they feel Nationalistic, they are unwilling to admit that some appalling events were caused by Nationalism, even when the perpetrators of the atrocity clearly state that their actions were caused by Nationalism. The Nazi Party was a Nationalist Party. Its name was the National Socialist German Workers Party (Hitler hated the nickname 'Nazi'

---

[39] Often misattributed to Clemenceau.

and always used 'National Socialist' or the German initials for the party, NSDAP, as the short form of its name). It said it was a Nationalist party and its policies were wholly based on the Nationalist programme. It was not a 'Fascist' party – Fascist was the name of its Italian sister Nationalist party, named after the 'Fasces', the symbols of power in the Roman Empire and only possibly appropriate to an Italian party – but the Nazi Party is often called 'Fascist', perhaps because people fear that admitting that the Nazis were Nationalists will pollute their own sense of Patriotism, which they think of as 'Nationalism'. But the distinction between Patriotism and Nationalism is clear and has been recognised many times: *'Nationalism is an infantile disease. It is the measles of mankind,'* said Albert Einstein; *'Nationalism is power hunger, tempered by self-deception,'* said George Orwell; *'Born in iniquity and conceived in sin, the spirit of Nationalism has never ceased to bend human institutions to the service of dissension and distress,'* said Thorstein Veblen, ornately. So we are not going out on a limb with this distinction between Patriotism and Nationalism.

In some ways we can compare the love of country, Patriotism, to the love we feel for our children. We love our children and see in them all the treasurable values of humanity. We support them and, while we are well aware of their failings, we hate it if others point them out. But we do not help our children commit crimes and we accept that our children are subject to the same rules of law as everyone else. We know other parents feel the same way about their children, and that all children, including ours, must accept the consequences if they behave badly. This is the natural feeling of parenthood and much the same feelings apply for many of us towards our homeland, our feelings of Patriotism. But Nationalism allows the Nation more power than we allow mere parents. It says that the Nation, unlike a parent, has permission to kill and lie in pursuit of its interests. Anyone who said – or acted out – '*My child, right or wrong*' would be considered to have taken a good and almost universal virtue to an unacceptable and dangerous extreme. A Patriot feels the same dislike of the Nationalist slogan '*My country, right or wrong*'[xxxvii]; it is a perversion of a natural urge.

The other visceral source of Nationalism is the tribal instinct: the feelings and behaviour derived from membership of a small group that lives, hunts and fights together. Humankind lived in tribes of extended families for hundreds of thousands of years and this has led to admiration for actions of individual self-sacrifice for the wider group benefit. It is this gut acceptance, especially among younger men 'of fighting age', that their individual interests should be subordinate to the group that gives Nationalism its vicious quality. Nationalism's twist is to take this primal instinct to protect and advance the interests of your 'nearest and dearest' and, instead, apply them to the Nation, a large group of people unknown to you, a group whose wishes you do not personally know and whose leadership may be completely indifferent to you and your loved ones.

Nationalists have the same Belief, whatever Nation they say they are, just with different groups of individuals and areas of land as their focus. Just because people live in different houses it does not mean that the concept of a 'house' is not a single concept; so it is with Nationalism.

A loose idea of 'nations' existed for centuries before Nationalism. It tended to refer – and it was always a vague term – to people who came from one large area or who spoke one language. Like 'region' today, this is the soft sense of nation with a small 'n', a group of people who come from the same (large) area and share some cultural characteristics. But before Nationalism was invented, no one thought that there were two completely different types of community: one type of community, a town or region, is informal, flexible and gently descriptive of origin and character; the other type of community, a 'Nation', is formal and hard-edged and superior to others. People did not think that Brittany, Bavaria or Andalusia were communities of a completely different kind to France, Germany or Spain. Before Nationalism, they did not think that the French, Germans or Spanish should always have armies and borders (because they are Nations), while Bretons, Bavarians or Andalusians must never have them (because they are not Nations). People before Nationalism would not have understood the reasoning behind the Nationalist thesis: that you should fight to obtain National borders and a National army and that you should fight, just as hard, to prevent regional borders or a provincial army. Borders before Nationalism, insofar as they existed, were the edges of the area ruled by a lord or king. There was no absolute difference between the areas called 'regions' and the areas called 'nations', although nations tended to be larger. But that was it; no other difference. Armies were not 'National'; they were the means by which a lord or king retained control of his area, both against external lords and internal wannabees. From time to time, they were also the means by which the lord or king might seek to extend the area he controlled. While there was often some level of fellow feeling, 'Us against Them', amongst the soldiers of these armies, whether Genghis Khan's hordes or Marlborough's infantry, they were essentially out to do their lord's bidding for their own gain, in pay and in loot.

Confusingly, though, the term 'National' is often used simply to describe a countrywide thing – a national newspaper or the Grand National horse race, for example. While no one is making claims about a separate, better Nation when they use the word this way, they are using a hard word for soft deeds, like saying 'I could murder a steak'. The Nation we are talking about is a hard, bitter term, as in: National Identity, National Security, National Guard, National Socialist, 'our aspiration is to National self-determination' and 'our Nation must be free!' The Belief of Nationalism is one of the biggest killers of all time and it is confusing that a country's soccer team is sometimes called a 'national' team.

The Nationalist Belief has only four propositions:

- That humanity is divided into different groups – the Nations.
- People of my Nation are better than the people of other Nations.
- That each Nation has an area of land that 'belongs' to it.
- That the Nation must have a separate country in that area: the Nation-State.

Nationalism has a second stage, after the Nation-State is achieved, where it believes that its Nation is not only 'better' but also should dominate other Nations. But let us look at how ordinary Nationalism works first.

People vary. They vary in height, in colouration, in aptitude for different activities and so on. These attributes vary between people fairly smoothly, going from short to tall, for example, without gaps where there are no people with those heights. Cultural elements also vary, although there tends to be a more geographical distribution to this. The types of hat worn in an area, for example, tends to be similar to neighbouring districts but can be quite different to the hats worn in areas far away. Before printing and mass literacy, it seems that language varied more or less smoothly from village to village. Neighbouring areas could easily understand one another and it got progressively more difficult to make yourself understood in your native dialect as you moved further away. The Chinese language is still like this. Where language families met, they blended together; so those in Bohemia, for example, spoke many varieties of mixed

Germanic/Slavic languages. Scholars and officials who needed to communicate across distances used separate, universal languages, such as Latin and Arabic.

David Bellos writes, '*The great explorer Christopher Columbus provides an unusually well-documented case of the intercomprehensibility and interchangeability of European tongues in the late Middle Ages. He wrote notes in what we now recognise as an early form of Italian but he used typically Portuguese place names... wrote his official correspondence in Castilian but used Latin for the precious journal he kept of his voyages.*'[xxxviii]

(In passing, the focus of this section is on Europe, simply because Nationalism started there and it had little effect outside Europe for its first hundred years or so.)

Nationalism denies this smooth variation. It imposes a border between people that, it claims, divides people into different Nations. In the Belief of Nationalism, the variations *within* the Nation are ignored as far as possible and the variations *between* the Nations exaggerated. The extent to which you are a member of any Nation should be flexible. How Irish you are, for example, depends on a complex of issues: family background, place of residence, self-perception, social and educational background, religious background, language, cultural perceptions, and many other things, including, importantly, how Irish you want to be. You can be more or less completely Irish, or you can be just a little bit Irish. Nationalism denies this and defines people as Irish or Not-Irish, black or white, friend or foe.

With this black and white separation of people into 'them' and 'us' agreed, Nationalism demands that everyone within the 'National borders' is a person of that Nation. Nationalism believes that you belong to a Nation, sometimes regardless of where you were born, and you should fight for an independent state co-extensive with 'your Nation's land'. All the people of your Nation should live in this area and no people that belong to other Nations should live there. The government of that area should be separate from any other political unit; it should be a Nation-State. People should fight and people should move to make this happen. Nationalism believes that everyone in the world should live in their own Nation-State.

The core of Nationalism is the idea that the people of each Nation are different from the people of other Nations. That mystical difference is why people of different Nations cannot share a common patch of land. The Nationalist believes that, because the people of the Nation are more like each other than they are like the people of other Nations, a separate Nation-State will better reflect the wishes of its people. Because people of my Nation are different to people of other Nations, they can be 'better' people; they can be more valuable than people of other Nations. It is assumed, normally just by implication, that people of the same Nation are more related to each other than they are to people of other Nations. In modern terminology, that they are genetically more similar to fellow 'Nationals' than they are to 'Foreigners'.

But how is each Nation defined?

Sometimes it has been suggested that the Nation is

the group of people speaking one language. But this works for very few cases. In the 1990s Serbs Nationalists fought Croatian Nationalists and both sometimes fought Bosnian Nationalists, yet all of them speak the same language, Serbo-Croat. Only a few Irish Nationalists ever spoke much Irish. At the other end of the spectrum, India includes so many languages that they are split into different families of languages. The first Nation-States created after 1793, France, Italy, Switzerland and Germany, all contained many languages and mutually unintelligible dialects within them. These separate languages and dialects are gradually disappearing in each country (except Switzerland) because a big effort was put into education to get to the one language that Nationalists sought. Sometimes minority dialects were officially persecuted or individual variant language speakers fled or were exiled. Sometimes, it was simply that minority languages have low status. There are around 8,000 languages in the world but fewer than 200 countries, so only the smallest, like Iceland, have only one language.

However, printing and mass literacy do seem to be pre-conditions for Nationalism because printing standardises language[40]. Before printing, language varies fairly smoothly from area to area, but printing tends to impose one official form of language across a whole

---

[40] Only alphabetic printing standardises language. Printing Chinese, where the characters represent ideas not sounds, tends to unify different languages: whatever language or dialect you speak, you can read the same material. Hence, in large part, why China is one country and Europe many.

kingdom, especially when laws and regulations are printed. So hard edges start: one area where the government is conducted in language A and, across an invisible but defined boundary, another area where government is conducted in language B – and that boundary is exactly where one king's land ends and another starts. Typically, the people either side of the boundary continue to speak their own argot, rather than either official language, but the idea of a boundary is made stronger. Originally, after printing became common in Europe, laws, government and religious material were often written in international languages such as Latin, so the arrival of a 'print border' was delayed. But popular pressure for laws and rules to be comprehensible to ordinary people led to vernacular languages being gradually introduced into government workings and publications. With that, borders started to mean a bit more than just the edge of the king's property. The end of the Hapsburg Empire started from the decision to change the legal language of the empire from Latin to Deutsch ('German') in the 1780s, unintentionally splitting the empire into full Deutsch-speaking citizens and the non-Deutsch-speaking 'other' citizens, citizens who mutated over the next fifty years into Nations.

But language is by no means the only way a Nation can be defined. Sometimes the definition of a Nation is geographic, like Italy, defined by borders of sea and mountains. But that does not work for Germany, Poland, Hungary, or any other country with long land borders.

Sometimes the Nation is defined by religion, like Pakistan, Israel or Lebanon.

Sometimes an uncomfortable and shifting concept arises, a bit linguistic, a bit religious and a bit geographical, like the Greek and Irish 'Nations'.

Sometimes Nationalism has required that many separate political units were brought together, like Italy or Germany, both created from a multitude of small states.

Sometimes Nationalism required that existing political units were pulled apart, like the Ottoman Empire or the Hapsburg lands.

Sometimes the Nation is little more than the product of a slogan: 'We must make our own decisions for ourselves.' In the Nationalist enthusiasm of the nineteenth century, few asked who this 'We' was, or why the decisions of this group would be better than those made by another group. Is it assumed by Nationalists that decisions made in Edinburgh, the capital of Scotland, will be better for people living in Scotland than decisions made in London, the capital of the United Kingdom. Yet the largest Scottish city, Glasgow, is physically closer to Liverpool in England than it is to Ullapool in Scotland. It is also more similar in size, better connected and closer in character and history to Liverpool.

Nations are mostly historical flukes. Often the decision on what a Nation consisted of was made without anyone at all realising that a decision had been made; the process had a huge element of arbitrary fortune. Belgians and Portuguese are, apparently, Nations, yet Sicilians and Bretons are not? Bosnians, Bulgarians, Croats, Czechs, Macedonians, Montenegrins, Serbs, Slovaks and Slovenes, who all speak varieties of Slav language, are nine

Nations? Yet Bavarians, Brandenburgers, Hanoverians, Hessians, Rhinelanders, Saarlanders, Saxons, Swabians and Thuringians who all speak varieties of Deutsch language are one Nation? But the Netherlanders, Swiss and Austrians, who also speak varieties of Deutsch, are not the same Nation? Or only sometimes. But once the mystic decision was made on who was in or out of a Nation, it had profound effects.

Before Nationalism in Europe, political areas and boundaries were defined by one man's or one family's power – kingdoms. Occasionally an area might be ruled by a group of families or by a committee of the wealthy. There were very few links between the area ruled by a king or duke and any kind of distinctive group that could be called a Nation. The area ruled by the Emperor Ferdinand of Austria, Bohemia, Hungary, Venetia, part of Poland, Croatia, etc., was not a Nation or nation. No more were the areas ruled by King George the 1st of England and Wales, Hanover, Scotland, Ireland, bits of America and the West Indies, in any way a nation or Nation.

Nationalism created Nations, not the other way round. Before Nationalism began in 1793 the only areas that came close to being Nation-States were both essentially islands: England (briefly) and Japan – and both those were only Nation-States if you gloss over a few exceptions.

Queen Elizabeth the 1st's (1558–1603) kingdom of England was close to being one country with one language, one shared history and one culture. Just before

Elizabeth came to the throne, her kingdom had lost Calais, its last bit of mainland Europe. After her death, the King of Scotland inherited the English throne and ruled both countries. So, for Elizabeth's reign, England was approximately a Nation-State… that is, if you ignore the queen's rule in Ireland and Wales.

Japan, then, is the only country in the world that has a long history of one state, one culture and one language. But that is also only true if you ignore the Ainu, a tribe of completely different origin and language, based in the northern Japanese island of Hokkaido and the Korean-speaking families who have lived in Japan for hundreds of years.

Practical Nationalism started in France. Before 1792, France was the name for a geographical area and the king that ruled it. It was made up of smaller areas – regions – such as Aquitaine, Brittany, Isle de France, and so on. People in France felt the usual attachment to each community they belonged to, with their attachment weaker as the groups got larger, from family to village to town or region, with loyalty to the kingdom the weakest of all.

This changed with the French Revolution of 1789 that swept away the king. Without a king, the government was left looking around for some reason for continuing to exist and, from the dark undergrowth, Nationalism emerged, filling the vacuum. The need for it was considerable because the former kingdom of France was under threat from the armies of other European kings, who were marching on it to restore the monarchy. In addition, some areas of the former kingdom wanted to take the opportunity to get rid of rule from Paris and were fighting for independence. With the king's authority gone, what reason was there for anybody to listen to anyone else's command? There was an army and a navy seeking reasons to continue to exist without a king. The problem was urgent: something had to be done before one side or the other executed the government leaders.[xxxix]

The solution, Nationalism, appeared from thin air, like a conjuror's rabbit. The temporary rulers of France at the time gained whatever legitimacy they had from an Assembly of Representatives from the whole of the kingdom and we can see almost the exact moment when the idea of a Nation, of a distinct and separate 'people', became a political fact. It was between the first and second constitutions of Revolutionary France. In 1791, with the king still present, a 'Constitution of France' was drafted, meaning a constitution for the area called France. Then King Louis was got rid of and, a year and a half later, in September 1793, the next constitution was called the 'Acte Constitutionnel'. This proclaims that the '*French Republic is one and indivisible*' and that it is based on '*French Citizens*' who collectively form the '*French people*' who elect the '*National*' representatives. The monster was born; the Nation and its Nation-State had sprung into existence.

The concept of the 'French Nation' explained – somehow – why the country's frontiers existed, why it was a defined area. It was not, at first, a very convincing explanation why 'France' was not just the name for the areas ruled by the previous king. But it was some explanation when one was desperately needed. These frontiers were the boundaries of the area occupied by the other new invention: 'French Citizens'. These French Citizens spoke a variety of languages. Some of these languages were related to Parisian French but mutually incomprehensible, such as the many varieties of Occitan spoken in the south of France. Other languages included in the new Nation were completely different: Breton, Basque and Flemish have no similarities to Parisian French at all. All these groups had in common was that, before the revolution, they all lived in the same political unit, a kingdom, known as France.

Nationalism, as an intellectual concept, had been thought about for some years. The question of where authority could come from, if not from a king anointed by God, had been discussed amongst European (and American) intellectuals before 1793. The intellectual movement that called itself, with ineffable smugness, 'The Enlightenment'[41], was leading to the idea of Nationalism before the French Revolution. The possibility of a 'German' people within the absurdly divided Holy Roman Empire had been discussed at an intellectual and emotional level before 1793. In the 'Declaration of the Rights of Man and the Citizen',

---

[41] The name Enlightenment (Lumières in French, Aufklarung in German) was first used by early eighteenth-century thinkers to describe their own thoughts.

formally adopted by the French Assembly in 1789, Article 3 stands out from the rest of the articles, which are about individual rights. It states, *'The principle of all sovereignty resides essentially in the nation. No body nor individual may exercise any authority which does not proceed directly from the nation.'* So the idea that there was a thing called a Nation, magically possessed of 'sovereignty' and 'authority', was newly in the air before its adoption as the basis for government authority, four years later.

In an odd twist, the leadership of Revolutionary France had acknowledged that they needed a new 'religion', without realising that they had already formed a new Belief with the invention of Nationalism. As part of their reformation of everything, they abolished the worship of God in November 1793 and set up the new 'Cult of Reason'. This was abolished in turn by Robespierre, who had become the holder of power around the same time, and replaced by 'The Cult of the Supreme Being' in May 1794. This was even shorter lived, dying, along with its founder, at his execution in July. These cults are much mocked today and their bombastic ceremonial and cod-services are often mentioned to point to mankind's capacity for folly while holding himself to be the embodiment of rationality. Perhaps we should mock a little more the Belief of Nationalism, with its laboured ceremonies and its vast pompousness; a Belief that arose at the same time as these, ludicrous, others.

This new idea of the French 'Nation', so weak at first, was forged and hardened in successful wars. These wars, which started as the 'Defence of the Revolution', came to be seen over time as the defence of the French Nation. Following military success, they moved from defence to attack and it became a war to strengthen the French Nation and bring 'Nationhood' to others. This happened without anyone deliberately deciding it, but, once the threat to the revolution itself had been seen off, there had to be some respectable reason to continue fighting, apart from fame and loot. Because people fought and died for the French Nation, they began to see it as an entity worth fighting and dying for – even though, unseen by almost everyone, the idea had been concocted so recently and so arbitrarily.

The states that the newly christened 'French' (*Français/Française*) were fighting against had even fewer 'National' qualities than France. There was the Hapsburg Empire, a collection of lands in the middle of Europe ruled by one family and often simply referred to as the Eastern Empire, the *Oster Reich* – Austria in English. There was Prussia, a random scattering of lands inside and outside the Holy Roman Empire, which had the King of Prussia as their ruler, and – with an official name that reflected exactly that it was not a Nation but a collection of areas under one rule – the United Kingdom of Great Britain and Ireland[42].

---

[43] In French, the word 'Bretagne' refers to both the island of Britain and the region of France called 'Brittany' in English. To avoid confusion, they called the larger of the two, 'Grand (Big) Bretagne'. This was translated into English as 'Great Britain'.

As the wars progressed, the idea of a 'Nation of the French' and of other Nations became hard and clear to people in France. There is nothing like violent death on a large scale for making something seem important. They started to see themselves as 'French' and as being 'Citizens of France': the ingredients of France, the stuff France was made of, not just people who were living in an area called France. Napoleon Bonaparte, who was born on the (then) Genoese island of Corsica and whose first language was Genoese[43], took the title 'Emperor of the French', not 'Emperor of France', after he seized power.

The difference between the new idea of a Nation and the old is elegantly illustrated by the history of National Anthems. The new French National Anthem, the 'Marseillaise', was written in the pivotal Nationalist year of 1792, explicitly to encourage soldiers to fight for this new idea, this Nation, and contains references to both the fatherland (*'patrie'*) and 'citizens' (*'citoyens'*). Two earlier songs have become National Anthems, the 'Wilhelmine' of the Netherlands and 'God Save the King', but they are both entirely about the ruler and have no mention of states or nations – so much so that it is still difficult to be sure which country or countries 'God Save the King' is the National Anthem of [44].

---

[43] His mother, who outlived him, never learned French.

[44] The Spanish National Anthem also preceded the 'Marseillaise' but had no words. The Japanese National Anthem is earlier as well and refers only to the emperor, not the Nation.

The French revolutionary wars exported the concept of the Nation, first to the peninsula of Italy. Italy had not been under one ruler since it was all part of the Roman Empire over a thousand years earlier. The languages spoken in the peninsula, although derived from the same Latin origin, had as little in common with each other as the language of Paris has with the language of Madrid, both also deriving from Latin. The concept of an 'Italian Nation' was completely novel, created by Napoleon as a tactic to rally support as he fought the Hapsburgs on the plain of the River Po. Napoleon decided on the Italian flag – identical to the new French revolutionary flag except green instead of blue[xl]. No one seems to have noticed the contradiction in having Nationality and the flag decided by the leader of another Nation. After that, the idea started to gain strength, a strength that led to the so-called 'unification of Italy' some sixty years later.

As Napoleon moved through Europe, the idea of Nationalism moved with him and his army. A unifying constitution was forced on the states that formed Switzerland. He also combined many of the principalities of the phantom Holy Roman Empire into one state he called the 'Confederation of the Rhine'. This was a key stage in turning an ancient literary error into a Nation.

The term 'Germania' comes from the classical Roman writer Tacitus. Around 100CE he had written a book called '*Concerning the Origin and Situation of the Germani*'. This used the Germani, a tribe based in the area of modern Belgium that Caesar had fought, as a name to describe, rather fancifully, a rough, manly race that covered all of Northwest Europe. Over the years, the peoples of Northwest Europe called themselves by any number of names: Teutons, Franks, Goths, Alemans, Vandals, Lombards, Burgundians, etc., but never 'Germans', since the Belgian tribe had vanished shortly after Tacitus wrote his book. Tacitus' work, which had been thought lost, was found again in 1455. Rather liking the description of this rough, strong and war-like people, the name 'Germania' was adopted as part of the propaganda for a 'crusade' against the Turks. At this period a need arose for collective words for bits of the increasingly theoretical Holy Roman Empire. The inhabitants of these regions used the word 'Deutsch' only to mean people who don't speak Latin and the term was already used at the time as a collective term for the people of the Netherlands – Dutch or 'Nederdeutsch', low Dutch. But a word was badly needed to cover the Holy Roman Empire's collection of dukedoms, principalities, free cities, etc. and the word 'Germany/Germania' simply fell into place, even though it was the name of a tribe living in a different area over a thousand years earlier.

Napoleon's Confederation of the Rhine fell with his fall and the area returned to its historic patchwork of principalities, but the idea of a Nation-State was planted and its name was Germany[45]. Before 1800 it had around five main, mutually unintelligible languages, but a huge

---

[45] Or Deutschland, Allemagne, Tyskland, Nemcko and Saksa; all are used to identify this Nation in various language groups.

effort was put into creating a standardised language as fast as possible. To this day, the shape of Germany reflects Napoleon's creation, leaving out Deutsch-speaking Austria and Switzerland, as well as the Dutch of the Netherlands[46].

After the fall of Napoleon, the newly invented Nations of Germany, and Italy, took over the torch of Nationalism. Nationalists saw these as real, complete entities, their history, which should have been that of a unified Nation, cruelly divided into many different states. It was in these areas that Nationalists fought for decades to 're-create' the imaginary unity of Nation and state. In the region that had become known as Germany, powerful influences, led intellectually by Fichte and Hegel, raised the German Nation to a new position as a real entity and one that, like polytheistic Gods, required human sacrifice. For Hegel, the Nation's right to call on the citizen to sacrifice his life was not for mutual protection nor to benefit the community but the righteous submission of the individual will to the needs of a spiritual entity higher than the individual[xli]. This vision of the Nation as a godlet, separate from and above the people that made it up, was the foundation for Nationalism's worst excesses under the Nazis who explicitly held it as part of their Belief.

---

[46] There was a very faint phantom of both Germany and Italy in the subordinate titles of the early medieval emperors. Frederick Barbarossa was crowned King of the Teutons and King of Italy as well as emperor (1155CE), but these titles had little more substance than his third regal title as King of Burgundy.

So, starting in 1793, Nationalism was the answer to the question of empowerment. People in nineteenth-century Europe felt they were disempowered, unable to affect political issues in their lives. By unifying previously smaller states, people would gain a stronger military force and be free to rule themselves – the early Nationalists believed that larger units, such as a unified Germany and Italy, would be better than the little, local states many of them then lived in. Few noticed that the definition of each Nation was largely arbitrary and, although many experienced the cruel consequences of creating separate and conflicting Nations, it often seemed safer to be quiet. Better to follow the crowd down the path of Nationalism, however absurd, than to make yourself and your family potential outcasts.

Existing monarchies were clearly unjustifiable and absurd and the ideas of Liberalism and Nationalism were intertwined to the extent that many simply assumed that a free society was only possible in a Nation-State. Nationalism, the first of the great modern Beliefs, was on the march. It was driven by people's desire to have more control over their personal destiny. By a terrible slip, the virtues of freedom and popular government became associated with the vice of Nationalism. In the popular uprisings of 1848, known as 'the year of revolutions', the cry of progressive elements in each country throughout Europe was for a Nation to be formed – except France, which had already been down that path and knew that being a Nation changed nothing and started to explore Communism instead. Over the next fifty years, many new Nations were created and the Nation-State system of Europe was set up, a system that put people into opposition with each other for no other reason than they 'belonged to' different Nations.

Although the Nation-State is an invention of Nationalism it is an invention that has shaped our world more than any other Belief. Millions of people have been forced to move from their homes to fit the patterns Nationalism decided were right: 'Germans', 'Romanians', 'Greeks', 'Turks', 'Armenians', 'Indians' and 'Pakistanis' and many, many others have tramped wearily or fled at speed to the strange land that Nationalism had decided was their 'National' home. Some moved in separate, family-by-family relocations, others in forced mass migrations. Languages have been standardised and local dialects suppressed. National teams have been set up and administrative units decided. Strange, contorted histories are written and heroic legends built up to fit the fantasy patterns of Nationalism. As a result, over the last 200 years, many countries have been created that almost fit the idea of a Nation: one language, one state and one culture. Creating these imaginary communities was often at great human cost, a cost that is still being paid in areas where some individuals or groups do not fit into the Nationalist mould.

But this cost is rarely attributed to a Belief because Nationalism is insidious and it is virtually never seen as a Belief; it is seen as a 'fact'. Nationalism has no official priests or churches, although political leaders often act as leaders in Nationalist services in buildings that are, effectively, Nationalist cathedrals. Nationalism has flags, symbols, music and songs and at least one day each year for its ceremonies. Nationalist songs, sung together, create a profound emotional effect on the faithful. Fervour for the Nationalist Belief is often strongest with those who express loud contempt for the unprovable ideas of the traditional religious Beliefs.

Because Nationalist Belief is so imbued in us that it seems as natural as gravity, it is necessary to labour the point that the concept of a Nation, capital 'N', is a recent, fictional construct, something that requires an act of faith to believe. *'Nation n. 1. large number of people of mainly common descent, language, history, etc., usu. inhabiting a territory bound by defined limits and forming a society under one government'*; as the Oxford English Dictionary puts it, it is an object that, as we have seen, did not exist anywhere before 1793. We are now so far gone in drinking the Nationalist idea that, if you want to join a Nation, you go through a process called 'Naturalisation'. In our mind, Nationality has become seen as almost a force of nature, so that joining a Nation is to be 'naturalised'.

Not all modern states are Nation-States. Citizens of the USA proudly come from many nations, using it in its old, pre-Nationalist sense of a group coming from an area and sharing certain attributes. The USA and other modern, multi-cultural states, such as Australia, show that Nationalism is not necessary. At their best, they are proud to be the common home to peoples of many different nations that elsewhere are told they need their own Nation-State and, if necessary, must kill others to get or keep it. Yet, even in such proud 'melting-pots' as the USA and Australia, some people adopt Nationalist attitudes at times, not just patriotic ones: 'Americans are better', not just America is better.

One of Nationalism's effects is to distort history before Nationalism, so that events are anachronistically put in terms of Nations, although Nations did not exist before 1793. A good example of this is the period 1337–1453 in Northwest Europe. In the nineteenth century, well after Nationalism had started, French historians invented the term the 'Hundred Years' War' for this period. In reality, conflict between the kings of France and England has gone on for centuries, with occasional pauses, until the kings of France ceased to exist. Yet the Hundred Years' War is presented as a war of a defined length, which it was not, between two defined peoples: the 'English' and the 'French', which it was not either. The Valois family held the title King of France; the Angevin family claimed that the title was rightly theirs. The Angevins had among their titles that of King of England. Both families had estates and often lived in France and spoke French. Henry IV in 1399 was the first King of England to have English as his first language since Ethelred the Unready in 1013. While the Angevins fought with troops from their lands in England, they also used troops from their lands in France as well as from their lands in Wales and Ireland. Local lords supported different sides at different times. Describing this period of hostilities as a war between the Nations of England and France is to completely misunderstand the culture and politics of the time.

In stark contrast, much of the history of the nineteenth and twentieth centuries can be seen as the working-out of the Belief of Nationalism. The Nation-States of revolutionary French imagination had first to be created. This made for unexpected Nationalist heroes like Giuseppe Garibaldi in Italy, leading the red-shirted peasants into Rome, and the huge, moustached Junker[47], Otto von Bismarck, in his spiked helmet, grabbing territory for his Prussian master behind the success of their army. Garibaldi, who was born in France[48], was the unlikely socialist-minded hero of an unlikely country, Italy. Bismarck, conservative to a fault, is credited as the even more unlikely creator of the completely novel German Empire.

One of the by-products of the Nationalist belief was the way religious differences could be smoothly turned into National differences, without anyone seeming to notice or comment. Disempowered Catholics in Ireland became disempowered Irish Nationalists (leaving the disempowered Protestants of Ireland in an uncomfortable position). Christians in the Ottoman Empire magically became Greek or Armenian nationals and the Muslims became Turks or Arabs and, wherever they lived, people of Jewish Belief and descent gradually lost their birth Nationality, as a phantom Jewish Nation arose they were

---

[47] 'Junker' is the term used for the Prussian aristocracy (the word comes from 'Jung Herr' meaning 'Young Lord').

[48] He was born in Nice in 1807.

'belonged to' by others, whether they wanted it or not, without a Nation-State.

The idea of disaffected groups splitting into a separate country gained strength as the nineteenth century progressed, notably in the case of Ireland. Throughout the United Kingdom of Great Britain and Ireland, Catholics were formally discriminated against until the mid-nineteenth century and they continued to be discriminated against informally even after their legal restrictions had been eased. But Catholics formed a majority only in the island of Ireland. Resentment of this religious unfairness amongst Catholics in Ireland magically transformed into the discontents of an Irish Nation – as usual, an entity with no previous existence or definition and which excluded the Protestant population of the island. The popular historian of Ireland Robert Kee put it that '*the undoubted ills from which Ireland suffered were those inflicted by a strong oppressor over a weak and alien people... a large enough distortion of events to amount to a historical untruth.*' Untrue, but believed with a fervour that still creates trouble today.

European intellectuals even invented the idea of a Greek Nation-State and pressed it on the, understandably surprised, local warlords of Epirus and the Peloponnese. In the 3,000 years of recorded Greek history, there had never been a Nation-State of Greece, or anything close to it. But officers in the Russian Army decided that the part of the Ottoman Empire that had contained some of the better-known city-states of the classical Greeks 2,300 years earlier was 'Greece'. Egged on by the Russians (and, later, by other

European romantics like the English Lord Byron), the 'Greek War of Independence' started with a thoroughgoing massacre of, it is said, every single Muslim in the Peloponnese, not because they were Muslims but because they were 'Turks'. The 'Greek War of Independence' was to continue with massacres as the principal technique on both sides, sides generated by transforming people of Christian family background into 'Greeks' and those of Muslim family background into 'Turks'.

Once formed, the new big Nations, Germany and Italy, like France before them, felt the need to pursue dominance, an empire. Before Nationalism started in 1793, acquiring other countries was the result of the rational, if unattractive, desire to grab their resources or to monopolise trade with them. The new idea of expanding the area of rule for a Nation's glory was a by-product of Nationalism. So Nationalism did not stop once the Nation-State it craved had been created; it moved on to a second phase. This 'second stage' Nationalism followed from the momentum of forming a Nation-State. It is not enough to have created the Nation; it must go on to glory and dominate other states. It is the same rationale as that of a team or gang: they are formed not just to exist but also to dominate rivals. Beating rivals then becomes their reason for existence. Rivalry with other Nations was often a key reason why the, often disparate, elements of the new Nation-States held together – especially since the creation of the longed-for Nation-State so often resulted in no change at all in people's daily lives.

This, expansive, part of the Nationalist idea was picked up by the Japanese, who moved into Korea and parts of China, and by the USA, who took over the Philippines intending, rather hypocritically, to start its own European-style colonial empire. It was also picked up by the United Kingdom, whose 'empire' before 1850 consisted only of Canada, for historic reasons, together with small trading posts, prison settlements and a few West Indian sugar islands. The Indian territories that later formed the centre of the 'empire' were so much a by-product of trading that they were still officially run by a trading company as a by-product of its tea business. After around 1850, however, chunks of land were declared to be colonies for little reason other than to prevent other European nations from doing the same. It made very little difference: apart from South Africa, the presence of a minute scattering of colonial officers had virtually no effect in the parts of Africa included in the British Empire before, during or after the label was used.

It was a triumph for the Nationalist Belief that the organisation intended to put an end to the wars caused by Nationalism was not called the 'league of countries' or the 'league of peace' but the 'League of Nations'. Previous peace systems had been called by their location – the Congress of Vienna, the Berlin Conference, etc. – but, by 1918, Nationalist Belief was so strong that the concept of Nations was included in the very title of the organisation intended to limit its malevolent effects.

With the exceptions of the civil wars of Russia and China, all the major wars of the twentieth century and

most of the minor wars were caused by Nationalism, with
the two World Wars directly and clearly caused by the
Belief. The Nazis, the German National Socialist Workers
Party[49], took the worship of their newly invented Nation
to its peak, with awful consequences. They were totally
defeated in a war of great horror; a horror compounded
by the discovery that, for Nationalist reasons, they had
deliberately slaughtered members of Nations who did not
have a Nation-State, notably the Jews and the Romani
(Gypsies). Yet, even then, few blamed the Nationalist
Belief for creating the disaster. This is possibly because it
is so easy to confuse with patriotism – love of one's
country – and patriotism was, understandably at the end
of a long and trying war, seen to be a shining virtue. So
the Nazi Party has been, ludicrously, categorised as
'Fascist'. This tortuous link, together with dumping much
of the poisonous content of the Nazi Party into 'Racism'
(see below), allows Nationalism, the name and
philosophy of the Nazis, to escape criticism.

The Nation-State was, for some, discredited by the
end of the twentieth century. But rather than putting
aside Nationalism as an inconsistent and dangerous
Belief, some people decided that the failure was with the
size of the units previously chosen to be Nations. What
was needed, it was argued, were smaller, more
homogenous states. So Belgium was seen as a failure as a

---

[49] The Nazis themselves hated the name 'Nazi' preferring the full party name
or its initials in German, the NSDAP. Apparently, 'Nazi' was the name of a
rural fool in a folk-tale given to them by their opponents.

Nation-State and the solution put forward has been to split it into two Nation-States on linguistic grounds: Flemish-speaking Flanders and French-speaking Wallonia. Earlier, from 1816 to 1839, when the fashionable Nationalist solution was for larger Nation-States, Belgium had been merged with the Netherlands on the grounds that they were the same Nation. In many European Nations, notably Spain and Britain, there are Nationalist parties claiming that there is a benefit – of largely undisclosed nature – to forming their own separate smaller states of Catalonia or Scotland. So it has worked out with Yugoslavia and the former Soviet Union, splitting into Nations defined quite arbitrarily. Fortunately, only relatively minor wars and terrorist campaigns have resulted so far from European sub-Nationalist sects and the Nationalist death toll since the Second World War has been relatively small – although still much larger than the death toll caused by all other Beliefs in Europe put together, over the same period.

The other, more considered, move was to link all the former Nation-States into a supranational European Union. So far this has had some optimistic results in diminishing European Nationalist aggressiveness. But it must be remembered that the most serious previous attempt to link separate states peacefully into a union, the USA, resulted, seventy years after its foundation, in a violent civil war.

Before 1900, a number of European colonies in the Americas had sought independence and had generally had to fight for it. But in none of them was there any serious appeal to Nationalism. The new countries formed did not initially see themselves as different Nations; they just wanted to be rid of remote and incompetent rule from Europe. Bizarrely, however, despite their new formation, it did not take long for some states, Paraguay, for example, to decide they were Nations. Paraguay was then able to enter into a Nationalist war. This, the War of the Triple Alliance (1864–70), was conducted with incompetence on the Paraguayan side, leading to its utter defeat and, it is said, to the death of almost all its men – more than half its total population.

In the litany of twentieth-century bloodshed caused by Nationalism, it is worth mentioning the splitting of the Ottoman Empire into Nation-States. Within the Ottoman Empire, Christians, Muslims and Jews had lived side by side for 400 years in the same villages and towns, separated into different religious structures, called 'Millets', but otherwise citizens of the Ottoman Empire. After the empire was on the losing side in the First World War, severe Nationalism struck, fuelled by the earlier horrors of the Greek Nationalist wars. Nationalism made it necessary for the population to divide into Greeks, Armenians and Turks. These now became separate Nations needing separate Nation-States (the Arabic-speaking part of the empire was dealt with separately, see below). This was achieved in a series of conflicts, mass migrations and slaughters from 1918 until 1922. The new Nation-State of Turkey, a Nation defined by the religion of the people – Muslim equalled Turk – was then made into a strictly secular state by its founding spirit, Mustapha, known as Kemal Ataturk[50], who was born in Salonika, now Thessaloniki in Greece.

Despite this, the bloodlust of Nationalism seems never satisfied and there continues to be a sputtering Nationalist war/insurrection in Turkey. People there speaking the three main Kurdish languages have been declared, by the unknown forces that decide these things, to be a Nation. Repressions, uprisings and the familiar troubles have followed.

The story of the southern, Arabic-speaking territories of the former Ottoman Empire was different. Keeping the whole Arabic-speaking region as one country would still have resulted in a smaller and more culturally homogenous country than, say, India. But Britain and France, to whom power in the area had been 'delegated' by the League of Nations, had the idea of creating states for somewhat fanciful Nations of their own devising, largely to spite each other. The border between Jordan and Iraq has a large kink in it, widely known as 'Winston's hiccup'. It is said that Winston Churchill (British Colonial Secretary 1921–22) had been drawing the boundaries after a particularly good lunch. While the specific tale is untrue, the story is true to the casual spirit in which the lines were drawn. Churchill certainly created the shape and size of the country we call Iraq by

---

[50] His given name was Mustapha, he adopted the name Kemal at military school; Ataturk is an honorific title, implying he is father of the Turks.

merging three Ottoman administrative areas into one. The Ottoman administrative area of Syria, on the other hand, was carved into pieces. One of these, the Lebanon, was designed by the French so that the area would have a Christian majority. The state of 'Palestine' was carved out of Syria for muddled reasons but, in part, to act as a Jewish homeland. The bad blood between the French and English colonial authorities, each determined to keep their 'own' bits as client states, largely shaped the countries we now see. A sad reason to arrange the Middle East into a jigsaw of conflicting, fictional Nation-States.

It was in India that the first avowedly Nationalist movement arose in a colonial empire. This was mostly after the First World War, which had taken a lot of the glitter off the British Imperium. Indian Nationalists like to date their movement back to the original Indian National Congress of 1885, but this is the usual Nationalist post-rationalisation. The original National Congress was founded by the, mainly English, members of the Theosophical Society – an eccentric semi-religious group – and led by an expert on birds, AO Hume. However, it did have the magic word 'National' in it.

After the Second World War, European countries, with the partial exception of France, simply lost interest in having an empire. It had become apparent during the war that they had brought no benefit to their 'imperial' governors during the crisis and had, instead, become a drain on the resources of the imperial power, especially if there was agitation for independence. Many former colonial territories were disposed of as they were acquired: as fast as possible and quite haphazardly. The former Indian Empire was crudely split into two countries along religious lines, with the Muslim state, Pakistan, consisting of two parts separated by 2,000 miles of India (they are now Pakistan and Bangladesh). It is estimated that this creation of Nations resulted in around one million deaths, as some people of the 'wrong' religion/Nation felt they had to move from their home into their new Nation-State. With minor exceptions, and very few sectarian deaths, the remaining Muslim population of India, 138 million in 2001, has lived in harmony with its Hindu, Sikh, Jain, Christian, Zoroastrian and neighbours of other religions since partition. Despite this, there is a continuing Nationalist squabble over which country should hold the area of Kashmir with its mixed religions but Muslim-majority population. Now both Pakistan and India hold nuclear weapons to defend themselves against each other and bicker about their border in Kashmir. Yet they were the same country in living memory.

One of the leading writers on Nationalism, Benedict Anderson, who first called Nations 'Imagined Communities', points out in detail the absurdities of post-colonial nations, commenting on Indonesia, for example, that '*Some of the people of* [Indonesian] *Sumatra are not only physically close to the populations of the western littoral of the* [Malaysian] *Malay Peninsula but they are ethnically related, understand each other's speech, have a common religion, and so forth. These same Sumatrans share neither mother tongue, ethnicity, nor religion with the Ambionese, located on islands thousands of miles away to the east. Yet during this century they have come to understand the Ambionese as fellow Indonesians, the Malays as foreigners.'*

Today, world opinion will consider very few excuses for war except where the excuse of Nationalism is given – 'National Self-determination' in the words of President Woodrow Wilson's tragic promise of 1919. Nationalism is still accepted as a principled reason for violence. Warlords in Yugoslavia and Eritrea, hoodlums in Northern Ireland and Sri Lanka, egotists and bandits in Scotland and Chechnya have exploited this quirk and more will arise.

Bizarrely, it was only in the 1980s with the publication of Benedict Anderson's book entitled *Imagined Communities* that the full absurdity of the concept of the Nation was brought to light. Once revealed, it rapidly became academically accepted. When it is pointed out that Nationalism is something we do not have to have, that the idea that people of one Nation are different to the people of another has no foundation in fact and that Nation-States are the result of Nationalism, not the other way round, it becomes difficult to take it seriously. Gradually, this is percolating through the system. But it will still be a long time before fantasies like the Hundred Years' War between the 'English' and the 'French' are removed from common understanding, and the general public becomes aware that Nationalism is a recent and deadly Belief.

One of the reasons for Nationalism's continuing strength in the modern world is the lack of alternative 'belongings'. The original change made by Nationalism was to put loyalty to the Nation above local loyalties to family, tribe or village. But these smaller belongings are disappearing with the gradual erosion of the extended family and smaller communities. Many people replace this loss of a sense of belonging with new ideas, such as supporting sports teams or Nationalism. As different parts of the world develop economically, we must expect them, too, to lose family and village ties, strengthening Nationalism there as well. This bodes ill for China, India, perhaps Indonesia and smaller countries.

The violence of Nationalism seems nowadays to be a little bit defused by peace, the consumer society and a more integrated world. But the Belief is by no means dead and, like the plague, it may be quiescent before another pandemic attack. The current Chinese leadership have found it too easy to use Nationalism to distract criticism when a grosser-than-usual corruption is uncovered. A faked-up squabble about a few uninhabited islands with Japan and attention is diverted, the Chinese people enjoying the idea of throwing their weight about after being bullied by others for 200 years. But it could yet be another ghastly import from Europe to China to follow the Christianity of the Taiping and the Communism of Mao Zedong. Nationalism could yet infect South America or Africa with one of its more virulent strains. Arab National unity has long been sought and it might be achieved, through methods and with consequences that are difficult to predict but not to fear.

Nationalism is a Belief that has brought few of the

comforts of other Beliefs. It is a Belief that despises conventional morality and that justifies violence, often on a huge scale. It has caused deaths by the million and continues to add to human misery today. Most of its adherents did not choose to be Nationalist but have, somehow, been invaded by the concept, never seeing it as a choice but as inevitable and unquestionable. There seems no reason not to regret its existence profoundly, worry about its future and condemn its spread.

The recent exposure of the unsubstantiated, modern foundation and grim record of this evil Belief may go some way to enabling us to get beyond it. But, for now, Nationalism continues to be seen as something different to a collective conviction, as something more than a Belief. Suffering will continue as people attempt to work out the contradictions of Nationalism on themselves and others.

Postscript: Racism

After the Second World War there was a concerted effort to re-characterise Nazi and Japanese concepts of National superiority as a new and distinctive Belief called 'Racism'[51]. This served to deflect criticism of Nationalism and let it escape much of the blame for the carnage it had created.

Racism is a variation of Nationalism; it is no more than a Nationalist sect. Both Nationalism and Racism split humanity into separate groups, groups that have a different 'human value'. Its only difference is that it splits people up into 'races', rather than Nations. A race does not require a state the way a Nation requires a Nation-State. There does not have to be a place for people of 'different races' to go to.

Racism follows the pattern of second-stage Nationalism, where people of different Nations, rechristened 'races', have a lower human value. The Racist defines what a race is however they like, most famously as people of different skin-colour. In just the same way as a Nationalist vaguely presumes different Nations to be groups with closer genetic links to each other than to outsiders, each race is vaguely presumed to share some genetic distinction.

---

[51] It was called 'Racialism' until the late 1960s.

One reason the term Racism came in was because Nationalists wanted to disassociate themselves from Nazi atrocities by changing the name of the Nazi ideology from Nationalism to Racism. Although the Nazis made clear that their objections to Jews and Roma were based on the idea of a superior German Nation, the Nazis used the term '*volk*', which can be translated into English as either Nation or race.

The new name of Racism was necessary as well to cover the situations in the southern states of the USA and South Africa at the time. In these areas discrimination on the grounds of Nation was difficult, as those discriminated against had no 'homeland' to go to – although the apartheid South African government made extensive efforts to create homelands for the different Nations they decided existed there.

In the anti-colonial movement of the developed countries that followed (not led) the dissolution of the European empires, much past imperial thinking and action was characterised as racist. This is unfair. Europeans mistakenly thought that they were superior to other peoples because, at the time, the evidence provided convincing support for the idea.

The extraordinary fact that Europeans, from 1492 to 1945, could simply step in, seize and rule any part of the world not already occupied by other Europeans led to an understandable superiority complex. From Hernando Cortez's takeover of the Aztec Empire with '250 men and horses' to Mussolini's Italian takeover of Ethiopia in the winter of 1935–6, Europeans simply came and took. In the whole inhabited world outside Europe, only Japan and Thailand, which was left as a buffer between British and French empires, were not officially ruled or unofficially dominated by European countries at one time or another[52]. Even Japan 'fell' culturally, if not politically, by submitting to the overwhelming power of the Commodore Perry's American warships and attempting to become more European than the Europeans.

Sometime in the eighteenth century, Europeans came to see this extraordinary dominance as proof of their intellectual or moral superiority over other peoples. The Arabs had felt the same in the eighth century, and the Mongols in the thirteenth, when they swept aside all opposition. It is unfair to see them as racists because they did not hold themselves above the 'natives' as a matter of Belief but as what they saw as a matter of demonstrable fact. When that 'fact' changed, so their opinions (mostly) changed appropriately.

One of the many reasons why Europeans were so dominant was that there was, of course, no Nationalism in the places they came to dominate. It was invented in Europe and did not spread outside until after 1900. It is simply a chronological error to ask why the Indians

---

[52] China was never technically part of any European empire, but in the later nineteenth century its (Manchu, non-Chinese) government had to do whatever the interested European powers wanted it to do, including giving them control of whatever areas they wanted and allowing the Europeans to administer 'its' border taxes.

before 1850 didn't want their independence of the British Raj – to go back to the previous, crueller and greedier 'local' rulers? Or back to the previous (non-Indian) Moghul emperors? A key reason why the British had come to dominate India was that they were less greedy than the rulers they replaced and had some regard for the rule of law. They may have stolen but did not steal everything they possibly could, regardless of the consequences for others, as many of their 'native' predecessors had done. Before the Europeans arrived in both Mexico and China, the ruling regime was loathed by the locals and seen by most of the population as being conquerors anyway. The Europeans were helped every step of the way by local people who expected any change to be an improvement.

As a lightning-conductor for anti-Nationalism, the idea that Racism is a separate and different Belief has been a true success. Many countries have fierce laws against Racist behaviour and sometimes against Racist speech. Both are socially unacceptable almost everywhere. In these same countries Nationalistic attitudes are acceptable: to demand a Scottish or Catalan Nation-State is as socially acceptable as the demand for a 'Whites-only' country is unacceptable and illegal. Yet the demand for a Nation-State has a far bloodier history than the demand for a 'Racially' pure state. Both depend on the same bogus distinction between 'us' and 'them'.

A problem that arises with both Racism and anti-Racism is the extent that apparently Racist attitudes depend on the exact words used. To *'discriminate between people of different races'* epitomises 'Racism'. It is widely disparaged and frequently illegal. To *'recognise people's ethnic diversity'*, on the other hand, is respectable and praiseworthy. Both phrases mean exactly the same thing. Not 'sort of' the same thing; exactly the same thing. The confusion arises because of a conflict in our basic human desires: we want to be treated exactly as others are treated, to have our basic human value recognised, but we also want our personal character and unique heritage to be recognised.

Nationalism made respectable the childish idea that the basic human value of one arbitrary collection of people is more than the basic human value of other groups of people. This idea polluted the egalitarian recipe for a stable and fair society. The Racist followed this idea. The only distinction between Racism and Nationalism is that the Racist cannot point to an area of land, a Nation-State, to which the 'lesser' people belong, whereas the Nationalist can.

.7.

COMMUNISM: INTELLECTUAL HEAVEN, PEOPLE'S HELL

C ommunism is a tidy Belief to describe. It has a well-defined start in 1848 with a simplified statement of its creed, called *The Communist Manifesto*, written by the Belief's principal founders, Friedrich Engels and Karl Marx. It also has a huge book with an extended statement of its propositions, *Das Kapital*, written later by Karl Marx, so we know in detail what the Belief stands for and holds to be true. Communists believed that it is inevitable that there would be a revolution, led by Communists, after which mankind would settle down to a world of universal prosperity and freedom. Following the revolution, the chains that tie mankind down will vanish and all will work to meet everyone's wants *'from each according to their ability, to each according to their need'*. The duty of the

Communist faithful is to hasten the date of this revolution and, when the day arrives, to lead the revolution safely to this glorious end.

The history of Communism has two stages: the first, the sixty-nine years from 1848 to 1917, when Communists struggled for power; the second stage, the seventy-four years from 1917, when Communists gained power in their first country, Russia, until the collapse of the USSR in 1991. That collapse effectively ended the Communist Belief. Not every country, or every individual, abandoned the label of Communism immediately after 1989, but the Belief was effectively dead. The results of trying to put the Communist Belief into practice had been found, even after extended and multiple trials, to be nearly the opposite of those forecast and desired.

Ideas of equality and the fair sharing of the Earth's resources have been around since the dawn of time. The principle of 'fairness' is one of the basic human instincts. Many movements have arisen in many lands seeking to establish a fairer distribution of wealth. These egalitarian (equalising) movements, often called 'peasant revolts', are almost always beaten back by the pre-existing rulers, mainly because, with all individuals treated as equals, the egalitarians suffer from weak leadership.

The unfairness of life in the nineteenth century was different, even when compared to the unfairness of earlier societies. For those living in European cities it was gross, in-your-face unfairness, not even softened by convention or tradition. Technical and economic advances were providing the prosperous with greater comfort, while the poor seemed to be worse off. They had traded their country hovels for equally unpleasant but filthier and more crowded urban slums. They had swapped the hard grind of agricultural labouring for the harder, grimier and more dangerous work of mining and the mills. For many, including Marx and Engels, the founders of Communism, it seemed as though a new class of completely alienated and miserable people was being formed. Marx called them 'Proletarians' after the Latin word '*Proletarius*', a member of the poorest class of Roman citizen whose assets, listed in the census, were only their children ('*proli*' in Latin)[53].

People living in the cities of Western Europe at this period of the 1800s were acutely aware that their world was changing. Eternal truths of the past were being cast aside. Steam power seemed to open a complete new world of possibilities. Western Europe was surging ahead and seemed to have the whole world at its feet. Old teachings did not work when the world was so different from the world the old teachers had known. New rules were needed for new times. But seeing the need for change did not lead automatically to showing what sort of change would work, the changes that would reduce the awful poverty and inequality.

But some were excited by the possibilities. They felt

---

[53] It is unlikely, on the evidence, that the poorest became worse off during the great change of the nineteenth century. There is no doubt, however, that many middle-class people thought the poor had become worse off.

that need for change was matched by the possibility of change. It was clear to people in the nineteenth century that the machinery of the future would be different, so it followed that the society of the future would be different too. Technical advances were moving alongside scientific advances. Chemistry was beginning to be a structured base for knowledge, not a collection of unreliable recipes. Science was developing a new understanding of the physical world, showing the ways materials related to each other. So it followed that we should have a new understanding of the social and economic world, showing the way humans relate to each other. There was a yawning gap for a new social 'science': a theory that would explain the causes of the current unfairness and the reasons behind the changes; a theory that would reveal what the future held; a theory that would guide idealists and show those who found the inequality unacceptable how they could help make it a better future. All this Communism provided.

The old monopoly Belief of Western Europe, Christianity, seemed to be steeped in complacency and structurally committed to the old order. It did not bother even to build churches for the rapidly growing population of the cities, so the poor were often as much deprived of spiritual comfort as they were of material comfort; there was just not enough room in the urban churches to fit them in alongside the pews reserved for the gentry. There were exceptions: evangelical Christian preachers who flourished in the cities as the century wore on. But, despite these efforts, many saw the old, God-based Belief as merely a palliative to the misery of the poor; a drug that gave temporary comfort but that utterly failed to address the problems of poverty and inequality. By the middle of the nineteenth century the new Belief of Nationalism was also beginning to show its weaknesses, especially to thinkers and idealists. It was crude, it had no logical structure and, above all, Nationalism made no attempt to address the gross inequalities of society. As the better off and the ruling classes increasingly adopted Nationalism for their own ends, its failings became increasingly obvious to those who cared about social justice. They sought a more rational solution, a more structured set of beliefs, and a 'science' of society. This science would explain the changes in the world and show how the grotesque misery of the poor could be ended.

The word 'Communism' (Kommunismus) seems to have arisen in Germany in the early 1840s along with a number of other similar words associated with 'levelling' ideas and groups. Only a few years later, in 1847, at the founding meeting of the Communist League in London, Karl Marx, a radical writer and activist, met Friedrich Engels, the son of a rich family of industrialists with interests in Germany and England. Engels had already written a book called *The Condition of the Working Class in England* and, as a published writer, the Communist League asked Engels to 'draw up a catechism'.[54] Marx

---

[54]   A catechism is the term for a short book explaining Christian belief, often in the form of questions and answers. The answers are often expected to be memorised.

collaborated with him and changed the name of the document from Engels' original title – *The Communist Confession of Faith* – to *The Communist Manifesto*. The founders of Communism never had any doubts that Communism was a Belief and borrowed Christian religious terms constantly. Even the term 'Manifesto' had originally meant a religious declaration.

Events in 1848, 'the year of revolutions', seemed exactly what Marx, Engels and other Communists were talking about. Everywhere the people were in revolt. To guide them, Marx and Engels rushed out *The Communist Manifesto*, a small booklet, to explain and guide developments. The Manifesto stated that a revolutionary takeover of power by the working class was inevitable. History, said the Manifesto, is purely the history of class warfare. In stage one, called the feudal system, a small group of aristocrats rules over many peasants. In stage two, the feudal aristocrats are replaced by a larger, middle-class group called the 'bourgeoisie', who live on the profits of employing the working-class in factories. In stage three, power is taken from the bourgeoisie in a revolution by the most numerous class: the industrial workers, the 'proletariat'. The revolution was certain to succeed, simply because the bourgeoisie were hopelessly outnumbered. The result of the revolution would be a society where private property becomes unnecessary, countries and borders would cease to have any meaning, the exploitation of women, children and men by others would cease, and even the town and country would become more evenly merged. Forever. This takeover could only be the result of a revolution – the bourgeoisie would never give up their privileges otherwise – and the Communist Party was there to lead the change. All this was written in an urgent, dramatic and exciting style; it reads like the trumpet-blast of a fresh, clean, good and true future.

And so it nearly seemed. All over Europe in 1848, revolts broke out. Simmering dissatisfactions were fanned into flame by a severe economic recession, flames fed by the knowledge that the world was changing. The recent (first) French Revolution showed that direct action could be effective in changing things; so initial riots were copied through the capitals of Europe and built into major insurrections. The closest revolt to Marx and Engels was in Paris. The poor (and shopkeepers and tradesmen) of Paris rose and seized power. They formed a provisional government for France and announced elections with all men able to vote. The election was where the script deviated from Marx's plan. The country voters, still very much the majority outside Paris and not at all proletarian, elected a group of conservatives. There was a period of struggle between the original revolutionaries and the conservative assembly, which ended, after a second election, in the rule of Louis Napoleon, the nephew and 'heir' of the former Emperor Napoleon. He returned France to its 'normal', semi-dictatorial government without any noticeable social change.

Across the rest of Europe similar patterns emerged, initial urban revolt falling to the more organised and countryside-based forces of traditional power. But, where it went beyond pure dissatisfaction, the driving idea behind the 1848 revolts outside France was Nationalism, not egalitarian theories. Nationalism was still seen as the solution to their problems by those who did not, like the French, already have a Nation-State, and did not, like the French, know that it achieves nothing by itself. In France the appeal of Nationalism had long since faded and new Beliefs like Communism could take hold in the popular imagination. But elsewhere in Europe, Communism and similar ideas were hardly mentioned in 1848.

Despite the setbacks, Communists had their views confirmed. Europe was not quite ready for the great Communist revolution, but, with the organising help of the Communist Party, the proletarian revolution would come soon and the freedom of mankind would follow.

Engels funded Marx liberally from the profits of the Engels family business interests that he managed in Manchester. Thinking about idle capitalists living on profit made Marx furious. In his view this is simply theft: taking the benefit of workingmen's output in return for nothing. But it was not at all hypocritical for him and Engels to live on the profits of the Engels family mills because they were intellectuals. Marx was not a role model for Communists in other ways: he boasted of his wife's aristocratic connections, when he had money he speculated on the stock-market (boasting again of his profits) and he got the maid pregnant. He used the time Engels' money gave him to work in the British Library, writing the grand, defining book of Communism. He called it *Capital* (*Das Kapital* – it was written in German) and it contained a comprehensive creed, covering history, economics and the theory of knowledge. It explained the world to many young idealists: why the world was so unequally shared, why there are repeated economic crises, and why being a Communist and observing Communist discipline was the solution that would inevitably bring about the transformation of human life.

Marx's theory of history was that the development from feudalism to bourgeois society leads to the development of factories able to make huge quantities of goods. But this is at the expense of the dissolution of old bonds between the members of society and their long-standing relationships. The result is the creation of the 'lumpenproletariat' (Marx's word), a disenchanted and poverty-stricken group at the bottom of society. The more capitalism advances, the more it destroys, not only the old aristocracy and peasantry but also the small shopkeepers and artisans, throwing them into the dispossessed mass of the proletariat and bringing closer the day of revolution. Inevitably, through many struggles and false dawns, there will be a revolution, as this huge, ever-growing mass of the dispossessed rises up against those who have taken so much from them: the bourgeoisie. The revolution will lead to a society where the masses are the rulers, not the minority. The revolution is inevitable, because the proletariat keeps on growing until it becomes the overwhelming majority. The bourgeoisie must, in the end, be too few to keep them down. The task of the Communist party is to speed the day the proletariat gets its act together.

Marx's theory of economics has the same crisp logic.

In a just world, if you do a day's work, you should be able to exchange it for someone else's day of work. Your pay for eight hours' work should be enough to buy goods that others have put eight hours' work into making. Your work is worth the same as their work. OK, they might have invested longer in education or you might have done so – no exact parallel is required – but the principle is clear. The average worker, working for one hour, should be able to buy the output of another average worker, working for one hour. But capitalism takes the value of some of your work and hands it to the capitalist, the owner of the company you work for. It is called profit. He has taken your work and given you nothing in return. The impoverishment of the worker is the direct result of his work being taken by the capitalist. Once the capitalist stops taking people's work in return for nothing and has to work himself, all will be better off on average. This is called the 'Theory of Surplus Value'.

(Before Communism the word 'capitalist' simply meant a person who had capital. The word Capitalism, meaning the system to which Communism was opposed, was first used by Communists (Blanc, Proudhon and Marx). Many people who wholly reject the Communist analysis unknowingly use their term, Capitalism, for the 'system' of commerce that arose in Europe in the eighteenth century and that led to so great an addition to human wealth and well-being. But it is not a deliberate 'system' at all and using the term Capitalism misleadingly implies it is. It arrived by accident; it is an 'emergent phenomenon' that came about without anybody planning it. It happened when powerful men were prevented from stealing at will. Sadly, there is no unloaded word to name this emergent 'thing'.)

Not all workers understand that they are a class, systematically oppressed by another class, and that their only opportunity lies in their combining to overthrow the system. They compete against each other for work, although the system exploits them all. They trust their bosses and so on. This is simply 'false consciousness', according to Marx, making the reasonable observation that the unlettered masses don't always know what will be good for them. They think they want something, but if they were better informed, they would not want it. Persuasion is not the answer; assertion and demonstration are the only ways for the Communist to change opinions. Progress, said Marx, echoing the earlier philosopher Hegel, is made not by reasoned argument but by 'dialectic', where opposed ideas, called 'thesis' and 'antithesis', generate a solution in a different plane, the 'synthesis'. ('Dialectic' simply means 'conversation' in ancient Greek. Marx picked up this use of the term from Hegel. Marx also got a lot of his ideas about history from Hegel.) 'False consciousness' means that progress cannot be achieved by reasoned discussion and voting does not result in government reflecting the true will of the people. Voting will, at best, only reflect their false consciousness. Only the government of the proletariat and its leaders, the Communist party, can lead to the rule of the many, not the few. Only the revolution can bring the end of class war, stop countries competing and avoid economic instability. Only the dawn of proletarian rule will deliver happiness forever, for all! To the barricades, workers!

Many of the increasingly well-read bourgeoisie were themselves transfixed by the scope and interlocking elegance of the theory: economics explained by history, disillusion by a theory of mind, a solution for the appalling inequality and for the suffering of the poor and, at last, a way to deal with the soul-crippling guilt of personal prosperity in the midst of mass poverty. All in one clear, coherent, modern, rational package. Or so it seemed.

This was presented both at huge length in Marx's book and in leaflets in question-and-answer format. These had a compelling vividness – here were the answers, the explanations and the actions needed. The presentation was also passionate, fired by fury at the class – the bourgeoisie – that brought all this misery, that had broken the bonds of trust. The workingman was reduced below the level of a slave: a slave's work was sold only once, the jobbing proletarian had to sell his work to the lowest bidder each day. Because class was the only true conflict, Nationalism was bogus, a distraction from the real challenge. Nationalism and traditional religions would shrivel away when they were no longer needed in the Communist dawn. This dramatic vision often had the effect of firing supporters with fervent energy and commitment to the cause. As a result, Communist parties always tended to be dominated by fanatical believers.

Fanaticism had much to work on, as the times were

turbulent in Western Europe. The revolutions of 1848 were suppressed, but uprisings, riots and attempted revolutions occurred repeatedly across nineteenth-century Europe. Of the many attempts made to bring on the final revolution, perhaps the saddest, in every sense, was the Paris Commune of 1871. After the defeat of the French Army in war and the capture of the self-proclaimed Emperor Napoleon III (formerly Louis Napoleon) by the Prussians, radicals rose up in Paris and, seizing power locally, declared the city an independent 'commune'. This ended in great bloodshed as the French Army reoccupied Paris and reprisals were taken. Marx, typically more visionary than sympathetic, saw this as the *'glorious harbinger of a new society. Its martyrs are enshrined in the great heart of the working class…'* He also observed that the takeover by the commune had not been ruthless or thorough enough. They had allowed time for the forces of reaction to recover. The message that Communist leaders such as Marx, Trotsky and Lenin took from the failure of the Paris Commune was to be utterly ruthless in achieving their great objective. Moderation, and even mercy, allowed the anti-progressive forces back in. The ends, the eternal benefit and happiness of mankind, justified the extreme means that would be necessary to establish the Communist paradise.

The informing character of Communism was its arrogance and associated intolerance. Converts were often fanatical: they knew they had the truth. If you disagreed with them, you were either ignorant or you were on the other side in the class war. The truths of

Communism were self-evident, so if you were educated and you weren't a Communist, it was because you were malicious: you wanted to carry on grinding the faces of the poor. All decent people would be Communists, if they were not greedy, self-interested and insincere. Communism, both when it was a small sect and when it had seized power, required orthodoxy of everyone. All must believe. It is not enough to do the right thing or to keep quiet and get on with daily life. You must believe. When out of power, Communism was highly sectarian, with different conflicting groups, each believing themselves free of error and sin. In power, Communist regimes were given to witch-hunts for splitters and counter-revolutionaries, those who did not believe with all their hearts. Often ordinary people were forced to recite Communist mantras, write pro-Communist letters and make speeches praising leading Communists and their achievements. This arrogance, this conviction of holding the complete truth, together with the conviction that all criticism came only from the malice of the critic, gave permission for Communists to engage in extreme acts: assassination, torture and massacre.

Communist parties arose in all the countries of Europe, and later worldwide, as the ideas hit educated and idealistic young people. In Russia in 1917, the first avowedly Communist group seized power under their leader, Vladimir Ulyanov, who called himself Lenin (apparently he needed a pseudonym and was living near the river Lena at the time). This was despite the fact that Russia and its huge empire was not at all at the cutting edge of development. It still had a very agricultural, peasant economy, in contradiction to Communist theory that required the most economically developed nations to lead the revolution. At the time the Communists took over the Russian Empire, it was still at war with Germany, so the Communists of Russia were forced to delay the arrival of the true period of workers' control. This delay was initially seen as caused by the difficulties in concluding the war and, at the same time, fighting a civil war against both Russian monarchists and troops sent by Britain, the USA, France and other former wartime Allies to help them. By acting with great clarity and utter ruthlessness, the Communist forces defeated all their enemies and achieved a form of peace after five years of hard fighting. Some 20 million or so died in these wars.

With the civil war over, harsh conditions were relaxed and the Russian Empire returned to a more normal existence with its name changed to the Union of Soviet (Committee) Socialist Republics, the USSR. The arrival of the period of true Communism was, and continued to be, delayed by practical issues. There was considerable debate among the Communist leadership on how best to hasten its arrival. Eventually, in 1932, Joseph Djugashvili, who had achieved supreme power under the name Stalin ('Steel'), moved to bring forward the day of complete Communism by removing all farmland from private ownership. Instead of the liberation of the people and eternal plenty, this led to mass starvation and a culture of terror. The failure of the future to arrive was blamed on sabotage by anti-Communist elements working undercover and mass purges of the leadership were conducted to remove these. It is fair to say that the period in the USSR from 1932 to Stalin's death in 1953 was one of the most terrible in history not caused by natural disaster. Poverty and deprivation were topped up with apparently random acts of government cruelty and all-pervading fear. Another 10–20 million or so died as a result of Stalin's policies. The outbreak of war with Germany in 1941 postponed further purges. For the USSR, the suffering of the war was terrible, with yet another 10–20 million killed, but it resulted in victory and the conquest of much of central and Eastern Europe. These countries were rapidly given puppet governments with Communist names and objectives.

Once an avowedly Communist government had arrived in Russia, many Communist parties outside Russia underwent a dramatic change. The authoritarianism of the Communist party in each country was completely subordinated to the authority of the Russian party and its leader. The change of the Communist parties from the pre-1917 style of a bottom-up 'Belief of the Book', with everyone arguing the fine points of *Das Kapital* to, after 1917, a top-down 'Belief of Authority' was astonishingly fast and complete. After 1917, every Communist party in the world held itself in grovelling subordination to the orders from the USSR. This was exploited by the USSR government, which dominated the 'Comintern', the organ of International Communism, and led to intelligent people with

Communist convictions to humiliate themselves by their knowing self-deception about conditions inside the USSR. In 1938 Stalin, the leader of the Communist USSR, signed a treaty with Hitler, the Nationalist leader of Germany, a treaty that allowed both countries to jointly invade and to annexe a half of Poland each. This led France and Britain to declaring war on Germany. The Communist parties outside the USSR obeyed Stalin's instructions to treat this as a Capitalist war that Communists should disdain. That is, until Hitler reneged on the treaty and attacked the USSR, whereupon the same Communist parties were instructed to support the war effort with all their strength. This they immediately did, reversing themselves overnight, apparently forgetting that they were the leaders of a movement based on logic, applied to eternal and unshakeable truths. A few Communist party members in the West became disillusioned by this cynical power play, but the majority of devoted Communists worldwide remained loyal to the party, despite its transparent reduction to a cypher of the USSR's foreign policy. Beliefs are often very hardy.

In 1947 the Communist party took over government in China and, under Mao Zedong, ruled with the utmost harshness. Over the next thirty years, Mao Zedong periodically initiated new internal campaigns that resulted in mass starvation and terror, challenging the USSR's record in creating a daily life of horror for ordinary people. Once again, tens of millions died. Not all Communist governments of this period were terrible, but, across all of them, they covered only the part of the spectrum that goes from depressing to vile. Only the Yugoslavian Communist rule under Tito (Josif Broz) can claim, in the light of subsequent events, that it at least kept the peace without excessive unpleasantness. Despite there being no doubt about the conditions in Communist countries, Communist parties remained strong in many democratic countries until the collapse of the USSR.

After Stalin's death in 1953, the USSR had a brief resurgence, epitomised by its achievement in launching the first man into space. But its government soon slumped into authoritarian stagnation and decline. From the early 1960s, there was the seemingly endless sight of elderly creeps spouting Communist slogans with complete insincerity, shivering in fear lest the ghost of Stalin return to reunite them with more honourable comrades who had perished under his rule. In 1989 governments in Eastern Europe claiming to be Communist fell to bits as soon as the USSR said that it would no longer force them to remain so. In 1991, the USSR itself fell to pieces. The weight of the complete failure of Communism to match even the lowest of its own objectives left the USSR government with nothing and it collapsed completely. The states of the former empire outside Russia itself declared independence and Russia reverted to an authoritarian semi-democracy. China, meanwhile, had abandoned all aspects of Communism, except the name, following the death of Mao Zedong. Under the Confucian regime that followed,

China's economy experienced dramatic growth.

Belief in Communism has now more or less petered out. Its allure has been snuffed out by the total contradiction between the theory and the experience of governments claiming to be Communist. But also the analysis depended on an oppressed class of manual workers rising against their oppressors and this class has diminished as fewer and fewer people are involved in manual labour in the developed economies. There are still some, generally elderly, diehard Communists, wedded to a Belief whose rationale was the liberation of the masses but which failed to do so in practice. Meanwhile, the masses have been liberated by economic growth.

Communism, like some Christian sects before it, promised the resolution of clearly seen wrongs and the arrival of a period of greater happiness. No blissful life after death was expected but a better life, in a better place, here on Earth was promised, in the arrival of the rule of the working class. Communism required the believer to join with fellow believers to organise action but also justified the use of methods that would otherwise be seen as morally wrong – assassination, arbitrary arrest and so on. Communism could revive, or a new Belief based on removing unfairness could start only if economic unfairness were again seen as the greatest challenge for mankind. But our real lesson from Communism is that any Belief, even if it has the kindest and most honourable intentions in mind, can end up committing and endorsing acts of wickedness. More than that, the greater the long-term benefit perceived, the more appalling the acts that can be justified to achieve them. If you are going to save the world forever, it is absurd to allow a few troublemakers or old-fashioned rules to stand in the way.

Postscript: Markets and Economic Theories

Communism is a Belief, capital 'B', because it is based on faith in a set of propositions, which it holds to be true. Are other socio-economic theories also Beliefs? Especially, are the right-wing, free-market economic theories Beliefs? Many people see them as equal and opposite theories to Communism and other left-wing theories. In addition, they are often presented, as Communism was, in semi-religious terms. Adam Smith's famous pro-free-market doctrine invokes a mystical 'invisible hand' of the market. Some economists have a misty-eyed reverence for markets and ascribe to them almost magic powers to enrich mankind. If trusting faith in free markets is not a Belief in the sense that Communism and Christianity are, why isn't it?

To 'believe in free markets' is to think that, in most circumstances, the best way to exchange goods and services between people is through a process where sellers and buyers haggle until a sale is made at an agreed price. Free-marketers believe that allocating goods through markets generates the most material well-being. The actual mechanism of markets varies greatly: shops with fixed selling prices, auctions, yard sales, contract tendering and many other price-setting mechanisms all counting as markets.

The most commonly considered alternative system to markets is to allocate goods through a planned system, whereby an authority, normally the government, determines who gets what.

Few doubt that markets can be useful in some circumstances. The traditional market stall has worked well for reallocating a farmer's surplus agricultural produce for thousands of years. However, markets can fail – they can sometimes simply not work as mechanisms for setting prices and distributing goods. Unconstrained, market systems can have a variety of malignant outcomes, from adulterated food to monopoly prices. Markets are also given to spectacular 'crashes', causing wealth to vanish suddenly, generating a variety of unpleasant economic after-effects.

There are cases where planned allocation is necessary, such as in funding and building roads (in cases where tolls are a practical impossibility). However, achieving a good planned distribution is more difficult than it at first appears. When planning systems have been applied widely in a society, they have been transparently inefficient. In addition, planning is always prone to corruption.

The argument about the appropriateness of markets in any situation depends on individuals' positions on the left/right political spectrum.

If you are inclined towards the right, it means you think:

- that society's well-being depends on its total amount of wealth more than its equal distribution.

- that good intentions can have bad outcomes and selfish intentions can have good outcomes.
- that individuals are the best judges of what makes them happy.
- that planners are often mistaken.

If you are more left-minded, you think roughly the opposite of these propositions.

These opposed ideas of the way the world works lead the left to prefer economic planning. Ideally, this consists of a wise and kind authority with the mission to make the best happen equally for all. The right's beliefs lead them to support markets because, ideally, markets allow individuals to decide for themselves what they want, which must be more accurate than someone else making that decision for them. The left sees planning as the default mechanism, the approach to be applied in every situation, unless there are clear and unambiguous reasons why a market will work better. The right regards markets as almost invariably better than planning and suggests them as a default mechanism in the same way.

Historically, both approaches have failed when applied too widely. Sometimes too much freedom has been given to market mechanisms, which has led to economic instability and a series of crashes. Sometimes planning has been given too powerful a role, leading to waste, corruption and abuse of power.

Ideally, there would be an applied science for the distribution of material goods and services, so that mechanisms of distribution could be optimised. Some would argue that the study of economics is just this, in which case economics is at a very early stage of development. We have not yet found ways to test theories of well-being optimisation. Even the way we measure a single individual's well-being (happiness, contentment, satisfaction, etc.) is disputed, let alone how we measure offsetting one person's gain against someone else's loss. Teetering on top of the theoretical void, practical constraints mean that we cannot construct tests that measure outcomes of different distribution mechanisms in real life. We not only can't tell whether to aim more at equality of opportunity or equality of outcome but we can't test methods for achieving either.

This inability to test theories of distribution leaves us with just the theories and arguments: arguments about the evidence of history, arguments about theoretical models, arguments about the causes of current problems, and arguments about future effects. In the absence of objective testing we are left with opinions, not facts. Decision-makers have to guess what is best, because they don't know what is best.

What makes a Belief is certainty: complete confidence in the basic propositions of the Belief. A free market or a planning enthusiast cannot (rationally) claim certainty. Their belief in their system is conditional: provisional until better evidence can be obtained. If new evidence were to indicate the other way, they would change their recommendation (or so they imagine, at any rate). So belief in free markets or planned distribution is simply an opinion about what the, sadly inadequate, evidence suggests is the better mechanism. It is not a Belief, capital 'B', based on a creed, independently held to be true.

.9.

ASIAN BELIEFS: THE BELIEFS WITHOUT TEARS

A part from Polytheism, all the Beliefs covered so far arose in the Middle East or Europe. All are associated at one time or another with intolerance and violence. But half of mankind has always lived in south and east Asia, worlds dominated by Indian and Chinese cultures. Here, too, major Beliefs developed, as large and long-lived as the Middle-Eastern and European Beliefs. But, without being completely free of religious violence, they have virtually never been the causes of violence themselves.

These Beliefs are also worth understanding because these two regions are returning to the world's centre stage, after a couple of hundred years on the side-lines. Both regions are in a phase of great change, when their traditional approaches are coming alongside Western ways in new combinations. China, in particular, has had a grotesque experience over the last two centuries at the hands of imported Beliefs. Tens of millions of Chinese have been slaughtered by pathological variants of Christianity, Nationalism and Communism.

The sages – or people – of Asia are not inherently less violent than those of Europe or the Middle East. China was briefly dominated by the profoundly violent Belief of 'Legalism', discussed below, and continued to follow, in theory at least, a draconian legal code for centuries. Buddhism was initially promoted by a man of great violence, Ashoka, in a Hindu (polytheistic) world that had often seen violence associated with the worship of Hindu godlets. Indeed, so violent was their world that Daoism[55] and Buddhism saw all life as a pain and struggle.

Buddhism and Daoism are both structured ways of looking at life, each leading to a programme of personal development. Because they see life as full of pain and misery, they offer similar solutions: to escape from this grim existence, individuals must free themselves of worldly desire and, through a process of learning and self-discipline, achieve a state of Enlightenment. With Enlightenment will come release from the pain and anguish of everyday life.

To understand these Beliefs, and the Greek philosophers who had the same basic view (see postscript), it is important for modern readers to

---

[55] Under the old system of transliterating Chinese characters into Latin letters, 'Daoism' was known as 'Taoism' and its key document was known as the 'Lao-tzu' rather than the term 'Dao-zi' used here. Sadly we cannot use the old system, not least because Confucius' name in that system is 'Kung-Fu'.

remember that life in these periods was, indeed, filled with pain, both physical and spiritual. There were few cures for toothache, sores or other chronic illnesses. Boils were a common affliction and it may be assumed that cystitis, fungal skin infections, warts and so on were endemic. There was little relief from pain; people simply lived with it. Children and loved ones died frequently, randomly and, often, in agony. Birth was accompanied by great pain and frequent death. Hunger was common and what food was available was often disgusting or deeply dull. Great cruelty was practised, both in war and in peace. So wretched was the lifestyle of humble folk that a quick or painless death was not a serious deterrent to crime. Grotesque processes of torturing people to death had to be devised to meet the need for something sufficiently nasty to discourage people from anti-social behaviour. Hanging, drawing and quartering (strangulation, cutting down while still alive, removing the guts and burning them in front of the person before chopping them – still alive – into four) was popular in Medieval Britain – both as a punishment and as entertainment. China practiced the 'death of a thousand cuts' that could make killing last many days. But the Roman system of crucifixion required less work to achieve a slow public death in agony and was more efficient when mass slaughter was required. When this background is remembered, it becomes less surprising that thinkers in China, India and the east Mediterranean came to the same profoundly gloomy view of the world.

Turning specifically to Chinese culture, some form of

continuing life after death had been assumed since pre-historic times and it was taken for granted that people in the afterlife had connections with the living. There was – and continues to be – the usual panoply of Polytheism: godlets and spirits, mystical rules such as Feng-Shui (wind-water) and the ancient process of divination known as the Yi Ching, the 'Book of Changes'. This held the idea of balancing the yin and yang and was later expanded into complex systems of hexagrams to divine the future. None of these affected the development of Chinese Beliefs, beyond providing a background and tools for use in analogies.

After 500BCE, writing started to be used for Chinese philosophical and religious concepts and the development of ideas was so prolific that they are known as the 'Hundred Schools of Thought'. But competition between them meant they reduced to just four main schools by around 300BCE.

The same three centuries, from 500BCE to 221BCE, when the schools of philosophy were developing, are known in Chinese history as the 'Warring States' period. Competing kingdoms fought wars that escalated in scale and cruelty over the whole period. This background of endless fighting created a need for thinkers to understand, explain and, perhaps, halt the slide towards bloody anarchy. This context set the tone for the four Beliefs that remained. Two, Legalism and Moism, were to vanish, destroyed by the effect of the first emperor's reunification of China and his rule, leaving the other two, Confucianism and Daoism, to dominate subsequent Chinese thinking.

Legalism was built on a loathing of the cruelties and disorder of the never-ending wars. It held that authority was all, that mankind was corrupt and that great severity was required to prevent the horrors of anarchy. To that end, totalitarian techniques were justified; indeed, they were necessary to gain the greater good of peace and order[56].

Legalism's leaders developed the mechanisms for imposing strict order. Informer networks and group punishments for individual 'crimes' were devised. Every individual was allocated to a squad of eight to twelve people. If any of them were found to have committed what the state saw as a crime, a wide term, everyone in the squad was punished. Often their punishment was exile to build the Great Wall. This grim doctrine justified these appalling techniques of oppression because the outcome, ordered rule, was seen as important enough for almost any method to be permitted if it helped achieve so vital a result. This was the Belief that helped enable the King of Qin to conquer the rest of China and, as the first emperor, impose a rule whose horror is remembered to this day. The first emperor is the one who is so famously buried with the army of Terracotta Warriors. At least part of the Chinese delay in further uncovering these is that they shed glory on a man whose rule, even now, is remembered with a shudder.

---

[56] The English writer Thomas Hobbs (1588–1679) developed a very similar set of ideas resulting from his experience of the anarchy and slaughter of the British Isles civil wars. Same solution to the same problem.

The other main school to vanish under the impact of the first emperor was Moism. This Belief had responded to the continual anarchy of the Warring States period by developing a knightly code of conduct. The code required that an individual should desire to benefit all mankind and that this should determine his behaviour. This was summarised under the title of 'All-embracing Love'. Moism has strong similarities to the 'Christian' code of Medieval Chivalry that grew up in Western Europe during the constant warring of the period 900–1400CE. A similar solution to a similar problem again, perhaps?

Mozi, the founder of Moism, saw it as 'the will of heaven' that we should all struggle for the benefit of mankind. Although Moist writings survived the first emperor, the school itself died. Moism's political stance of utter obedience to authority was probably too close to some Legalist ideas to be accepted in the revulsion against totalitarianism that followed the death of the first emperor.

Ironically, the two schools that survive to this day, Confucianism and Daoism, while not exactly opposed, resemble the yin and the yang of world-views: Confucianism worldly, cynical, authoritarian; Daoism escapist, striving, personal.

Confucianism centres on society and how the individual should govern their lives in a social and political context. Its focus is on the relationships between individuals, groups and government and achieving the good life through fitting in with others. Daoism is about personal spiritualism, gaining individual peace and achieving the good life through a thoughtful withdrawal from distractions. Although both philosophies can live side by side, they do have conflicting implications: Daoism encourages withdrawal from the world; Confucianism insists on involvement with it. The development of Daoist thought was influenced by the existence of Confucianism. The Daoist emphasis on the individual and on personal freedom can be seen, in part, as a reaction to the emphasis on society and on self-control in Confucianism.

The great and varied outpouring of Chinese thought over the centuries is often collected up by analysts and teachers and lumped under one or the other of these two headings, rather as if they were categories in a library: Confucianism is 'Politics and Sociology' and Daoism is 'Mind, Body, Spirit'. So there are writings that are commonly filed under the headings of Confucianism or Daoism that are not compatible with the mainstream of these philosophies. It seems that any abstract writing must be categorised as one or the other by later Chinese scholars and this leads to confusion.

It has been said that a week is too long to see Rome and a lifetime not long enough. So it is with Confucianism and Daoism. A volume that sought to cover all the thoughts under these two headings could not be read in a lifetime. So we will take a very brisk tourist trip round the central area of each, noting only the postcard sights.

Confucianism is a profoundly conservative set of

principles and sayings, originally collected together (long after Confucius' death) in a book called *The Analects*. Order, virtue, respect for seniors, care for dependents and juniors, preference for righteousness over profit, self-discipline and respect for ancestors, respect for the family and respect for community godlets and ceremonies – these are all strong themes. Around these ideas, Confucians weaved complex justifications in terms of man's essential goodness fighting his animal crudity and so on. But the central personal guidance is always the concept of 'proper' behaviour. Proper behaviour is the centre of a well-lived and rewarding life. The central political concept of Confucianism is the respect for authority required of individuals and the matching care for individuals required of authority. This is expressed in a central analogy of Confucianism: the state's relationship with the individual and the individual's relationship with the state should be as a father's relationship to a son – care and nurturing on the father's or state's side matched by respect and support on the side of the son or citizen.

Perhaps unsurprisingly, Confucianism was adopted as the official state 'religion' of China after the death of the first emperor and the establishment of the long-lived and largely successful Han Dynasty. Even today, Chinese politics can be understood as a restoration of paternalist Confucian thinking far more than it can be understood through any connection to the Communism it still uses as a badge.

Confucius did not believe household godlets existed or that ancestors had an influence on this life. Despite this, he stressed the importance of conducting the appropriate ceremonies and sacrifices to godlets and ancestors because the ceremonies had benefits for social and family order and cohesion. Effectively, Confucianism is a thoroughly worldly Belief that sees the possibility of achieving a good life through proper behaviour and through fitting in with the social and political world we have to live in. It sees life as, at its core, good and the way to live best is to fit in with it.

Daoists, on the other hand, believe that every life is fundamentally one of pain, loss and discomfort. You can only escape from the suffering life brings by self-discipline and mental exercise. The objective of these is to achieve an enlightened state of withdrawal from worldly desires. 'Dao' means 'The Way', the way to achieve this liberation. The only struggle in Daoism is the personal struggle to achieve a state of peace. Hence Daoism has no political stance, except withdrawal from politics.

A famous story illustrates the Daoist approach. A great statesman has retired, but the emperor sends two senior officials to persuade him to return. After a long journey, they find him sitting, fishing by the side of a pond. They try to persuade him to return, talking of his importance, the emperor's need of him and the distinction he will gain. He listens politely. When they run out of arguments, there is a silence and a little turtle slides down the opposite bank of the pond and into the water with a 'plop'. The statesman says he is now like the unimportant, little, muddy turtle in the pond. In the capital, he says, there is a turtle in the palace, with gold and jewels on its shell, held in great reverence. The difference is that the little muddy turtle is alive. They leave him still fishing.

The book of poems called the *Dao De Jing* (*Way Virtue Classic*) is seen by most as the foundation of Daoism. It dates from some time before 300BCE and may be based on much older spoken material. Its legendary author, called Dao-zi (Lao-Tzu) is seen as the founder of Daoism. The poems are mystical, enigmatic and thought provoking. It has been said that paradox is at the centre of Daoism. A well-known example gives a feeling for the style:

> *'In Dao the only motion is returning*
> *The only useful quality, weakness.*
> *For though all creatures under heaven are the products of being,*
> *Being itself is the product of non-being.'*

Daoists have followed many paths to find release. One aspect of Daoism, drawn from Chinese tradition, is the idea of striving to balance the elements, the yin with the yang, and much Daoist thinking stresses ideas of balance. Daoism was generally happy to include godlets and ancestors in its thinking, but it is the tone of Daoism more than any specific idea that is its distinctive feature. It has a gentle, mystical feel that seeks a calm kindness and an unostentatious generosity.

When Buddhism 'arrived' in China – and the process was a slow one over many years – it became intimately fused with Daoism. The two approaches were seen as different presentations of the same truths. Buddhist writings[57] and traditions added the concept of monasticism to Daoism and provided an extra body of thought on the paths to enlightenment. After 700CE, and with imperial favour, Buddhist temples and monasteries grew rapidly in numbers until 845CE, when the emperor changed his mind, turned against Buddhism and destroyed the monasteries and temples (as well as the, much smaller, Christian and Zoroastrian churches)[58]. After the 'Forfeiture', as it is called, the religious situation reverted to the previous pattern. But now it was with the combination of Buddhism and Daoism as a personal Belief, rather than just Daoism, competing against Confucianism for what has been called 'the greater share-of-mind'.

Both Confucianism and Daoism set their face against strong passions and raw, animal energy. This sets the tone for the official presentation of Chinese history and the shock and horror when it is interrupted by periodic outbursts of religious fanaticism. These, fuelled by social discontent, have periodically led to extremely violent internal wars.

Two examples, covering a wide span of years, illustrate why, to this day, China's rulers have a lively fear of

---

[57] Some of the main Buddhist Sutras were translated into Chinese by the Christian Bishop of Chang'an, then the Chinese capital, around 790CE. *A History of Christianity in Asia,* Moffett, Orbis Books, Vol. 1.

[58] His motivation was mainly financial, not religious.

fanatical religious sects. This aspect of Chinese history, along with the surprising fact that many of these cults start as exercise groups, explains much of the current Chinese government's apparently disproportionate reaction against the Fulan-Gong exercise group/sect. The highly destructive revolt of the Yellow Turbans (184–202CE) involved a fanatic religion called the Way of Supreme Peace. (Although the Yellow Turbans are sometimes described as a sect of Daoism, this appears to be a prime example of tidy-mindedness, requiring that all thinking is categorised as either Daoist or Confucian, however implausible.) Although the rebellion was eventually defeated after sixteen years of war, the destruction caused brought to an end the 400 years of the Han Dynasty.

In the nineteenth century CE the Tai-Ping revolt, which cost over 20 million lives, was inspired by Christian ideas. It, too, was fuelled by social discontents and a perception of the failure of the government. Finally, it was put down – with European help – after fourteen years of war and starvation. But, as with the Han Dynasty, many see the effort required to put an end to the revolt as leading directly to the fall of the Ching Dynasty.

However, the sheer incompetence, as well as the corruption and venality, of the nineteenth-century Ching governments cannot be overstated. They were loathed by many of the people. It is now fashionable to decry the wicked ways of the West in forcing 'unequal treaties' on China, but they would not have been so one-sided had there been any competence at all in the Ching court. Nor were the Ching emperors Chinese – they took care to emphasise the fact that, as Manchus from outside China, they were above the Chinese – a fact often forgotten in anti-colonialist rants. The 'Forbidden City' in Beijing is so called because the Chinese were forbidden to enter it.

In the twentieth century CE imported Beliefs affected the course of China's history. A weak form of Nationalism supported the deposition of the last emperor, but it failed to provide the impetus for unity and the country fell into anarchy as separate warlords built fiefdoms. Then the Japanese marched in under the impetus of their own Nationalist Belief. After the country had suffered twenty years of anarchy, invasion and warfare, a Communist sect under Mao Zedong, aided by the defeat of the Japanese at the end of World War II, seized power in China. Communist Belief and the desperate nature of the struggle that had got him to power inspired Mao Zedong's political programmes after his victory. While Mao created political stability, it was sometimes at the expense of totalitarian misery for the population and a grotesque loss of life from his cruelly implemented political ideas. Many in China today take comfort from the fact that the first emperor's reign unified China and was followed by almost 400 years of relative peace and prosperity under the Han Dynasty. They hope that the same will follow the similar unification and reign of Mao Zedong. So far, the dramatic improvement in Chinese material wellbeing over the last decades is seen in China as more then compensating for the harsh methods used by Mao to gain and consolidate Chinese unity

The difference between the patterns of Chinese and Western Beliefs, before the two systems met each other in the seventeenth century CE, is that the Chinese had open and tolerant Beliefs, occasionally interrupted by outbreaks of intolerant, prescriptive and violent cults. By contrast, the European tradition was of intolerant, prescriptive and violent Beliefs. These were imported into China over the nineteenth and twentieth centuries: charismatic Christianity with the Tai Ping in the 1860s, Nationalism at the end of a Japanese gun in the 1920s and Communism after 1947. All had horrific consequences for China and its people.

Having been so burned by Western Beliefs, China has now reverted to de facto public Confucianism, despite keeping the name of Communism. As China basks in a long period of internal and external peace with rapidly advancing prosperity there is, understandably, a great fear of anything resembling a Western Belief. This includes democracy, which has been far from universally successful in nearby Japan, Thailand, Malaysia, Russia, Iran and India. The Chinese ideal is much more like Singapore: a Confucian, paternalist government that has made its, mostly Chinese-speaking, people some of the richest in the world. (Although Singapore has a free vote, only one party has ever held power and it has never held fewer than 90% of the parliamentary seats.) For the moment, however, the idea of democracy in China holds the fear of conflict, of disunity, of a descent into anarchy. All are recent memories in China. Setting up a conflict, even of votes, seems a great risk to take, simply to earn smiles from patronising Western governments and critics. The current system works and works the traditional way, the Confucian way, the Chinese way. The British ruled Hong Kong that way for 150 years with success, so the West seems hypocritical in criticising China for continuing the system they used themselves for so long.

China has always preferred 'Belief Lite': Confucianism and Daoism, both bookish and as far from the electoral battle as they are from the battlefield. China cannot see any reason to adopt the kind of populist electoral system typical of Europe and America, a system that they see as forcing governments to borrow unsustainably to retain popular support.

On the other hand, destructive Beliefs have repeatedly bubbled up in Chinese history; the sheer coolness of Daoism and Confucianism leaves room for more warm-blooded, passionate Beliefs. Perhaps the living memory of the horrors of Mao Zedong's (extreme) Communism will inoculate them against a new Belief – although that memory is astonishingly faint already. On the other hand, some new form of modern Chineseness will come from this huge and rich land as it develops, so when a new Belief arrives looking different and Chinese, it will be vital to catch it before it develops into an aggressive phase.

Hinduism is the name applied to the polytheistic sea of beliefs, practices, legends, traditions, art and magic of India. Attempts to describe Hinduism conventionally are doomed to failure. If you get through the original Vedas (Hymns) of the pre-historic Aryan invaders, the

Upanishad commentaries, the immensely long stories of the Mahabharata and Ramayana, the very many godlets (traditionally 330 million), the current three principal godlets, Vishnu, Brahma and Shiva, with their many divine aspects and human avatars, you have contemplated the relevance of the mystic monosyllable, Om, and you have understood the sub-religions such as Shaivism and Vaishnavism, you still have barely begun to describe it.

You cannot become a Hindu; you have to be born one. But, all that said, what Hinduism has beyond a 'simple' Polytheism is a social and communal structure: caste. Caste is India's private obsession. It shapes and reflects how people in a group should relate with each other and to the group as a whole. Hinduism's one consistent quality, over the millennia, is that it retains the dominance of the caste system with the priestly (Brahmin) class at the top of it. The background of Hinduism, its powerful priesthood clan and its strong social mechanisms are the original context of Buddhism.

Around 500BCE – and the dates of early Buddhism are both vague and largely irrelevant – a number of religious teachers, Gurus, arose in India with world-view philosophies that resemble those of Daoism or the Hellenistic Philosophies. They, too, saw the world as full of pain and anguish. These Gurus saw, as well, the need for self-discipline and structure to an individual's struggle, the struggle to break free of the desires and needs that drag the soul down into this tormented world. But on top of the struggle to be free of the world's pain, Hindu thinking had incorporated the idea of reincarnation. This is the idea that life is an endless cycle of death followed by rebirth (*Samsara*). The form of rebirth, from the lowest form of life to the highest, depends (in some but not all visions of Hinduism) on how an individual had done in the life before, the amount of good or bad 'karma' accrued. The concept of karma, which means, literally, 'action', can be looked at with vast complexity, but, in practice, boils down to the accumulation of good or bad marks for good or bad deeds (and, sometimes, thoughts). Which actions attract how many good or bad marks varies in different sects. The Gurus saw reincarnation as adding an extra level to the problem of escape from the grossness of the world. For them, you have to seek enlightenment, possibly through many cycles of life and death and life, before you are finally free from the miseries of this world.

The best known of these teachers were Siddhartha Gautama, who became known as the Buddha (the enlightened one), and Vardhamana, who became known as Mahavira (great warrior), whose followers formed the religion of the Jains. There were others, but their thinking later merged with mainstream Buddhism or Hinduism. Although there are differences between Jain and Buddhist thinking, Jainism is enough like Buddhism to be included with it. The notable, practical difference is that Jains take even more extreme efforts to avoid taking animal life than most Buddhists.

Buddhism's great strength, like the other expansive world-Beliefs of Islam and Christianity, is that it can be approached in different ways. Each approach connects to the others to form a complete, multi-level Belief. Buddhism can be approached through the stories of Buddha's life, through the Canon of Writings (Tripitika), through Bodhisattvas (explained below) or, simply, through the practice of meditation. Hinduism and Buddhism fit together as a pair similar to the way Confucianism and Daoism relate to each other: Hinduism, outward and social/political; Buddhism, inward and personal.

The simplest way for everyday people to understand Buddhism is through the legends of the life of the Buddha. There are many variations of these, so a summary here may not exactly fit someone else's version. These legends of the Buddha start with the famous story of a prince, Siddhartha Gautama, who was sheltered from exposure to the bad things of life by his father until after he was fully a man and married. After accidentally seeing an old man one day and learning of the decay in the world, he left his palace and became an austere holy man. After years of struggle and contemplation he finally achieved enlightenment and became the Buddha. Thereafter, for forty-five years, he travelled and taught. Many tales are told of events in this period of the Buddha's life, stories that help the unlettered to understand the ideas that are also expressed in the more intellectual 'Tripitika' (Canon).

Although the historical accuracy of these tales is irrelevant to Buddhists, the fact that nothing of Buddha's life or teaching appears to have been written down for 300–400 years after the Buddha's death poses a challenge for those looking for the authentic teaching. The Emperor Ashoka (c300–232BCE), who ruled much of India, decided to take Buddhism as his religion before any aspect of Buddhism was written down. It is said that Ashoka converted to Buddhism in reaction to the violence of the wars that took him to his throne. It would probably be more accurate to say that it was his support that defined Buddhism as a separate Belief, changing it from just another strand of Hinduism. He sponsored its teaching inside his empire and sent missionaries to take Buddhism to lands outside. It is recorded that one of the Greek kings that followed after the split up of Alexander's empire adopted Buddhism around 200BCE. Buddhism's development as the leading 'brand' of Indian contemplative Belief is due to his support.

Part of Buddhism's early appeal in India was its rejection of the caste system. This ironclad hierarchy, splitting the population into hundreds of different, ranked social classes from birth, is integral to Hinduism and dominates India to this day, despite repeated attempts to lessen its grip on people's lives. A Belief that rejected caste had appeal to those lower down the ladder. Even some of those higher up the ladder chafed at the social restrictions caste imposes and took to the freedom Buddhism offered.

Well before the first Buddhist material was written down, 200 or so years after Ashoka and some 500 years after the life of the Buddha, the religion had already split into two different branches: Theravada and Mahayana. Theravada, which means 'ancient teaching', is the underlying form of Buddhism practised in Sri Lanka and most of Southeast Asia – Cambodia, Laos, Myanmar (Burma) and Thailand. It is, in theory, the relatively austere form of understanding and behaviour that sticks closely to the approach of the first written Buddhist material, the Pali Tripitika. The emphasis is on personal enlightenment, rejection of worldly desires and the monastic tradition. Theravada Buddhism is essentially a philosophy and self-improvement programme with very little to say about God, godlets or their equivalents. Despite this theoretical simplicity, in practice much polytheistic practice has been introduced and some very ornate Theravada temples have been built in competition with the Mahayana branch.

Mahayana Buddhism – 'Mahayana' means 'great vehicle' – is the branch of Buddhism that dominates in China, Korea, Japan and Vietnam. Mahayana Buddhism has godlets of myriad variety, some, but not all, called Bodhisattvas. It has legends of the supernatural and of other worlds and has multiple schools, varying in practice and belief from exotic Polytheism to austere asceticism.

The theoretically simpler Theravada Buddhism rests on early verbal teachings, captured in the first written Buddhist works, the Pali Tripitika[xlii]. The Pali Tripitika, (it means 'three baskets' and refers to the containers which held the Buddhist writings) was written in Sri Lanka about 30CE. It is called 'Pali' because it was written in the Pali language of northern India, where it was memorised, probably long before it was committed to writing. The Pali Tripitika covers the gloomy Buddhist view of the world as the abode of miseries and presents Buddhism as a practical programme of self-discipline and self-improvement, resembling a modern self-improvement book in its structure with clear, numbered headings and defined programmes of action.

It leads with the Four Noble Truths and the Eightfold Path to enlightenment. The Four Noble Truths set out the rationale for self-improvement: suffering exists; suffering comes from the craving for existence; suffering ceases when the craving ceases; freedom from craving is possible by practising the Eightfold Path.

The Eightfold Path is a practical course of action to deal with the challenge presented by the Four Noble Truths; it provides you with the ways to liberate yourself from craving and move to enlightenment. To achieve this you need to follow a programme with two mental aspects: 'Right View' and 'Right Intention', that is, understanding Buddhist teaching and following its precepts. You must be ethical in your everyday life: 'Right Speech', 'Right Action' and 'Right Livelihood' and you must meditate using the three keys to successful meditation: 'Right Effort', 'Right Mindfulness' and 'Right Concentration'.

Theravada Buddhism is a personal Belief and a central part of its teaching relates to meditation (yoga), using concentration and self-discipline to liberate the mind from the drudgery and pain of the world. This is linked to what is called, for lack of a more accurate term in English, 'monasticism', a central concept of Buddhism. In Buddhist monasticism, individuals give up, normally for a period only, daily, practical jobs and family life and follow a contemplative, celibate existence under the monastic rules of Buddhism, separated from everyday life and, generally, sustained by the alms of others. Their existence alone, following this holy 'lifestyle', brings goodness and peace.

Theravada Buddhism, like Daoism and the Greeks, has next to nothing to say about God, godlets or creation. This form of Buddhism is not centred on believing but on doing. Godlets are accepted in much the same way as the Prophet Mohammad accepted the existence of djinns (desert spirits) or some people today accept ghosts; whether they exist or not is irrelevant to the issues of how you live your life. Buddhism started with monks and poor, wandering teachers, not priests or ceremonies.

Mahayana Buddhism saw the process of self-improvement by itself as too limited – possibly as too self-focussed as well. In Mahayana, those who achieve enlightenment are moved by compassion to put off their own final salvation to help others. This is what the Buddha himself did, remaining alive after his enlightenment for many years to help others. These enlightened ones are known as Bodhisattvas – Buddhas-to-be. It is an easy step to go from admiration of the enlightened to worship of them and, effectively, the Bodhisattvas became godlets. (In the Jain tradition the equivalent enlightened ones are the Jinas, from whom the religion gets its name.) By the first century CE, a wide number of Buddha and Bodhisattva figures were being worshipped and the idea of merit that could be gained by the worship of these figures had arisen and even the idea that salvation could be granted from above by these godlets.

Mahayana added not only the Bodhisattvas but also new 'Sutras' to its form of Buddhism. These are additional teachings – the word Sutra means 'thread' and early Sutras were literally added on to scriptures with a string. Later the word 'Sutra' was seen as metaphorical, a thread of thought. The Sutras started being added around 100CE – long after the time of the Buddha – but are seen by some as representing the Buddha's thoughts. No one agrees on the number of Sutras, which vary in length from a few lines to complete books. Some estimate that 600 Mahayana Sutras survive written in both Sanskrit, the ancient language of India, and in Chinese. In Mahayana, the value given to different Sutras varies, so that, for example, the Nirichen school only accepts the Lotus Sutra, which is completely ignored by some other schools.

Over time the number of Bodhisattvas multiplied, so that, soon, twenty, thirty or forty were being worshipped, all with complex interrelationships, associations with legends and different areas of life they patronise. A couple of examples of Bodhisattvas may give an idea of their nature: Sitatapatra is the Goddess of the White Parasol and protector against supernatural danger; Manjusri is the Bodhisattva of keen awareness and wisdom. Some, like the Amitaba Buddha of the Pure Land sect seem virtually to replace the original (Gautama) Buddha. This confused whorl of beliefs gave people a desire to hold onto something tangible in their religion. To meet this need, a cult of relics built up, with profitable temples of pilgrimage being built round the main relics such as the tooth or hairs of the Buddha. The resemblance to Medieval Christianity and later Sufi Islam is very close. The Beliefs had reverted to Polytheism in all but name and their lost intellectual structure was replaced by veneration of magic places and objects.

This anarchy did, however, allow each culture that experienced Buddhism to shape it so that it suited local traditions and needs. Schools started, developed, split and multiplied. In the West a well-known school is called 'Zen', derived from the Japanese Zen Buddhism, which was derived from the Chinese school of Chan Buddhism (which also gave rise to the Vietnamese Thien school and the Korean Seon school). In most areas where Buddhism was imported it both sat alongside local Polytheism and merged with them to some degree – there is very little religious intolerance associated with Buddhism.

By around the year one, Buddhism was well established across India and had a presence in Southeast Asia. But it had also split many times and was beginning to be reabsorbed by Hinduism in India, which had already accepted the Buddha as one of the avatars (earthly incarnations) of the godlet Vishnu, alongside Rama and Krishna.

In China, Buddhism was greeted as an enrichment of Daoist thought and practice, adding a much stronger monastic element to previous Chinese practice. After a complicated history of imperial support and then imperial destruction, Chinese Buddhism effectively split in two. The Chinese state decided to regulate Buddhist monasteries, limit their numbers and supervise their theology. This state-Buddhism, unsurprisingly, started to resemble Confucianism in its role as a promoter of 'proper' behaviour.

On the other hand, for individuals in China looking outside the nationalised religion, Buddhism linked into and merged with Daoist ideas. Both share an emphasis on seeking personal enlightenment, aided by writings, contemplation, meditation and spiritual exercises. Away from state control, a number of different schools of Buddhism developed in China – the best known are probably the Chan and Pure Land schools – and extended, further altered, into Korea, Japan and Vietnam. Although the different 'schools' vary widely in their beliefs and practices from the very polytheistic to the austerely intellectual, they all centre on the search for enlightenment and release from craving.

In India, separate Buddhism simply faded away. Without a Church hierarchy or a rigid doctrine, it was unable to avoid being absorbed by the flexible approach and stronger social structure of Hinduism. But Hinduism itself had also adapted to the demand for a more satisfactory spiritualism.

For Hindus moving in the direction of a deeper Belief, the key text is an eighteen-chapter passage from the great Hindu saga of the Mahabharata, a passage separately called the Bhagavada Gita (Song of the Lord). This was written after Buddhism had become a major influence but is difficult to date with accuracy closer than sometime between 200BCE and 200CE. In the story, Arjuna, the hero, is waiting for the start of a battle that will involve fighting relatives, friends and former teachers. He worries about the morality of his action. The Lord Krishna, an avatar of Vishnu, here in the role of Arjuna's charioteer, addresses his concern and gives an extended revelation on the nature of life, the meaning of existence and the path to personal peace. The Bhagavada Gita reveals a complete religion/philosophy of life. It covers the immortality of the soul (Atma), the duties of humans and the different types of yoga that can be used to transcend material existence. (The meaning of the term 'yoga' is, as with everything in Hinduism, complex and variable. The best average translation into English is something like 'personal discipline in pursuit of spiritual insight'.) The Bhagavada Gita also explains Vishnu's role as the creator of the universe and the devotion to him needed to raise a human from the sea of death and rebirth. For some Hindus, the Bhagavada Gita on its own provides a complete and satisfactory religion, with Krishna/Vishnu as the only God. The 'Hare Krishna' movement (more properly the International Society for Krishna Consciousness) takes the Bhagavada Gita as its key text. But, for most Hindus, it is just one part of an almost infinitely complex interlocking set of writings, practices and beliefs.

In Tibet, Buddhism was imported by order of its secular rulers and became a state religion, associated with power. This small strand of Buddhism is known as

Vajrayana (diamond vehicle) and is the source of 'Tantric' practice and the speculative *Tibetan Book of the Dead*. Apart from the fact that it allows the worship of living individuals and that some of its elements are secret, this is an obscure and complex set of teachings and practices. Its similarity to other forms of Buddhism has been compared to the similarity of Orthodox Judaism to other forms of Buddhism.

Under the Mongol rulers, the heads of monasteries, known as the Grand Lamas, were made governors of Tibet, with the Mongol ruler, Altan Khan, creating the position of Dalai Lama. This became seen as the senior position in Tibet after Gushi Khan, of the neighbouring Khosut tribe, killed all the Dalai Lama's rivals in the seventeenth century, leading to a more or less continuous history of violence, poisonings and politics associated with the title (until the present incumbent's re-invention of the title as a contemporary, if political, Vajrayana saint). So involved with power were the monasteries that some became, in effect, garrisons for fighting 'monks'. This association of the Tibetan Lamas with political power remains today.

In Japan, Buddhism developed, as so many aspects of Japanese culture developed, by taking Chinese learning, drying it out and giving it an austere beauty. The most influential school of Japanese Buddhism, Jodoshinshu, has been described as closest in feeling to Protestant Christianity. It emphasises the futility of human action to achieve Grace; Grace being only in the gift of Amida Buddha (or Amitaba Buddha). Amida Buddha is a different Buddha to the original and is the principal Buddha of the Pure Land School. His origins are described in the Larger Sutra of Immeasurable Life, a typical polytheistic legend. Quite uncharacteristically, the Japanese abandoned the celibacy required elsewhere of Buddhist monks as part of their renunciation of the world and allow Buddhist 'priests' to marry and have families.

Buddhism in all its variations is defined by its role: almost every strand of Buddhism offers a programme to help individuals achieve enlightenment and escape from the wretchedness of the world through self-discipline, meditation and mental exercise. Apart from this core, though, Buddhism is too varied to be treated as much more than a label, prominent because it was promoted by the power of the Emperor Ashoka and attached to beliefs that are as varied as the people holding them. In the end, there does not appear to be a philosophical position or moral stance or social practice that has not, at one time or another, been presented as Buddhist, so, while there is a core of what Buddhism is, there seem to be no limits to what people can make it.

It is a disappointment that the more Buddhism is inspected, the less definite it becomes. There are deep thoughts, written and spoken in a Buddhist context, and there are great Gurus teaching and helping people under the Buddhist label. But there are also trivial thoughts presented as Buddhism by inept teachers. Given that the only element that is almost consistent across most strands of Buddhist Belief is a rejection of worldliness, it seems unlikely that it will develop a violent strand. However, there have been several past Buddhist practices of beating unworldliness into people and it is not impossible it could happen again.

Postscript: Greek Philosophy

Greek[59] Philosophy has two main connections to Beliefs: the way it started, resembling Buddhism and Daoism in its view of life, and the way that it ended, developing into something close to a Belief itself, before its main themes were absorbed by Christianity, which then closed it down.

It is less absurd to compare the Ancient Greek civilisation with China and India than a glance at a map might suggest. The classical Greek civilisation covered a much larger area than the current country called Greece. Across all the eastern Mediterranean Greek was the primary language of culture and commerce for nearly 2,000 years. Alexander (the Great) took Greek influence as far as India, an influence that continued across the region until well after the rise of Islam.

Athens became the intellectual centre, the university, for this broad culture. This was a direct by-product of its democracy, allowing the freedom of speech and the open discussion necessary for higher education – as well as the huge wealth generated by its silver mines. Athens remained the principal university of the Mediterranean for almost 1,000 years, from the period of Socrates and

---

[59] The 'Ancient Greeks' called themselves 'Hellenes' or 'Ellenes'. 'Greece' comes from the Romans confusing the Hellenes with a tribe from modern Albania called the Graeci. We are, as with the Germans, stuck with the wrong name for the wrong people thanks to the Romans.

Plato, around 400BCE, until 529CE when the Byzantine emperor closed the schools of Athens because they were not Christian.

Over this nearly 1,000 years there was a huge range of thought and we know very little about most of it. Much was deliberately destroyed because it was non-Christian and much was lost just through the normal processes of aging and confusion. A great deal of our information comes from later writers, many of them hostile criticisms by later Christian sources or from popular, gossipy summaries. We use these because we have no alternative sources of information. It is like trying to understand the nature of modern Philosophy when your sources are only the writings of Karl Marx and *Hello* magazine.

In its early phase, Greek Philosophy divided into a number of schools, the best known of which are Stoicism, Cynicism, Epicureanism and Platonism. (The names of the schools are purely labels: Stoics were taught in a porch, 'Stoa' in Greek; Cynics means 'the dogs', no one really knows why; the founder of the Epicureans was called Epicurus, etc.)

Although these schools bickered with each other and held themselves to be providing completely different insights and typical modern summaries emphasise their differences, in practice they had very similar underlying assumptions. They all took it for granted that our messy world caused misery that needed a programme of personal action to resolve. They all addressed the question of how to live a satisfactory life and, although they did their best to conceal it, came to similar answers: the need for a self-disciplined escape from desire. The same basic analysis and same fundamental conclusion as the Daoists and Buddhists.

These schools also speculated about the creation of the world. Summarising drastically, all of them except Plato's school saw the universe as the creating spirit itself. Just as we see only the physical aspect of a person although they have an invisible mental or spiritual part, so it is with the universe: while we see only its physical aspect, it also has an invisible mental or spiritual aspect. (Spinoza came to a very similar view in the seventeenth century.) However, for all their ingenuity, the Athenian schools allowed that this was pure speculation and gave little time to the issue of creation.

Plato and his later followers took a different but equally speculative path. They proposed that there was a world of perfection and our world was merely the sadly battered replica of this perfection. Plato used the vivid image of shadows cast on the back of a cave wall: we see only the shadow shape of the much richer real object casting the shadow. This world of perfection could only be in the mind; its perfect objects could only exist as mental images. In our mind we can envisage a perfect circle, but in our world we can only draw a flawed replica – however carefully the circle is drawn, it will be flawed at some level.

Our understanding of what Plato's later followers thought about the creator is complicated by four things: much of their writing is lost, they are writing about very abstract ideas, they argued a lot and the words they use

– words like 'logos', literally, 'word' – often have complex meanings difficult to fully comprehend now. Some of Plato's school saw the creator and presiding spirit of the world as a Trinity, made up of 'the One', 'the Word' and 'the Soul'. In other versions the One and the Word created the craftsman (Demiourgos) who, in turn, made the material world. These ideas, and their variants, were very influential in shaping the Christian (Orthodox/Catholic) understanding of God as a Trinity. The most direct example of the Neo-Platonist use of 'the Word' in the Bible is Chapter 1 of the Gospel of St John, which begins *'In the beginning was the Word and the Word was with God and the Word was God'*.

The schools, summarised here, were much more than just philosophies of life. Each school had not only a speculative cosmogony and the recommended ways to approach a happy life but also had views on logic, the reality of experience, ethics and so on. They also linked with the ideas of the Sceptics, a group who asked for high levels of evidence before they would accept assertions, to create views about what existed and about the relationship of words to objects. (Almost all we know about Scepticism comes from the much later writings of a Roman, Sextus the Empiricist, named after the term 'Empiricism' (derived from the Greek *'Emperia'*, experience) meaning scepticism with a college education.)

Alongside the austere intellectualism of the Athenian schools of Philosophy, mystery religions flourished, becoming more influential as the period of political domination by the Greeks gave way to the Roman

Empire. Some of the best known were the cults of Isis and Dionysus and there may have been many others. But if our knowledge of Greek Philosophy is limited by the destruction of written records, our knowledge of the cults is even more limited. The few commentaries we have on the cult of Dionysus, you will be saddened to hear, focus more on the sexual and other sensational activity of the cult, than on their cosmology. As a result we know virtually nothing of their beliefs. [60]

The style and some of the substance of Greek philosophising went into the development of early Christian theology (ideas about God). The very idea that discussing the nature of God is a worthwhile activity is probably the principal Greek legacy to Christianity. But the key flaw of Greek Philosophy as a set of Beliefs was its pure intellectualism. Buddhism started with a similar take on the world to the Greek Philosophies but combined its abstract analysis, attractive to literate scholars, with the rich legends of the Buddha's life, legends that illuminated Buddhist teaching for the less literate. The schools of Athens deliberately lacked any common touch because they had to teach to make money, so they failed to build a Belief. But when their bloodless abstractions were combined, by Saint Paul, with the more emotional and visceral qualities of Judaism, it created the fireball of Christian theology.

---

[60] To spare you unnecessary research, we don't actually know very much about their sexual practices either, apart from the fact that they were shocking.

.10.

ENVIRONMENTALISM: THE PURITAN BELIEF

The Environmentalist Belief is that humanity is destroying or using up the earthly resources needed for human life to continue in the future. Hence, humanity needs to change its lifestyle – now – to avoid a future catastrophe. The biggest changes to lifestyle need to be made by those who consume the most and so destroy the most; that is, the richer countries and richer individuals most need to change their ways.

During Environmentalism's brief history, the theories that have been used to link humanity's current behaviour to its future problems have changed again and again. But, whatever the theory, the end result is always the same: future disaster. The underlying cause of the disaster is always the same: humanity's rapacity and carelessness. The remedy for the disaster is always the same: self-denial and compulsory austerity.

Like Communism, which people often took up in reaction to the sight of gross economic injustice,

Environmentalist Belief rests on an accepted wrong: that humankind can make a mess of its surroundings, a mess that can be both offensive and dangerous. But Environmentalism does not emphasise local issues, such as urban smog or polluted rivers. These are small-scale, so they can be – and often are – solved with practical action. They also diminish with rising wealth, as society can afford to put more resources into cleaning them up. The focus of Environmentalist Belief is on possible future worldwide problems, problems no individual can avoid or escape, problems whose scale and impact call for an immediate and powerful response. These theories all share the same characteristics: changing individual behaviour could have some small effect, changing collective behaviour could have a larger effect, but community-wide change, enforcing the direction set by the Environmentalists, is the only solution that could, possibly, avert the problem altogether.

Environmentalism shares with the other modern Beliefs of Communism and Nationalism, the pattern of taking a natural, generous instinct and building a complete Belief onto it. Nationalism built a Belief on love of our country and community, but develops it into a world of conflicting groups. Communism came out of sympathy for the downtrodden, but built a Belief that trapped people under a grim and sadistic government. Environmentalism builds on our dislike of waste, ugliness and greed and makes from them a Belief with large and immediate demands of all of us. All these

Beliefs gain great strength because criticism of them can be seen as criticism of the attractive drives that underlie them, not the negative results of converting these into a Belief; criticise Nationalism and you are unpatriotic, criticise Communism and you are selfish, criticise Environmentalism and you are uncaring.

Like Nationalism, Environmentalism is not often seen as a Belief, although it is widely recognised that many enthusiastic Environmentalists often become 'Green' because of their personal disposition, rather than the persuasiveness of the case. Many people support Environmentalists in a general way, because they see it as a pressure group, fighting waste, ugliness and greed, rather than seeing it as a Belief. The feeling is that, while the 'Deep Greens' are prone to exaggeration, their cause is good, they do no harm and some benefit is likely to come from their campaigns.

Environmentalism is also, like Nationalism, a near-universal Belief; most people in the developed world support it to some extent. Few people doubt the general proposition that humankind is creating long-term problems – of some sort – by its current behaviour and consumption. Most agree that the greater the consumption, the sooner the problems will arise and the larger they will be. Many people with moderate Environmentalist beliefs build up 'Green' habits, intending to reduce their personal environmental impact. They buy products with Green credentials, they carefully sort their trash for recycling, they use water with care and they choose their car with thought for its energy consumption. These people value their Environmentalist beliefs. They see their concern about our common future and our common planet as part of what makes them ethical, caring people. Their personal response – the sacrifices they make, the everyday care they take – makes them responsible, decent individuals.

Low-level, popular Environmentalism does not rely on any specific, individual mechanism to generate the future problem. If a new mechanism arises that links today's behaviour to problems tomorrow, the public by-and-large accepts it, and adds it to the previous mechanism. Most people at the time of writing assume that the threat to the Ozone layer is intimately linked to Global Warming, although the two are independent and largely unconnected concerns.

One of the great strengths of Environmentalism is that it includes people of both right-wing, conservative attitudes and left-wing, liberal/progressive attitudes. On the conservative side there are dedicated conservationists, often keen hunters, typified by the Sierra Club and the original WWF, World Wildlife Fund; on the left there are hippy types, like the original Greenpeace team, and 'anti-capitalist' campaigners. They make for uneasy partners, normally supporting different aspects of Environmentalism. The right-wing types may stress preserving nature and preventing destruction of wildlife habitat, while the left-wing will attack large corporations and wealthy individuals for the damage they do. Mostly they avoid each other, but campaigns in areas they are both interested in, such as preventing development in the rainforest or population control, are sometimes hindered by temperamental clashes between the two different 'wings'.

Criticism of Environmentalist concepts is often seen as coming from the personal failings of the critics, their lack of concern or imagination, rather than any scientific or rational doubt about the problem-causing mechanism itself. Environmentalists believe that any informed, rational person must see that the problem exists and that to deny it is irrational. Scepticism or doubt can only come from ignorance or, more often, wilful self-deception. Like the Communists before them, they see their opponents as wicked people and themselves as leaders in caring and understanding. The leaders of the Environmentalist Belief are strongly evangelical, seeking to convert others to their Belief, some of them admitting to occasional deliberate exaggeration of potential problems, as well as the strength of the evidence for them, in order to attract attention.

Interest in environmental themes and the degree that environmental threats are taken seriously vary in line with the economy. When economic growth is strong, environmental worries are given a high priority. Extreme Environmentalist opinions are listened to. The claims of leading Environmentalists in the boom of the late 1960s and early 1970s may seem absurd in retrospect, but books such as *Only One Earth*[xliii], which demanded urgent international political action to avoid a world disaster caused by pollution, were required high-school reading in many areas. *The Population Bomb*[xliv], whose exaggerated forecasts make for amusing reading now, was treated quite seriously. When economic growth fades, the enthusiasm for the Environmentalist causes falls, as more immanent problems seize the headlines and as personal problems of finance and employment become more urgent.

Over the history of Environmentalism, humanity's careless or self-indulgent behaviour has been linked to serious future problems by a series of different mechanisms. The first such mechanism was God's anger at man's selfishness, indulgence and neglect of proper worship. At various times, Jewish and Christian Puritans (and, occasionally, Muslim ones) have forecast doom to come, resulting from God's righteous anger at mankind's wilfully disobedient behaviour. Although many think this religious Puritanism is completely different to Environmentalism's secular Puritanism, the psychology, the language and the type of changes they seek are the same. Both groups demand that luxuries and pleasures be reduced and seek power to enforce these demands. The difference between them, of course, is that religious Puritans believe that they know, from their interpretation of the sacred texts, what the consequences will be if people refuse to change their ways. In stark contrast, Environmentalists believe that they know, from their interpretation of the scientific texts, what the consequences will be if people refuse to change their ways.

The first secular mechanism that would lead to doom was the 'Population Explosion', a term that refers to the ability of mankind to grow in numbers at an ever-increasing rate. The argument was that this growth would continue, accelerating all the time, until the mass death caused by the inevitable food shortages intervened. Two people can have four children, each of them has four children and each of them has four and so on, with ballooning numbers as the generations pass. Logically, this process must lead to shortages somewhere along the line, before the weight of all these people is greater than the weight of the Earth. Alternatively, disease or natural disaster would interrupt this process. But, one way or another, catastrophe looms. There is practical evidence to support this concern. The population of the world has grown rapidly in the last 200 years, from around one billion in 1800 to around seven billion by 2012. Death rates, particularly among children, came down from the start of the Industrial Revolution and population numbers started to surge ahead from that point.

It was early in the Industrial Revolution and at its centre, Britain, that people first became widely aware of this concern. A hugely influential book called *An Essay on the Principle of Population* by Thomas Malthus, a clergyman, was published in 1798[xlv]. Its thesis was that starvation was an inevitable consequence of population growing faster than food supplies possibly could. Adding data to theory, the first UK census took place in 1803, shortly after Malthus's book was published. This measured the UK population at 8.3 million, an estimated increase of 77% over the preceding 100 years. More tangibly, it was impossible not to see that the cities were growing at an increasing rate year by year, swallowing the countryside around them. The population of Birmingham, England, for example, grew from 15,000 in 1700 to 74,000 in 1800 and to 522,000 in 1901.

As a result of Malthus' theory and seeing the evidence of uncontrolled population growth, many educated Victorians saw mass starvation as inevitable (unless a great plague reduced the population first). So there was no point in attempting to alleviate the hunger of the poor: they were doomed anyway. So much was the theory accepted that it even dissuaded some key members of the United Kingdom government from providing help to the starving during the potato famine that started in 1845/6 in Ireland. What was the point of attempting to fight the inevitable? Providing relief could, at best, only postpone starvation. Some saw the famine as '...*a direct stroke of an all-wise and all-merciful Providence*'. The famine was barely mentioned by Irish politicians in the election of 1847[60], nor did the substantial Irish bloc in the UK Houses of Parliament take any action.

The next human action seen as the possible cause of the end of the world came from the development of nuclear weapons after 1945. The existence of these raised the possibility of an end to the human race as the unintended consequence of an atomic war. In the early days, after the first hydrogen bomb was tested – 1,000 times more powerful than the first atomic bombs – it was believed that the bombs alone could accomplish the end of the human race. After the initial shock at the scale of possible destruction had worn off, it became apparent that the stock of nuclear weapons was several orders of

---

[60] There were full voting rights for Catholics and an Irish electorate of around 5% of the population.

magnitude (thousands of times) too small for nuclear weapons to accomplish the destruction of all humanity by themselves. A good part of humanity might go – those in the cities that were bombed – but not anywhere near all, not by bombs alone. However, some speculated, a nuclear war might be accompanied by a 'nuclear winter'. This would be the result of the nuclear explosions raising a dust cloud that would remain in the atmosphere for a long time, reflecting the sun's heat away from Earth. This idea arose after the discovery that the end of the dinosaurs might have been caused by a large meteor striking Earth and raising just such a dust cloud. But, on inspection, it became apparent that the bombs were, again, nowhere near powerful enough to raise so large a cloud and the idea faded.

In the late 1950s and 1960s several organisations were set up to challenge the possibility of the deliberate use of nuclear weapons, with the Campaign for Nuclear Disarmament, CND, the best known. These organisations can be seen as connected to the Environmentalist movement, although they had a more directly political agenda at the time. Greenpeace, one of the leading Environmentalist sects, founded in the early 1970s, reflected the agenda of that period, covering both pollution ('Green' issues) and nuclear weapons ('Peace' campaigning).

Later, as the long-term dangers of radioactivity became clear, the safe disposal of man-made radioactive material became an Environmentalist issue. It emerged that some nuclear waste dumps would not be safe to open for 100,000 years – a shocking time-scale, vastly longer than any comparable waste problem. This, almost everlasting, side effect of mankind's use of nuclear energy and weapons disturbed many. But, although it is long lived, there is not a great quantity of high-level (very dangerous) nuclear waste. There are currently about 200,000 tonnes of such waste worldwide, which may sound a lot but would fit inside a cube of fifty metres each side. The amount is growing at around 12,000 tonnes a year. This is a minute fraction of the natural radioactivity in the world, only dangerous because of its concentration. The small scale of the problem, away from the immediate locality of a few high-level waste dumps, meant that it lacked wide relevance as a problem.

In the mid-1960s, the next scare to come to the forefront of Environmentalist thinking was atmospheric pollution on a continental scale (air pollution in cities had a long history and was starting to improve at this period). This concern started to increase during the 1960s as consumption – particularly power consumption – increased. Various gasses and processes have been put forward at different times as the possible causes of long-term disaster, but, at this period, the focus was on the gas by-products from electricity generation, notably sulphur oxides and nitrogen oxides. In the developed economies at the time, coal was the main means of electricity generation and coal produces a lot of unpleasant gasses when burned, especially as the careful burning processes and 'stack-scrubbers' used now to decrease pollution were not then available. That such processes were developed and made compulsory in the developed world owes a lot to the actions of the nascent Environmentalist movement and served to diminish pollution problems in richer countries. In less wealthy countries, however, the local pollution problem from coal burning for electrical power can still be severe (although it remains much less severe than in those cities where cow dung is the primary fuel used for cooking and heating).

There were also more specific threats to the environment raised during the 1960s. The most powerful concerns focussed on a widely used insecticide called DDT (DichloroDiphenylTrichloroethane). This followed the publication of a book called *Silent Spring* by Rachel Carson (1962) in which she drew attention to the side effects of the large-scale and indiscriminate use of insecticides. DDT was one of these (although Rachel Carson objected to the careless use of some other insecticide chemicals much more). Her objection was not to the use of DDT by itself but to its widespread and indiscriminate use, for example, in whole-area spraying to prevent crop pests. *'It is not my contention that chemical insecticides must never be used. I do contend that we have put poisonous and biologically potent chemicals into the hands of persons largely or wholly ignorant of their potentials for harm,'*[xlvi] she said. Rachel Carson's work made a huge impact and the controls on some of the more dangerous chemicals she mentioned were rapidly improved. But, because she died sadly young in 1964, she was not able to prevent or discourage others taking up her original campaign and pushing it to a tragic extreme. As a result of the campaign,

DDT, which, used carefully, safely saved many lives by the control of insect-borne disease, was completely banned in the USA in 1972 and worldwide use of DDT became, effectively, forbidden. Stopping the use of DDT resulted in a large increase in the incidence of malaria and other insect-borne diseases. The best recorded case was in Sri Lanka, where recorded instances of malaria increased from just 29 cases in 1964 to over 600,000 in 1968, after DDT was withdrawn from use. It seems likely that similar, but less well-recorded, increases in disease and death occurred in other areas as well. Such was the demonisation of DDT that it took over thirty years, and uncounted millions of preventable deaths, before this important and safe (when properly used) chemical could be re-introduced, in 2001, to reduce disease[58].

In the mid-1970s there was a dramatic increase in Environmentalist concern with the 'Energy Crisis'. Energy crises have a long history. The first such crises were brought about by the exhaustion of local wood stocks. This was probably very common in unrecorded history but is first recorded on a large scale during China's Song Dynasty (960–1279CE) and in England after 1600. Both these crises led to the development of coal mining as an alternative source of energy to replace the vanishing stock of wood.

Returning to the 1970s, the Arab states, which included

---

[61] DDT was once again allowed to be used in controlled circumstances (no whole-area use) following the Stockholm convention of 2001, organised by the UN Environmental Program and the World Health Organisation.

many of the dominant oil-producing nations, embargoed the sale of oil during and after the 1973 Egypt/Israel war. This caused an immediate shortage of oil in Western countries, bringing into sharp focus the fact that fossil fuels have a finite supply. This, in turn, led to speculation that the end of modern lifestyles would be brought about by oil running out, albeit that some dates for the complete exhaustion of all oil, such as the early 1990s, which were widely quoted in relatively serious journals, were absurdly pessimistic. The concern about oil supplies raised a more generalised concern about the depletion and final exhaustion of natural resources: we were using up materials and, logically, there would come a point where there was no more of any particular material. Copper, used for electrical wiring, was an often-cited example.

In the same period, the 1970s, there was also the fear that the production of gas pollutants from electricity generation, especially nitrous oxides and sulphur dioxide and their presence in the atmosphere, would reflect solar energy, bringing forward the arrival of the next Ice Age[xlvii]. This concern faded as the apparently cooling phase in climate records, which had been going on since 1945, was replaced, after 1979, by a period where global temperatures appeared to be rising[62].

During the 1980s, fears were raised about acid rain

---

[62] Technically, Earth is still in an Ice Age – in an 'Interglacial Phase of an Ice Age'. This is because there is now permanent ice at the poles. For 80–90% of the Earth's history, it has been warmer than it is now and there has been no permanent ice anywhere on Earth at sea level.

killing forests downwind of power stations. Acid rain is an effect created by the pollutants coming from the chimneys of coal-fired power stations and other coal-burning factories forming acids when dissolved in atmospheric water in clouds – mostly the same sulphur and nitrous oxides as in other concerns. Acid rain caused by coal burning had badly affected soils close to old industrial centres, notably in the hills downwind of Lancashire in England, where much of the early, and most polluting, industry had started. But the evidence for any large-scale effect on trees much further away was found initially to be inconclusive. Later the theory was abandoned as mistaken. The forests that had been said to be affected by acid rain were found to be suffering as a result of several dry years and, when wetter years returned, the excess deaths of trees stopped.

A subsequent concern of the 1980s was that the gases used in refrigeration and certain types of packaging, known as CFCs (ChloroFluoroCarbons), might destroy the Ozone in the atmosphere. This concern was raised by satellite observations that, after winter at the poles, there were large areas over the Arctic and Antarctic where Ozone was more or less absent in the atmosphere and that these 'holes' might be extending down to lower, more populated latitudes. The loss of this ozone, if it occurred, would have increased the penetration of ultra-violet light to the surface of the Earth. Changing the gasses used in refrigeration and aerosol packaging to ones that have no effect on Ozone, an agreement made in Montreal in 1987, averted this possible risk.

During the 1990s, the progress of DNA-splicing technology led to the development of plants with specific attributes achieved by inserting new DNA into their existing sequences. Environmentalists objected to this process and its products, which they called 'GM', genetically modified, foods. Other related issues, such as the fear that large corporations might end up controlling the supply of seeds, added to their objections.

As the 1990s progressed, a concern built up that the production of carbon dioxide (CO_2), made by burning fossil fuels as sources of energy, might become a problem because the extra CO_2 would have the effect of trapping more heat from the sun, warming up the Earth. This theory became known as 'Global Warming'. Since the start of the industrial era the average amount of CO_2 in the atmosphere has increased from around an annual average of 280 parts per million (ppm) to 380ppm, an increase that appears to be largely caused by burning fossil fuels. In addition, it was feared that the reduction in the area of the tropical rainforests might add to the problem of higher atmospheric CO_2 because it would reduce the amount of CO_2 absorbed by plants. As a result of these and other processes, it was thought that carbon dioxide's increased presence in the atmosphere might lead to an increase in the temperature of the Earth by what is known as the 'Greenhouse Effect'.

(Technically, the theory is that additional carbon dioxide would lead to an *enhanced* Greenhouse Effect. The overall Greenhouse Effect, allowing energy from the sun to pass through the atmosphere but preventing its return to space by heat radiation, is essential to making the Earth warm enough to support life at all.)

Carbon dioxide is the second most important contributor to the Greenhouse Effect, accounting for about 10–12% of the warming effect. Atmospheric water vapour accounts for more than half of the total Greenhouse Effect, probably 70–85%[63], with minor gasses, such as methane, making up the remaining amount. Environmentalists believed that an increase in global temperature, even if it was as small and slow as around two degrees a century suggested by some, would have a negative effect on human life.

The theory that global temperatures would rise because of man's production of atmospheric carbon dioxide was originally called Anthropogenic ('man-made' in Greek) Global Warming but this name became less frequently used as global temperatures stopped their nineteen-year upward trend after 1998 and was often replaced by the term 'Climate Change', often with less focus on the specific mechanism of CO_2 heating or global temperature increase.

The theory of Global Warming/Climate Change achieved the strongest and longest impact of any of the mechanisms linking current human behaviour to future problems. Even after the Western financial crash of

---

[63] This figure is so politicised that it is impossible to find a consensus. However, all sources agree that water vapour accounts for more than 50% of the Greenhouse Effect. Most of the lower figures (50–70%) treat clouds as having a separate, additional Greenhouse Effect on top of other water vapour effects, so the overall numbers are not so different.

2007/8 and more than a decade of stable temperatures, it continued to be widely believed.

Finally, from time to time other mechanisms have been suggested for the link between thoughtless or careless human activity and a retributive doom for humanity but have achieved less prominence. The acidification of the oceans (as a result of extra carbon dioxide in the atmosphere) and the battle for finite water supplies are two less publicised future challenges promoted by some Environmentalists.

Like the history of environmental concern theories, the history of Environmentalist organisations is relatively short. The predecessors of the current Environmentalist organisations were founded primarily with a concern for preservation of areas of natural beauty and wildlife. Both the Sierra Club in the USA, founded 1891, and the National Trust in the UK, founded 1894, focused more on conservation than on worries about the future sustainability of humanity. Similar conservationist movements and clubs were founded in several European countries around this period, with a focus on preserving the pristine qualities of areas where the influence of man was limited.

Environmentalism is also associated with a broader agenda of concern about the indirect effects of man's activities, including those that do not have a direct implication for the long-term survival of humanity. The most prominent of these is the risk that species of animals and plants will become extinct as the direct or indirect result of (careless) human activity. Another proto-

Environmentalist group, the WWF (now the World Wide Fund for nature, originally the World Wildlife Fund), was founded in 1961, focusing on endangered species and with a worldwide, rather than national, interest.

The first fully Environmentalist sects were Friends of the Earth, founded in the USA in 1969, and Greenpeace, also founded in the USA in 1970. These both started after a period of sustained economic growth. In Europe at around the same time, a number of Environmentalist organisations were growing up, many of which later fused to become Green parties in different countries.

These Environmentalist organisations faced the challenge of keeping environmental concern at the forefront of attention as some of the early Environmentalist concerns lost their potency.

The exponential increase of population stopped for reasons yet to be fully understood but, perversely, is directly correlated with increasing wealth: wealthier people and wealthier countries have fewer children. It is said that the mechanism is via the education and full inclusion of women in economic activity in the wealthier economies – that fully emancipated women choose to have fewer children. Whatever the intermediate mechanisms, as the wealth of the world increases, so population growth falls towards or below zero. Currently, world population is expected to peak at around 11 billion, about 50% more than it is at the moment. The rate of population increase is slowing and some countries, mainly in Europe, have birth rates below those needed to replace the current population, albeit that numbers in those countries are kept up by immigration.

The risk of widespread nuclear war has very much diminished compared to the height of the period known as the 'Cold War', when the USA and the Soviet Union did actively contemplate the massive use of nuclear weapons. The more recent increase in the risk of smaller scale nuclear attacks by terrorists, or by some of the less stable states with nuclear arms, is alarming but does not present a threat to humankind as a whole.

DDT is now sparingly used where it is needed to prevent the serious spread of disease. Agricultural pesticides have been made much less toxic than formerly, although the use of some types still causes concern. Other serious pollutants, such as nitrous oxides, sulphur dioxide, lead residue from leaded fuel and so on, have been successfully decreased or eliminated by regulation in the richer countries – a positive outcome, aided by Environmentalist activity. It seems clear that, as developing countries get richer, they also follow this path to lower emissions, after an initial surge in pollution as energy demand increases.

General chemical pollution is diminishing as the regulation of chemical pollutants continues to be tightened. Atmospheric or oceanic pollution cannot be seen any longer as a problem that is out of control. Both exist, but at levels that do not appear to pose any global threat and that continue to diminish.

Acid rain has been shown to have only localised and relatively small effects and these are being reduced by regulations on the amount of pollutant gasses allowed to be emitted.

Genetically modified plants (ones where the DNA has been systematically altered, rather than the process of random mutation and selection used in the 1950s and 1960s) have been introduced on a huge scale with no adverse effect at all. They have also reduced the usage of insecticides substantially. Were the continuing constraints on such plants reduced to normal levels, insecticide usage would fall more and malnutrition would be reduced, substantially in some areas. In fact, the genomes of virtually all food plants are modified – they are mutated variations of their non-food varieties. Moreover, a generation before the GM food scare, some leading food crops had been artificially genetically modified by nuclear irradiation followed by selection. These include leading varieties of Thai, US and Basmati rice, the main British barley crop, as well as chickpeas, grapefruit, pears, wheat, etc. In all, over 2,500 such radiation-modified seeds were released over fifty years for cultivation before the GM food scare started.

Any risk there may have been to the Ozone layer has been eliminated by the replacement of the Ozone-destroying CFCs with compounds that have no effect on the Ozone layer – an Environmentalist achievement but also one more mechanism of environmental concern eliminated and needing replacement if Environmentalist Belief is to flourish.

Removing the possible problem of the expanding hole in the Ozone layer left Environmentalism with only one worldwide issue: Global Warming. This rapidly outgrew all previous issues and has become almost synonymous with the Environmentalist Belief itself. The theory of Global Warming has, in a vague, generalised form, now become generally accepted by the public in the West, albeit that there is a group of vehement objectors. The British media organisation, the BBC, for example, now holds the theory of Global Warming[64] as an official Belief of the organisation, seeing the evidence for it as overwhelming and criticism of it is discouraged. It is worth seeing how the theory achieved this position.

The existence of a man-made process of Global Warming or any other Climate Change can, at this stage, only be a matter of Belief. There is no scientific way at present, or in the foreseeable future, to predict future weather or climate, any more than there is a way to predict future stock-market levels. The best current forecasts of future weather, beyond a week or two, are no better then complete guesses[65]. 'Climate' is, technically, a thirty-year average of weather and is as unpredictable as other weather periods. One may believe or disbelieve in the possible effects of additional CO_2 in the atmosphere on temperatures but there is no current scientific basis for such belief or disbelief.

---

[64] We have to continue to use the term 'Global Warming' as there is not a 'Theory of Climate Change', other than that related to carbon dioxide induced Global Warming - although there are many theories as to why the climate has changed historically and may do so in future, none command any kind of consensus.

[65] Weather here means variation from the average for the time of year

The theory of Global Warming first became widely publicised with the setting up of the Intergovernmental Panel on Climate Change (IPCC) in 1988 and public awareness has been led by the regular series of reports it produces. It was during the smooth Western economic growth of the late nineties and early two-thousands that followed, that the support for the theory of Global Warming grew, backed by the generally warming trend in world temperatures that started in the late 1970s. Many governments attended a conference on Global Warming at Kyoto in 1997 and signed a protocol promising future reductions in their national CO_2 output. Although the theory of Global Warming meant that the undertakings agreed were too small to make a difference to future Climate Change, it was felt to be a demonstration of serious concern. The USA, which refused to participate, was severely criticised.

During the 1990s, organisations started to adopt a stance towards Global Warming, mostly based on self-interest. Some oil companies took a stance opposing the theory, while atomic energy companies and alternative energy concerns supported it. The administration of the European Union saw Global Warming as a prime example of an issue that needed the kind of multinational administration they provided and took it up with vigour. They combined with financial traders and energy companies to develop tradable CO_2 emissions permits for Europe. When these were launched, it turned out that they had created an unintended windfall profit for European energy companies, but a substantial business has subsequently grown up trading the permits and they have continued since, albeit with mixed reviews.

By the year 2000, the theory of AGW had, for most people, overcome the initial obstacles to its acceptance. The main criticisms and responses were:

- The theory of Global Warming was far from new. It first had been put forward by the Swedish scientist Svante Arrhenius in 1896 (as a good thing – he looked forward to warmer Swedish winters) and again by Stewart Callendar in 1938. However, it had largely been ignored during the long cooling-trend period 1945–79 and because an influential paper by Knut Angstrom in 1900 had shown, experimentally, that increasing CO_2 levels in a column of air had virtually no effect on radiation capture[xlviii] (a result retested and confirmed). However, the rising trend in world temperatures 1979–98 revitalised the suggestion and reopened the question of the practical effect of CO_2.

- Because we cannot long-term forecast any other aspect of weather or climate, some people find the idea that we can predict temperature change long in advance difficult to accept. But all that the theory of Global Warming predicts is that, other things being equal, adding CO_2 to the atmosphere increases world average temperature. By analogy, it may be difficult to predict the taste of a complex dish with many ingredients while cooking it, but it is fair to predict that adding more chilli will make it hotter.

- The weather/climate is known to vary across every timescale, by years, decades, centuries, millennia, 10,000, a million, 100 million years, and more. The Ice Ages are geologically very recent, the last ending only 10,000 years or so ago, and showed dramatic changes in climate, sometimes over very short periods. One well-known Greenland ice core suggests that the temperature increased by 10°C in fifty years at the end of the last Ice Age. A cold period, known as 'the little Ice Age' and running from about 1400 to about 1800, ended only very recently. There is little or no agreement as to what caused these changes; but they certainly have not stopped.

- Many meteorologists saw the model behind Global Warming as gross over-simplification of an immensely complicated subject. Only a small amount of infrared radiation is absorbed by atmospheric CO_2 compared to the amount absorbed by water vapour. CO_2 has a critical role in dissipating heat and cooling the thermosphere part of the upper atmosphere[xlix] and an increase in it may actually enhance this cooling effect. Feedback loops are caused by cloud cover and other issues little understood, even by specialists. In the analogy, they see adding more CO_2 into the atmosphere as more like adding a complex herb like thyme to a dish rather than adding a one-dimensional spice like chilli: effect on the outcome cannot be simply described.

- World temperatures have risen less than might be expected. It is agreed that the rise in the twentieth century was around 0.7°C, which in itself would make the century unusually stable. For comparison, when a band of warmer water develops off the coast of South America (El Nino), it is believed to raise world temperatures in that year by around 0.4°C – and is around thirty times less than the rate of warming in some areas at the end of the last Ice Age. Since 2000, world temperatures are recorded as having no discernible trend towards warming or cooling.

The IPCC sometimes did not help build faith in the theory of AGW by being seen to be over-partisan in its favour. They famously included a graph, known as the 'hockey stick', several times in their 2001 report with insufficient checking. Its failings were used later to criticise the whole report. Later, ill-judged statements by the chair of the IPCC defending statements in the report (to the effect that the Himalayan Glaciers could melt within thirty years) were shown to be badly unfounded and added to the IPCC's reputation for low standards and one-sidedness in the pursuit of publicity.

In the 1960s there had been the hope that it might be possible to forecast the key weather variables over the longer time periods suggested by the term 'climate'. But, ironically, it was in weather forecasting that Edward Lorenz developed the key advances in the mathematical Theory of Chaos. He showed that it is mathematically impossible to forecast complex systems, such as weather, by progressing from measurements of past weather. Lorenz specifically looked to see if there could be an averaging effect over longer periods – whether, at least in theory, climate-length periods were forecastable. He found that they are not and his findings, showing that climate was no more forecastable than weather, were announced in the opening address of the 'Causes of Climate Change' conference at Boulder, Colorado, in 1965, causing some shock[1] (the 'Climate Change' referred to in the conference's title was natural Climate Change). Lorenz showed long-term climate predictions cannot mathematically be better than a complete guess. Although this has stood as a finding since, it has not prevented people hoping that long-term, computer-models of future weather may, one day, have improved on pure guesswork.

Despite these challenges and difficulties, faith in the theory of Global Warming and fear of the consequences of doing nothing to prevent Climate Change became almost universally accepted in Europe, and widely believed in the USA and Australasia.

An almost desperate desire to do something arose and measures were introduced by governments over the late 1990s and 2000s to lower energy consumption and diminish reliance on fossil fuels. It became apparent, however, that these measures would be ineffective, not least because they would diminish CO_2 output in the developed world more slowly than it was increasing in the less developed world. So even ideas that were known to be ineffective, such as the development of 'biofuels' and wind turbines, were promoted in order to be seen to be doing something. 'Biofuels' was the name given to foods that were processed into alcohol and refined so that they could be used in engines to provide power. These fuels were originally commercially developed and subsidised in Brazil as part of an agricultural support and import reduction policy. Using biofuels does not reduce CO_2 output or increase its absorption, compared with consuming fossil fuels. Whatever else would have grown on the land used for biofuels would have absorbed a similar amount of CO_2 and making biofuels absorbs almost as much energy as it provides (harvesting, fermentation, etc.). Subsidies for turning food crops into biofuels were introduced by the US in the late 2000s[li], unfortunately coinciding with a series of poor harvests to raise the prices of basic foods.

Wind turbines were also essentially symbolic. It had long been known that the power they could realistically supply would be minute compared to that from other sources, that it would be intermittent because the wind is intermittent and that even the energy input in building and connecting the turbines would take many years to recover. However, the desire to do something, even if it was more of a gesture than a solution, proved overwhelming and a large number of heavily subsidised land and offshore turbine farms have been built. Their impact on fossil energy consumption has been even less than forecast.

At the time of writing, world average temperatures have been stable for over a decade and the nineteen-year period of rising average temperatures up to 1998 is beginning to fade from popular memory. This, combined with the Western economic recession, is diminishing the sense of urgency attached to the theory of Global Warming.

However, the Environmentalist Belief is now strong enough to override delays in the arrival of Global Warming itself. The IPCC exists; it has a staff, a bureau, an agreed forward plan of action and is firmly committed to the concept. Academic positions in 'Climate Science' are funded; Carbon Emission Permits are a traded financial asset with their own market. Government departments have changed their name (e.g. the UK Department of Energy and Climate Change). Environmental sects, such as Greenpeace and Friends of the Earth, have staffs and systems and, at the moment, no alternative world-affecting issue to campaign about. There are now large industrial sectors that depend on continuing subsidy and price distortion in favour of 'low-carbon'. This sector naturally promotes the theory of Global Warming and lobbies governments accordingly. Many scientists working in climate and weather studies owe their posts, their future careers, possibly some of their sense of self-worth and certainly their budgets to the theory of Global Warming. It is clear that the promotion of the theory of Global Warming – under the less specific banner of 'Climate Change' – is in strong hands and will continue vigorously, even if it faces further obstacles in the future.

The theory has now long been outside the norms of scientific discussion, having become involved in a highly politicised and often bitter struggle carried out on the internet and in the media. There is a move among supporters of Climate Change, aware of the growing challenge of stable temperatures to their theory, to claim that extreme weather events will increase in frequency (although there is no mechanism for this other than the theory of Global Warming). This concept allows any unusual weather event to be linked to the need for Environmentalist action and for publicity every time an extreme event happens. As we tend to perceive recent events as more extreme than past events, regardless of their actual size, this works well to promote the Environmentalist cause, although it can be over-worked. In 2010, some Environmentalist commentators linked the UK's coldest winter for thirty years to the theory of Global Warming via this concept and the same has been suggested for the harsh winter of 2013/4 in North America.

Environmentalism has a central emotional appeal, a desire to clean up the mess we make, extended further by the Puritan urge, an urge that seems to be triggered in part by guilt at prosperity. Its core thesis is that doom is inevitable, unless mankind repents now and adopts a programme of austerity. Environmentalism is not a rational response to the negative effects of humanity's by-products any more than Communism is a rational response to inequality or Nationalism is a rational response to disempowerment. It is a Belief that seeks to redirect the modern world, with its 'dependency on limited natural resources' and its waste production, and to return mankind to a simpler, more natural life.

While the Environmentalist Belief has had some positive effects, it is far from free of negative effects on humanity. In banning the use of DDT for so long, Environmentalism increased the levels of sickness and death through preventable insect-borne disease. In delaying crops with targeted DNA modifications and in the higher food prices caused by biofuels, Environmentalism has added to malnutrition. Fear of Global Warming is causing governments to increase consumer energy costs and divert resources in an attempt to reduce 'carbon' output. On the positive side, Environmentalism has helped develop and strengthen many anti-pollution laws and conservation causes and helped save endangered animals. Sadly, the Belief largely prevents separating the beneficial aspects from the damaging – even charities originally dedicated solely to animal conservation, such as the WWF, have been taken over by a broader, Belief-based agenda.

Environmental Belief has now institutionalised the theory of Global Warming under the Climate Change brand, so that the perceived problem continues, despite stable average world temperatures. There is no reason to believe that rising average world temperature, if it happened, would have an exclusively negative impact – there may be many positive benefits of such a rise, as the man who invented the concept, Arrhenius, saw but it is often presented as a threat to all human life on Earth. Such a dire threat may, in future, be used as justification for more extreme ideas than windmills.

It is disturbing to reflect that Environmentalism is the only Belief dedicated to deliberately making people poorer and fewer. Could it end up, like Nationalism and Communism, the other two modern, non-deistic Beliefs, generating and justifying mass slaughter? It already has financial resources and full-time staffs and personnel, some able and willing to take direct action. Greenpeace alone has twenty-eight offices in forty-five countries with 2,400 full-time staff, 15,000 volunteers, three ocean-going ships and around three million members. Friends of the Earth claims seventy-four countries but discloses less about itself. Both are international, unaccountable to any external body and decide themselves wholly what their agenda is, taking account or putting aside scientific or humanitarian issues as they wish. The IPCC has a full-time secretariat, chair and strong governmental links. These people are not going to go away just because the problem does.

Like Buddhism, Environmentalism has no central control and it has already developed some very small violent sects, creating the term 'Ecoterrorism'. A sect calling itself the Earth Liberation Front has firebombed a wide range of, sometimes surprising, places, including the Vail ski resort in Colorado, USA, because, they said, *'putting profits ahead of Colorado's wildlife will not be tolerated'*. A connected group, the Animal Liberation Front/Animal Rights Militia, has bombed homes and has ambushed and physically attacked people they saw as involved in using animals to test new medical products.

For the moment the existence of 'underdeveloped' countries is something of a constraint on extreme Environmentalism. States that still suffer deep poverty are unwilling to hear the wealthy cry that 'tomorrow we die', until they, too, have had the chance to eat, drink and be merry. But this constraint will lessen as global wealth continues to rise. As the poorer countries catch up, the next wave of environmental fervour may go further than the last.

Hopefully, the benign side of Environmentalism, its desire for conservation and its delight in the natural world, will prevent the third modern Belief from following the path of its slaughtering predecessors. But we should all be aware that Environmentalist Belief might, at some future time, be in a position to impose the drastic measures it promotes: impoverishing humanity and creating, in part at least, the doom it predicts.

Legend has it that Kelvin Mackenzie, doyen of tabloid journalists, suggested that Environmentalists, given power, would act as violently as the Communists had done when they had power. But he expressed it differently: *'Give that lot [Environmentalists] one sniff of power and they'll turn from Green to Red faster than a frog in a liquidiser.'*

Postscript: Fanatics and Puritans

Beliefs are inspiring: they lift the eyes and the spirit from the dustiness and dullness of the daily world to great visions of God, freedom from want and a better future for you, your children and their children.

But, as they inspire, so they create fanaticism – the more extreme version of inspiration. Inspiration turns into fanaticism when people find the power and nobility of their Belief is strong enough to prompt and justify actions outside social norms; it provides a justification for violence to yourself and to others.

There is a disposition to group violence in some young men. Violence was the largest cause of death among young men until quite recently. So, although we live in more peaceful times, the instinct of some young men (and a few young women) to find an attraction in violence still exists. One of the ways it expresses itself is in fanatical devotion to a Belief. Fanaticism exists without Beliefs – history is full of periods when societies divided into opposing groups, some of them fanatical, without any serious Belief. The 'Blues' and 'Greens', originally different chariot team supporters, whose vicious confrontation almost destroyed Byzantium, the poisonous struggles of the 'Guelphs' and 'Ghibellines' in Medieval Italy and even some modern football team supporters have shown that Belief is not necessary to fanaticism. Beliefs can, however, help build and sustain fanaticism to a level non-Belief fanaticism cannot reach, even when, as in Islam, their faith deplores it.

Fanaticism is largely independent of the Belief it seems to be part of – some people seem to have a disposition to become fanatics, regardless of their specific Belief. Over the last 200 years, Nationalism has been the main cause of fanaticism. Nationalism institutionalised fanaticism and created mass armies, such as those that dominated the First World War, where whole groups became fanatical and effectively suicidal behaviour was compulsory. In the last fifty years the decline of the most violent forms of Nationalism and the vanishing of Communist fanatics have put Islam and, possibly, Environmentalism in the driving seat for straightforward fanaticism.

Fanaticism can take the form of self-sacrifice. Sometimes fanatical self-sacrifice does not directly affect others. For example, self-deprivation (asceticism) leaves everyone else alone. Sometimes self-sacrifice is combined with extreme violence to others, as in the figure of the suicide bomber. Most commonly, however, self-sacrifice fanaticism shows up as Puritanism.

Puritanism is not the same as asceticism. Asceticism is self-deprivation in an attempt to achieve purity or freedom from desire. Puritanism is the insistence that everyone should deprive themselves and those who fail to deprive themselves voluntarily should be deprived by force. Puritanism occurs at two levels. Level one Puritanism is just about sex. It sees the sexual act as disgusting and, unless ritually consecrated, as an offence against godlets or God. This Puritanism sees sexual desire as pollution and sexual variation, especially homosexuality, as sin. For these Puritans, sexual abstinence is admirable, pure and spiritual: the defeat of the animal body by the spiritual mind. Support for a Puritan view of sex has ebbed and flowed in many religions, although sects that reject sex altogether no longer exist or, like the Shakers in the USA, are reduced to three members (Jan 2011).

Beyond the purely sexual Puritanism is the wider, second-level Puritanism. This rejects many or all forms of overt pleasure as offensive and continued popular indulgence in them as abominable and bringing forward the end of the world. Such Puritans often find reason in their Belief to dislike laughter, enjoyment of food, attention to appearance, activities performed just for pleasure such as dancing or singing, or any other overt or physical pleasure at all. Depending on the specific Belief, they see enjoyment of these things as against God's rules, lacking in Communist seriousness or damaging the planet's ability to sustain life, etc.

Most Beliefs are linked to some level of self-denial; if your Belief does not discourage you from doing anything you want to, it is difficult to see what importance it could have. But second-level Puritanism has a much stronger effect, one that requires everyone to deprive themselves substantially.

Like violent fanaticism, second-level Puritanism seems to be a psychological disposition that many people are capable of, but one that only comes out in response to certain events. Sometimes a natural disaster seems to call for repentance. The appalling effects of the Black Death in Europe, which killed one-third to half the population, brought on a flood of repentant sects. The Flagellants were especially prominent in Catholic Europe in the 1350s, after the first attack of the Black Death. They wandered the countryside in parties flogging themselves, often to extremes and sometimes to death.

Sometimes a guilty prosperity will bring symptoms of Puritanism to the fore, as it did in Victorian England. Only the Environmentalist Belief has Puritanism at its core, as, without the need to reduce consumption to avoid the apocalypse, Environmentalism does not exist. In other Beliefs, periodic attacks of Puritanism, like periodic attacks of fanaticism, occur only sporadically and regionally.

All Beliefs can be inspiring and so can develop fanatics, some violent, some self-harming and some Puritan. These are aspects, by-products, of every Belief. To condemn any particular Belief because it is linked to a type of fanaticism, or to a horror caused by fanatics in its name, is a mistake. Beliefs are vehicles for fanaticism and Puritanism in the same way as they are vehicles for art, music and charity.

.11.

THE NEXT BELIEF?

To become a mass phenomenon a Belief must meet a core human psychological and emotional need, a need that may be particularly cogent in society at the time they start.

- Nationalism originally gave individuals the hope that they would be empowered. Now Nationalism and its Racism variant give a sense of self-worth to those who cannot find it elsewhere.
- Communism promised to end gross economic unfairness and helped individuals handle the guilt of being richer and suffering less than others.
- Environmentalism also assuages the guilt of an easy prosperity and makes it a virtue to attack the lifestyle of the wealthy or complacent.
- Judaism meets the need to belong and/or to feel special.
- Polytheism gives the apparent ability to make a difference, at least sometimes.
- Confucianism and Hinduism reassure the well-off that their position is merited and necessary.
- Daoism and the simpler forms of Buddhism provide tools to deal with depression, loss, grief and pain.

- Christianity and Islam succeed by meeting multiple psychological and emotional needs:
  - the promise that existence is fair. After death there will be joy for the good, however wretched they may be now.
  - self-esteem because the creator of the universe cares for each person.
  - a means to relieve guilt.
  - for some, as with Polytheism, a means to gain favours in this world.

The success of a Belief depends on delivering these psychological and emotional benefits; it does not depend on the Belief's faith being true. While the truth of religious faith is impossible to assess objectively, the faiths of the three secular beliefs are dubious at best: Nationalism's faith in the existence of distinctive types of people, uniquely bonded to an area; Communism's faith that history has a determinate drive; and the Environmentalist faith in the theory of Global Warming. For Nationalism and Communism their faith in mistaken propositions may not have been obvious at first, but, even as it became unmistakable, the obvious falsity of their faiths had little effect on their appeal for many years. Environmentalism is unaffected by the complexity of atmospheric science, the unpredictability of the weather or the continuing lack of Global Warming and there is no reason to believe it ever will be.

Once established, Beliefs are robust. Judaism has an appalling history of generating suffering for its adherents; but it persists. Nationalism has an appalling death toll, yet continues to appeal – although in Europe, where the Nationalist slaughter was worst, its appeal does seem to have diminished a little. To reduce Communism to virtual extinction took decades of repeated, disastrous and complete failure to deliver on any aspect of its promises.

The existence of widespread literacy, modern science and worldwide communication has proved no barrier to the creation and spread of new Beliefs. On a small scale, new Beliefs arise every day. Some grow large enough and last long enough for us to recognise them as Beliefs and call them 'cults'. Far more arise but don't get a popular name and, when we run across someone with an unknown Belief, we are at a loss to understand their motivation and end up simply calling them rude names. 'Single-issue nutter', 'obsessive' and 'weirdo' are epithets applied to someone under the influence of a minority Belief. The vast majority of mini-Beliefs will get nowhere, but when one hits the right psychological and emotional need, a new major Belief will arise. A Belief that suddenly harmonises with the structure of society is like a particular wind speed – not necessarily a very strong wind speed – that harmonises with the structure of a suspension bridge; the bridge starts to writhe and shake itself to bits. Although we cannot see its form in advance, given time it is certain that a new major Belief will arise. It may be completely new, as Communism was when it started, or it may be a mutation of a previous belief, like the Reformation of Christianity. It will build on a decent or noble emotion and take it further. It may be benign, but it could be as deadly as post-Reformation Christianity, Nationalism and Communism all proved to be, wiping out a significant proportion of the population.

It is alarming that three of the last four major developments in Belief (the Reformation, Nationalism and Communism) were quickly pathological – especially when the fourth and most recent, Environmentalism, is still in its youth. If Environmentalism follows the same path as the last Belief to develop, Communism, it will take over its first country in 2038, sixty-nine years after it was founded (taking Greenpeace and Friends of the Earth, founded in 1969/70, as the start of formal Environmentalism). After that Communism had seventy years of terrorising its people…

More immediately, Islam is the prime candidate for the next existing Belief to develop deadly mutations. Arguably, it already has. Al Qaeda, ISIS and other 'Islamic' terrorist groups have shown that the explicit ban on religious compulsion[lii] in the Qur'an and the many ahadith of the Prophet forbidding war on women and children can be talked away as easily in Islam as the similar bans were in Christianity.

Or there could be a completely new Belief, maybe in rapidly developing China. It has happened there before, several times, but, in the past, the disruption and deaths were confined within that vast country. This limitation seems unlikely to be repeated with any new eruption. The rise of a new pride in China, seeking a new outlet, is fertile territory to plant a Belief. It is one of the few parts of the world, for example, where a homegrown Nationalism has not had a killing phase yet.

Perhaps understanding Beliefs will help us to recognise their dangerous elements as they appear, so that deadly variations can be dealt with before they kill people. Perhaps people of religion can work against the tribalism and intolerance that twist their faith into Beliefs with deadly potential. Perhaps improving communication and knowledge will enable humanity to leave behind the dangerous aspects of collective convictions. Perhaps we can escape and get beyond Beliefs.

Perhaps.

Notes on terms, names, periods, etc.

Bible is used to cover not only the Christian book but also the Jewish Tanakah, which is very similar to the Old Testament section of the Bible (see chapter 5). The King James Bible/Version (KJV) is used for quotations as the most widely read English translation.

Church A structured organisation based on a Belief, originally a top-down corporate organisation of the Christian Belief. Used here, by extension, for any corporate organisation of any Belief.

Country A term referring to a large region in Europe, generally larger than a duchy (dukedom) or county. Until the advent of Nationalism, 'country' was a loose term – much as the term 'region' still is a loose term – unless there was a sharp geographical border, like a coast or mountain range. Saxony, Sweden, Muscovy, France, Burgundy, Bohemia, Prussia and many more were countries that varied in time and space. Many modern countries did not exist – Italy was a peninsula, as was Spain (until it was adopted as the name of a state and the peninsula had to be changed to Iberia to accommodate Portugal), Greece was a misnomer for a part of the area that had been occupied by the Hellenes; Ireland is an island, not a country.

The USA muddled the issue because it took independent states and united them in one country, so a 'state' in the US means what a 'province' means elsewhere. Now 'country' is normally used for an independent political unit of the type that used to be known as a state and is muddled with the concept of a Nation as well. Here 'country' is used to mean an independent state having nothing to do with Nation.

Dates are given as years BCE and CE. These stand for 'Before the Current Era' and 'Current Era'. The dates in this system are the same as those using BC (Before Christ) and AD ('Anno Domini', Latin for 'Year of the Lord'). The BC/AD system was devised around 540CE by a monk called Little Dionysius (Dionysius Exiguous). He took an earlier guess of the year Jesus was born in and gave that year the number 1. But, according to the Gospels, which are the only evidence we have, Jesus was born during the reign of Herod (Hordos), who died in 4BCE, so it seems desirable to avoid the BC/AD terms for their inaccuracy, as well as their origin in one specific Belief. We are, however, stuck with the fact that, due to the Roman numbering system, there is no year 0. The years go from 1BCE to 1CE the next year.

Names Where the name of a person, people or tribe is well known in English, the conventional English form is used. So, although the names 'Kong Fuzi' and 'Yeshua' are close to the way these individuals pronounced their names, the conventional English form of their names are used here, Confucius and Jesus. This includes all Biblical names where the King James Version of the name is used.

Otherwise names are written to be as close to phonetic as possible.

Titles or honorifics are only used where it is necessary to make clear who is being referred to; so just Paul is generally used instead of Saint Paul (or Saul, his Hebrew name), but Dao-zi is used, not just Dao, because 'Dao' has many other possible meanings. For Chinese names the modern Pin-yin spelling is used rather than the older Wade-Giles spelling. For example, 'Daoism' is what used to be known as 'Taoism' under the old system. (It also avoids the inevitable disillusion of discovering that the man we call 'Confucius' was, in the Wade-Giles system, called 'Kung-Fu'.)

For geographic terms the phonetic spelling is normally used for countries and areas that no longer exist and the standard name in English if it still exists today. Exceptionally, the term Judea is used instead of Yehuda or Judah or Judas, as many early readers complained that 'Yehuda' disrupted their reading. The name 'Israelites' is used for the tribe that the Jews referred to as the Samaritans. 'Israel' is used for the kingdom that ceased to exist in 722BCE and also for the modern state, founded in 1947.

Patriotism is an emotional and rational desire to support the state you live in, especially in war and through the use of arms or money.

Qur'an The 'Recitation' of the Prophet Mohammad. Muslims see it as the direct word of God. Quotes from the Qur'an are avoided as far as possible. Mohammad disapproved of using quotations out of context, especially quotations from religious sources. Despite this, those wishing to claim that its message is one of violence or of peace often quote the Qur'an out of context. It seems worthwhile to avoid adding to this problem. In passing, Muslim writers in English tend to follow any mention of the Prophet Mohammad's name with '(PBUH)', short for the full 'Peace be upon him'. This will not be used here, mainly because this is the sort of pompous flummery that the Prophet particularly disliked.

Sect A group within a Belief with a particular and distinctive creed in which they differ from other sects of the Belief.

Sectarian Adjective referring to discrimination, war or murder because other people belong to a different sect.

State Originally, a political unit owing no higher allegiance. So, for example, the kingdoms of Poland and France, China, the Grand Duchy of Muscovy and the Osmanli (Ottoman) Empire were states.

The situation became complex after thirteen, formerly British and separate, American states combined to form the United States of America, keeping the name 'state' for each of the units making it up. This has been widely copied, so now many countries use the term state' to apply to what had formerly been called provinces or similar. For clarity, here 'state' is only used in its earlier meaning of an independent political unit of whatever size.

Endnotes

[i] The faiths of the different Beliefs are discussed in detail in various chapters. However, as a brief summary:

- The polytheistic faith is that there are invisible people who can grant magic favours.

- The Judaic faith is that they are the chosen people of a godlet.

- The Buddhist and Daoist faiths are that you can escape the misery of life by mental discipline.

- The Confucian faith is that proper behaviour will bring happiness and success.

- The Christian faith is there is one God who created the universe and who judges and sentences people after their death according to rules very opaquely outlined by his human avatar, Jesus.

- The Islamic faith is in the same God as Christianity and that his will is revealed in the Holy Qur'an and the life of Mohammad.

- The Nationalist faith is that people come in different types and need to live, separated from other Nations, in their own area.

- The Communist faith is people are split into different, conflicting classes and that victory by the workers is inevitable.

- The Environmentalist faith is that thoughtless behaviour by humans will result in terrible future consequences via a variety of mechanisms.

ii   Why are Nationalism, Communism and Environmentalism the only modern '-isms' that are 'Beliefs' (or ideologies) when there are so many more – Socialism, Conservatism, Feminism, Liberalism, Egalitarianism, Mercantilism and Internationalism, to pick just a few? These '-isms' in practice come into three categories, none of these achieving the status of a Belief, 'a structure of thought, behaviour, tradition and practice, based on ideas a group hold to be true: a collective conviction'.

      The first category are those '-isms' that are so vague as to defy analysis. Socialism and Conservatism are examples. Both imply a point of view: Socialism, that the perspective of society as a whole is more significant than the perspective of the individual; Conservatism, that a cautious approach should be taken to change. Neither has the definition or complexity of a Belief.

      The second category is the '-isms' that simply name a campaign: Feminism, Egalitarianism, Mercantilism and Internationalism. Feminism, Egalitarianism, Mercantilism, Internationalism and the like are names for the formal or informal promotion of, respectively: women's interests; equality; trade discrimination and something to do with smoothing national boundaries.

      Some of these, such as Feminism and Egalitarianism, are linked to the more complex third category of modern '-ism', exemplified by Liberalism. Although Liberalism has many definitions and sub-categories, it centers on the belief in respecting the equal dignity of each individual, regardless of their origin, their status or, largely, their behaviour. The flag of Liberalism is a desire for the legal implementation of the strongest form of Human Rights declaration. Although, like smacking children or not, this is often presented as a starkly moral choice; it is prompted by a more logical analysis. Liberals believe that a peaceful, safe and prosperous society is best built on the free support of individuals, that support achieved by the respect given to their individual dignity, regardless of their differences of origin, status and, largely, behaviour. They are opposed by those who believe that society should more strictly define and enforce what it is acceptable for individuals to be and do. Liberalism is a belief in one specific mechanism as the best way to achieve the same end, a peaceful, rich and free society, as their opponents think is best achieved by other means. It is not a Belief in the purpose or role of life.

iii   2 Kings 2:23 and 24.

iv   See Heroditus, *Histories*, VII 54 and Dionysius of Halicarnassus: *Roman Antiquities* 38.2.

v   2 Kings 21:16.

vi   Roughly contemporary with Homer was Hesiod, who wrote several books. They may have been orally transmitted for some time, but some feel strongly that they were written by Hesiod himself, probably as prompts for his performance of them because he could not remember his recitations without them.

vii   Plato, *Phaedrus*

viii   1 Kings 11:5-7.

ix   2 Kings 17:6.

x   Amos 7:14.

xi   2 Kings 21:3 onwards.

xii   2 Kings 22:8.

xiii   2 Kings 23: 22.

xiv   Two of the sources of the Torah, 'J' and 'E', had already been edited together before the Exile.

xv   Genesis 1:26.

xvi   In this instance the editor put the J version of the story after the
E version of the story and appears to have smoothed the
changeover from 'Elohim' in the first version to 'Yahweh' in the
J version by using a combined 'Yahweh Elohim' name for this
section, a form used nowhere else.

xvii   Ezra 4:3.

xviii   Sacrifice was not the whole animal, most of which was taken
home and eaten, but was the ritual slaughter of the animal with
bits given to the godlet as a gift – notably the kidney fat.

xix   There is no agreed definition or origin for the term 'Sadducee',
but it is probably derived from 'Zadok', the high priest in David's
time.

xx   Isaiah 45:1. It is possible that the Messiah/Christ referred to in
the book of Daniel (Daniel 9: 24–26) that is normally seen as the
key prophesy of a new anointed saviour is also referring to Cyrus.

xxi   Matthew 26, Mark 14, Luke 7, and John 12.

xxii   Matthew 13:55 and 56, marginally different in Mark 6:3.

xxiii   John 2:12 and John 7:5.

xxiv   The act of crucifixion was a Roman form of execution that means
that it was for a crime judged by the secular Roman authorities.
The Jewish authorities were empowered to execute heretics but
their method would normally have been death by stoning. The
Gospels claim that Jesus was judged by the Jewish authorities as
a heretic but handed to the Roman authorities for execution as a
rebel. They say that the Roman governor, Pontius Pilate, a man
elsewhere described as violent and impulsive, dithered in
allowing the execution until impelled by the demand of the
(Jewish) crowd. This does not stack up and the more probable
explanation is that the Roman authorities arrested Jesus (as the
Gospels say) and executed him as a rebel. The Gospels may have

wanted to exculpate the Roman authorities of his death as they lived in a Roman-dominated world and to blame the Jews, who had persecuted Christians.

xxv   Acts 13:9–13.

xxvi   Matthew 24:30 and 31.

xxvii 1 Corinthians 11:24 & 25.

xxviii Romans 4:29.

xxix   Paul's preaching in Acts 17:23-32.

xxx   Leviticus 16:21.

xxxi   Romans 3:25, 7:3.

xxxii There are many examples. One specific case: 'Canon 14. We prohibit also that the laity should not be permitted to have the books of the Old or New Testament; we most strictly forbid their having any translation of these books.' – The Church Council of Toulouse 1229CE. Source: Edward Peters, *Heresy and Authority in Medieval Europe*, Scolar Press, London. ISBN 0-85967-621-8, pp. 194–195.

xxxiii Genesis 3:16–19, Qur'an 20:122.

xxxiv *Decline and Fall*, chapter L.

xxxv   John 8:7.

xxxvi Surahs 24:30 and 33:53 and 59.

xxxvii Romans 2:27.

xxxviii Surahs 7, 11, 15, 26, 27 and 54.

xxxix Originally *'Our country – In her intercourse with foreign nations may she always be in the right, and always successful, right or wrong.'* A toast in 1816 by Commodore Stephen Decatur of the US Navy.

xl   *Is That a Fish in your Ear?* David Bellos, Allen Lane 2011

xli   The British Isles revolutions of 1650–60, which also removed and executed the king, did not result in the development of Nationalist ideas. While there were other factors, this seems principally because it was an era when differences between peoples were seen almost entirely in terms of their religious Beliefs, which Christian sect they followed. With so much sectarian hatred around there was little room left for Nationalist hatreds. A very similar problem faced the States of America when they decided to reject the authority of the King of England. In contrast to France, however, each state already had its own system of authority. The joint continental army and navy of the United States were created as an alliance of necessity between separate entities, each with their authority intact. So, while proto-Nationalist ideas abounded – the slogan 'no taxation without representation' is part Nationalist, part Democratic, for example – the full Nationalist thesis was impossible.

[xlii]   11 Oct 1796

[xliii]   Hegel, *Philosophy of Right* (323–325).

[xliv]   Benedict Anderson, *Imagined Communities*, revised edition Verso 206, p120.

[xlv]   Karl Marx, Critique of the Gotha Programme 1875, 'Jeder nach seinen Fähigkeiten, jedem nach seinen Bedürfnissen'.

[xlvi]   Mozi Ch35.

[xlvii]   The Tripitika was originally written in Pali but some of it was later translated into Sanskrit. It is normally broken into three sections, the Sutras, some of which are seen as the sermons of Buddha, collected at the first assembley after the Buddha's death, the Abhidharm, philosophical interpretation of Buddhist doctrine and the Vinaya, the rules and regulations of monastic life.

[xlvii]   Barbara Ward and Rene Dubois, Andre Deutch, 1972.

[xlix]   Paul Ehrlich, Ballentine/Friends of the Earth, 1968.

[l]   To be fair to Malthus, he was unfortunate in his timing, as the

factors that would make his prediction false, commonly called the 'Industrial Revolution', were coming into play just as he was writing. His influence was critically important, nevertheless, since it was in reading his work that both Darwin and Wallace worked out the theory of natural selection.

li Diary of Sir Charles Trevelyan, the civil servant in charge of famine relief.

lii *Silent Spring*, Chapter 2.

liii Harrison, Gordon A, *Mosquitoes, Malaria, and Man: A History of the Hostilities Since 1880*, Dutton, 1978.

liv Kukla and Matthews, 'When will the present interglacial end?' Science 178, 1972.

lv Knut Angstrom, 1900.

lvi http://mccomputing.com/qs/Global_Warming/Atmospheric_Analysis.html

lvii The average world temperatures for the last fifteen years (1997–2011) in degrees Celsius are given as: 14.39, 14.52, 14.30, 14.29, 14.43, 14.49, 14.49, 14.44, 14.53, 14.49, 14.48, 14.38, 14.49, 14.53, 14.35. Source: Met Office Hadley Centre (HadCRUT4).

lviii Spencer R Weart, *The Discovery of Global Warming*, Harvard University Press, 2003, p62.

lix B. A. Babcock – *The Impact of US Biofuel Policies on Agricultural Price Levels and Volatility,* International Centre for Trade and Sustainable Development (ICTSD), 2011

lx Surahs 2:256, 10:99, 15:2-3, 18:29, 109:1–6 and many others requiring fairness, moderation and forgiveness in and after war.